D1393987

English Court Theatre, 1558–1642

Several famous playwrights of the Elizabethan and Stuart periods, including Shakespeare, wrote for open-air public theatres and also for the private indoor theatres at the palaces at which the court resided. This book is the first full account of such court theatre, and examines the theatrical entertainments for Elizabeth I, James I and Charles I.

By contrast with the now-vanished playhouses of the time, four of the royal chambers used as theatres survive, and the author attempts to draw as full a picture as he can of such places, the physical and aesthetic conditions under which actors worked in them, and the composition and conduct of court audiences. He both confirms the role of royal patronage in the growth of professional theatre, and offers a new definition of the function of theatrical occasions in creating the cultural profile of the English court.

The book includes plans and illlustrations of the theatres and an appendix which lists all known court performances of plays and masques between 1558 and 1642.

JOHN H. ASTINGTON is Associate Professor of English at the University of Toronto. He is the editor of *The Development of Shakespeare's Theater* (1992) and author of several articles on the private court theatre of Shakespeare's time.

English Court Theatre 1558–1642

John H. Astington

CAMBRIDGE
UNIVERSITY PRESS

PUBLISHED BY THE PRESS SYNDICATE OF THE UNIVERSITY OF CAMBRIDGE
The Pitt Building, Trumpington Street, Cambridge CB2 1RP, United Kingdom

CAMBRIDGE UNIVERSITY PRESS
The Edinburgh Building, Cambridge, CB2 2RU, UK http://www.cup.org
10 Stamford Road, Oakleigh, Melbourne 3166, Australia

First published 1999

Printed in the United Kingdom at the University Press, Cambridge

Typeset in Bembo 10/13 pt [VN]

A catalogue record for this book is available from the British Library

Library of Congress Cataloguing in Publication data

Astington, John
  English court theatre, 1558–1642 / John H. Astington.
    p.   cm.
  Includes bibliographical references and index.
  ISBN 0 521 64065 2 (hardback)
    1. Theatre – England – History – 16th century. 2. Theatre – England – History –
  17th century. 3. Theatres – England – History – 16th century. 4. Theatres – England –
  History – 17th century. 5. Great Britain – Court and courtiers – History – 16th
  century. 6. Great Britain – Court and courtiers – History – 17th century. I. Title.
    PN2590.C66A88 1999
    792'.0942'09031 – dc21
  98-39968 CIP

ISBN 0 521 640652 hardback

To the memory of my parents

Contents

Illustrations and acknowledgements

Acknowledgements

Permission for the reproduction of photographs has been kindly granted by the
Cambridge University Library (Map), Courtauld Institute of Art (1, 7 and 18),
Mr R. J. G. Berkeley, Berkeley Castle (1), The Royal Collection © Her Majesty
Queen Elizabeth II (2 and 11), The British Library (3, 10, 12, 14, 15, 17, 19), The
College of Arms (4 and 5), The British Architectural Library (6), The Provost
and Fellows of Worcester College, Oxford (7), The British Museum (8, 13, 16
and 20), The Ashmolean Museum, Oxford (9), The Duke of Devonshire and the
Chatsworth Settlement Trustees (18), and the Victoria and Albert Picture
Library (21).

Preface

This book grew out of studies begun many years ago; it was first proposed in something resembling its present shape at the close of the 1980s, and I can only thank those who have encouraged me to persevere with it for their patience when it must have seemed unlikely that these pages would ever materialise. I have incurred many debts during its slow progress, and I have particularly benefited from a great deal of excellent scholarship on the English court which has been published during the 1990s, and which has made my task, eventually, easier to complete.

While I was a student my curiosity concerning the performance conditions of early plays was satisfied by many lively and stimulating books about the Elizabethan and Stuart actors and their playhouses, but I found it difficult to understand the place of theatre at court. On the one hand, one was told that the connection between the court and theatrical activity elsewhere was of great significance, while on the other there seemed to be no satisfying and coherent account of the conditions of court theatre itself, beyond the rather special and restricted area of masque performance. While I have taught drama and theatre history for the last twenty-five years this odd gap has remained, and it is as an attempt to fill it that this book has been written.

My indebtedness to other scholars and researchers over a long period is so great that it would be tedious and probably impossible to acknowledge with individual thanks, but I would like particularly to express my gratitude to colleagues in the annual theatre-history seminars of the Shakespeare Association of America, who have winnowed a good deal of the material which now appears in this book. I am grateful for financial support during the preparation of the work from the Social Sciences and Humanities Research Council of Canada, from the Folger Shakespeare Library in the form of a Fellowship, and from the

University of Toronto, in research leave and grants. Sarah Stanton has been a wise and consistently encouraging editor, and I am very grateful for her guidance. My wife and daughters, whose love and forbearance I have severely tested over the course of this study, have repaid me beyond my own deserving and my power to thank, other than through this simple record.

Abbreviations

Ceremonies	Albert J. Loomie, ed., *Ceremonies of Charles I. The Notebooks of John Finet 1628–1641* (New York, 1987)
CSPV	*Calendar of State Papers, Venetian, 40 vols. (London, 1864–1947)*
Diary	V. Sackville-West, ed., *The Diary of Lady Ann Clifford* (London, 1923)
ES	E. K. Chambers, *The Elizabethan Stage*, 4 vols. (Oxford, 1923)
Feuillerat, *Edward and Mary*	Albert Feuillerat, *Documents Relating to the Revels at Court in the Time of King Edward VI and Queen Mary* (Louvain, 1914)
Feuillerat, *Elizabeth*	Albert Feuillerat, *Documents Relating to the Office of the Revels in the Time of Queen Elizabeth* (Louvain, 1908)
Henry VIII	David Starkey, ed., *Henry VIII. A European Court in England* (London, 1991)
Herbert	N. W. Bawcutt, ed., *The Control and Censorship of Caroline Drama. The Records of Sir Henry Herbert, Master of the Revels 1623–73* (Oxford, 1996)
HKW	H. M. Colvin, gen. ed., *The History of the King's Works*, 6 vols. (London, 1963–82)
JCS	G. E. Bentley, *The Jacobean and Caroline Stage*, 7 vols. (Oxford, 1941–68)

MSC	Malone Society *Collections* series (see Bibliography for details of individual volumes)
O & S	Stephen Orgel and Roy Strong, eds., *Inigo Jones. The Theatre of the Stuart Court*, 2 vols. (Berkeley and London, 1973)
PRO	Public Record Office
Thurley, *Palaces*	Simon Thurley, *The Royal Palaces of Tudor England* (New Haven, 1993)
WS	E. K. Chambers, *William Shakespeare. A Study of Facts and Problems*, 2 vols. (Oxford, 1930)

Introduction

Then did the worthies of that famous Age,
Make me the constant, the continued stage
Where they did act their Revels, Mirth, and Sport,
Being the harmlesse Genii of the Court
Henry Glapthorne, 'White-Hall, A Poem', (London 1643)

The English court under the Tudors and Stuarts was a political and administrative institution which retained the mobile character of medieval kingship. The court was simultaneously the monarch's residence, the centre of national administration and of communication with foreign powers, but – remarkably to a modern understanding of how a state fulfils these functions – it was not necessarily fixed in any one place. As the king or queen moved from Whitehall to Greenwich, or to any of the other royal houses around London (see map), the central executive government moved also. The institution of the court carried on its business in a variety of royal palaces in and about London, and indeed elsewhere if need arose; the monarch's residence was the physical focus for the administrative functions of the chief nobility and their servants. The court represented an impressive concentration of governmental, administrative and legal power, civil and military, domestic and foreign, but it also continued to be the place where the reigning monarch carried on his or her everyday life, with its mundane functions of eating, sleeping and keeping clean. The court was therefore simultaneously a public and a private place: the rituals which arose around the boundaries between the public and the private mark out the history of much court ceremonial and etiquette. The English court at the close of the sixteenth century has been compared in size and character to 'a luxury hotel', with up to 700 'guests' and roughly 1,000 staff members, but since these people moved from one palace to another through the course of the year it was also 'a hotel on

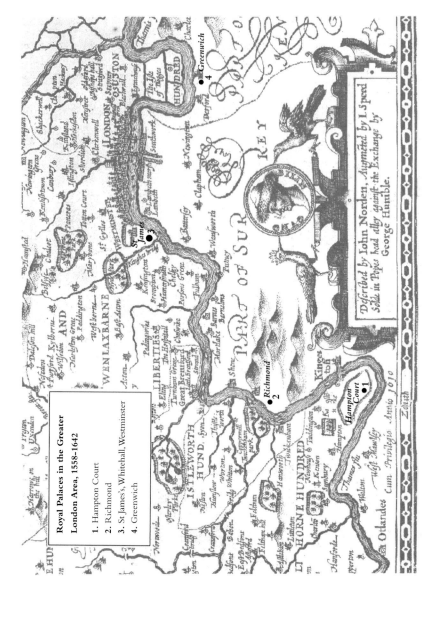

Royal Palaces in the Greater London Area, 1558–1642

1. Hampton Court
2. Richmond
3. St James's, Whitehall, Westminster
4. Greenwich

Court locations, based on John Speed, c. 1610.

wheels'.[1] The strain of living in public must partly lie behind the various stories of Queen Elizabeth's irascibility, and equally behind those of King James's similarly short temper, as well as of other indiscretions – at least as his reporters have it – on public occasions. The crisis over governmental rule from the court, a complex descendant of a far simpler medieval original, came in the 1640s, but the tensions had been felt for many years before that.

James may have been impatient with the constant pressures of such a life, and he certainly sought relief from the administrative demands of a court that was increasingly based at Whitehall by taking off to relatively remote corners of south-eastern England for hunting trips. Equally, however, he was consciously proud of his position, and in the book of royal statecraft written for his son Henry, *Basilikon Doron*, he restated what, in the context of the present study, is one of the most interesting contemporary commonplaces about the monarch's function in the court: 'A King is as one set on a stage, whose smallest actions and gestures, all the people gazingly do behold.'[2] The court as a kind of theatre, in which the serious business of civil order, prosperity, national interest, and state power is symbolised by rituals involving the enthroned monarch, rituals which, if not exactly open to public view, were at least an impressive show to which those involved might feel privileged to be admitted–all this was familiar to Shakespeare, and makes itself apparent in his plays.

Whatever James and Charles might have claimed, government was not centred in the king alone, but the king or queen alone symbolised its authority, and, wherever the monarch appeared at gatherings involving more than his or her personal attendants and close advisors, national and frequently international prestige were involved. So, from a relatively early date, the monarch's 'pastime' – the recreational events which were meant to relieve the stresses of governing the commonwealth – potentially provided occasions of political significance. The assembly of the whole court – the chief representatives of the English nobility, and hence of the executive government – let alone foreign ambassadors and visiting notables, at performances of plays, masques, ballets, and concerts naturally lent such occasions a hierarchical meaning. The presence of the enthroned monarch in the audience complicated the relationships between the observers and the performers; various literary manifestations in the texts of some plays and, markedly, of masques bear witness to the complex theatricality which would have been in the air at all court shows. Even hunting, into which Henry VIII and James threw themselves with personal athletic gusto, could be turned into a ceremonial occasion to symbolise the power of the monarch and his or her munificence. Large companies still flatter senior executives or important customers with rituals of fishing and shooting which retain associations of privilege, as having been the pursuits of the moneyed Edwardian gentry. The intent is the same as it was in Elizabethan or Tudor times: to signal status, and to confer prestige on those with whom it is shared.

Certain other court ceremonies were far more accessible to a wide and general public. Processions through the public streets in times of progress, royal marriages, funerals, and coronations, were so; but also the annual Accession Day tilts at Whitehall under Elizabeth, with their elaborate pageants, speeches, and armorial trappings as accompaniment to the contests themselves, all mounted in a large arena, must have done much to widen the apprehension of the splendour and rather self-conscious romance of the court.[3]

The importance of 'magnificence' – the conspicuous and self-advertising display of wealth and cultural sophistication – was well understood by the founder of the Tudor dynasty, Henry VII. While his political intent seems partly to have been to signal a continuity and conformity with the late-medieval monarchs he succeeded, and hence to legitimise his rather tenuous claim to the throne, his cultural taste included new continental influences, and signified the cosmopolitan power of an England which depended for a good deal of its wealth on trade with northern Europe. Henry's great new palace of Richmond, an ambitious and splendid architectural undertaking, appears to have been designed on French models, while the cultural sophistication of the Burgundian rulers and their entourage seems to have underlain Henry's patronage of artists and craftsmen, and the pageants and ceremonial shows of his court.[4] His son Henry entered with vigour into the role of munificent patron as well as that of skilled participant in the fashionably noble accomplishments of horsemanship, fighting, dancing, and music. Henry VIII was by far the most ambitious builder of all the Tudor and Stuart monarchs, aided by the money and estates of dissolved monastic establishments, and the acquisition and expansion of two large palaces taken over from Cardinal Wolsey: Hampton Court and Whitehall. Henry also largely rebuilt the palace at Greenwich, erected the fantastic and elaborate Nonsuch, and added enormously to royal property generally. His aggressive foreign policy, not particularly effective in terms of successful warfare, was accompanied by grandly elaborate, and what one can only call theatrical, displays of diplomacy, proclaiming the king and his national power in heraldic splendour.

Following the short reigns of his children Edward and Mary, the long rule of his second daughter, Elizabeth, established the fame and prestige of the English monarch on an unprecedented scale. Although never able to be as free with money as her father had been, Elizabeth maintained a court which lacked nothing in expansive magnificence when she chose to display it, and her followers and supporters carefully fostered images of their ruler which emphasised her power and almost mystical authority, perhaps to compensate for the usual symbols of personal military prowess commonly assigned to male leaders. Good fortune and good government strengthened the political and economic power of the kingdom during her reign to such an extent that, in the seventeenth century, under the Stuart rulers James I and Charles I, the English court had become a major centre of European diplomacy. As a leading Protestant power, England had a considerable role in international politics, and James, committed to peace though he was, enjoyed his position as something of a broker between the major Catholic powers of France and Spain. Conscious of their European significance, both Stuart monarchs cultivated a personal style and a court taste which were more internationally fashionable. The renaissance in graphic art and architecture in particular was finally acknowledged and absorbed into English culture during their reigns; their foreign queens, Danish and French, successively, helped broaden the sophistication of taste of the Stuart courts.

Patronage of the arts was therefore part of a quite deliberate programme of royal propaganda, and those arts which advertised royal magnificence more obliquely, or were less utilitarian, were less favoured. Henry VIII's building programme was directed as much to defensive fortification as it was to splendour, and even the style he favoured for his palaces has more than a hint of the castle about it; he was as interested in securing the services of foreign armourers, gunnery experts, miners, and other technicians as he was those of the distinguished foreign painters and craftsmen who decorated his chambers. Patronage of writers and scholars by the crown at any point between 1485 and the 1640s, could at best be called nominal and occasional. Musicians fared somewhat better, as the need to maintain royal choirs at Windsor and Greenwich provided a number of official posts which were filled by a succession of distinguished composers and performers; instrumentalists were also maintained by the monarch to provide suitable music at feasts and dances. The post of Sergeant Painter – which was certainly filled by accomplished portraitists – seems on the whole to have leant more to the utilitarian pole, certainly under the Tudors, and as late as the Restoration the post is described in terms of a series of applied tasks the incumbent is expected to fulfill, more or less as a superior interior and exterior decorator.

It is in this context of 'tied' patronage that we must consider the theatrical arts at the Tudor and Stuart courts. Dramatic shows, of various kinds, evidently provided the kind of splendid advertisement of cultural sophistication that monarchs wished to foster, apart from having a strong appeal for their own sake. Kings and queens themselves performed: Henry VIII in costumed 'masks', Queen Anne as a dancer in Jonson's masques, Queen Henrietta Maria and her ladies in French (and English) plays, as well as dancing, with her consort, in the masques. The future Charles II danced before his parents as 'Prince Britomart' in a masque at Richmond in 1636. These 'amateur theatricals' of royal and noble enthusiasts may be firmly distinguished from the professional theatre which the court patronised when plays were brought to the palaces by the commercial companies. To a degree these extremes met in the masques, which involved some professionals as coaches and in speaking parts, but dramatic entertainments at all levels of skill and finish were presented at court in the same places before similar audiences. Plays and masques were shown in the same court rooms, and in the earlier Tudor years they shared costumes, properties, and scenery.

Otherwise, the court maintained an arm's-length relationship with professional actors, whose activities underwent such a remarkable change between the accession of Henry VII in 1485 and the opening of the Rose playhouse just over a century later. Henry maintained his own troupe of actors, about whose activities we know very little. When Elizabeth gave order in 1583 for an acting troupe to be formed under her name, bringing together the most famous and accomplished performers in London, she evidently did not expect them to be resident at court as exclusively royal entertainers, and they probably received very little as direct emoluments from their title apart from their livery, the clothes in scarlet cloth which would designate them to be servants of the queen. The Queen's Men continued to act commercially in London and throughout the country; while more prominent, their career is similar to those of the numerous troupes who bore the names of leading noblemen. The function of a nominal patronage which served as official protection for the commercial career of actors has often been commented on in histories of the development of the Elizabethan theatre, and the troupes which bore royal names, as all major companies did after 1603, were no different in any essential respect from those patronised by the nobility.[5]

The licences or letters patent which the acting troupes carried with them stated that their professional career, the exercise of their quality, was in fact practice, in order that they would be ready to entertain the king or queen when so required. Royal performances, therefore, though they were relatively infrequent events in the company's annual activities, had a particularly important place in its well-being. Aside from that, performance at court was a sign of favour and prominence, frequently touted on the title-pages of published plays, for example, and was well rewarded financially. The court has traditionally been viewed as one of the major supports of the professional stage, despite the very oblique relationship that obtained between theatre artists and their patrons.

Because of the social nature of theatre, plays were particularly a feature of the royal calendar in feast seasons, when the court was full, and given over to celebration. The old festivals of Christmas, celebrated over the full twelve days between Christmas Day and Epiphany, and the two or three days of Shrovetide, the festival preceding Lent, remained the particular times of year at which plays were seen, although increasingly under the Stuarts plays were commissioned throughout the year. The association of theatre with feasting, dancing, and other communal celebration is interesting in itself, but the demand for the actors also corresponded with their own professional season: it was in the period between the autumn and the early summer that playing in the London theatres was most usually carried on.

My aim in this study is to concentrate attention on the physical and aesthetic conditions under which actors worked when they performed at the Tudor and Stuart courts. What was the relationship between the stages on which actors performed in their playhouses and other regular playing venues, and those built for them in the temporary theatres which were made in court halls and chambers? How, if at all, were playing and staging adapted to such conditions? How did the stages for professional plays – *Much Ado About Nothing*, *Othello*, *King Lear* – differ from those built for masques? In attempting to recreate these important early performances in our imaginations there are many matters about which we need guidance. Modern readers can consult numerous excellent books about conditions in the contemporary playhouses, but it remains more difficult to understand the 'theatres' in which the English monarchs and the leading nobility saw many of the plays which interest us today. By contrast with the now-vanished playhouses, however, four of the royal chambers used as theatres in the sixteenth and seventeenth centuries survive, and can still be visited. In the chapters which follow I will attempt to draw as full a picture as I can of such places, and of the conditions within them during the years when audiences watched plays and masques there. As in most areas of theatre history in this period there are probably more questions than available historical information can reliably answer, but I shall attempt to indicate the boundaries of reliability in any of my own answers. We must begin with some understanding of the organisation of the court, then of the external influences which might bear on court performances, before passing to the actual wood, paint, canvas, and candlelight of the stages within the royal palaces.

1 The royal administration

Where is our usual manager of mirth?
What revels are in hand? Is there no play
To ease the anguish of a torturing hour?
Call Philostrate.

William Shakespeare, *A Midsummer Night's Dream*, 5.1.35–38 (London, 1600)

In order to understand the functioning of the court under Elizabeth, James, and Charles, one must grapple with the historical accretions of administration which had grown from a far simpler medieval system. The conservative and traditional instincts of monarchs and civil servants had retained titles and divisions of influence and responsibility from previous centuries, but changes in the practices of rule and in physical living arrangements, and chiefly the enormous expansion of the court as an administrative centre in the 1500s and 1600s, resulted in often eccentric and Byzantine methods of organisation, at least to modern eyes.[1]

Much of what we know of the details of court life in the sixteenth and seventeenth centuries comes from records of expenditure, preserved in the Office of the Exchequer. The head of each administrative subdivision of the royal household completed a variously detailed annual account, making claim on royal funds for money laid out and detailing the defrayment of cash advances. These surviving records provide many instances of outlay on dramatic activities. Two departments in particular were involved in theatrical activities at court: the Office of the Revels, which, after its beginnings under the early Tudor kings, grew into a full-scale production team, subsequently being reduced to a rather less expensive operation; and the Office of the Works, a major royal department charged with building and maintenance on a very wide scale, among the responsibilities of which was the provision of stages and seating for plays. The papers of the Office of the Wardrobe, which supplied cloth and furnishings for all kinds of state occasions, might also be expected to provide information pertinent to theatrical events, but, although the Wardrobe certainly was crucial to court plays and masques, its accounts for the period considered in this book are disappointingly meagre, providing only general summations of annual activities, with tantalisingly more detailed information on occasion.[2] Other records pertinent to theatre occur in the accounts of the Treasurer of the Chamber, historically the department of the royal household which dealt with costs connected with the monarch's immediate environment, and which was presided over by the Lord Chamberlain.

In fact 'the Chamber' is a more or less specific term, depending on how it is applied. Originally it represented one part of the binary division between the private and public lives of the monarch: the Chamberlain administered the king's chamber, where the king slept, ate, and conducted business. The more public side of the court, centred in the hall, included all the supporting offices of kitchens, workshops, stables, and so forth, and was administered by the Lord Steward or the Master of the Household, which is what this part of the court, again rather confusingly, could be called, since the whole royal entourage was also known as the household. The word 'household' could therefore also be applied generally and loosely, or specifically to refer to a particular administrative division with particular areas of responsibility. The more complex courts of Tudor and Stuart times had introduced architectural divisions, as we shall see, between chamber and household, which might be reflected in the still understandable division between the household above stairs and the household below stairs: the monarchs lived on upper floors, with service buildings at ground level. A third division, between purely domestic offices and the stables, was reflected in the Tudor post of Master of the Horse, although this had become more of an honorific title than a practical responsibility by Queen Elizabeth's reign.

To return to the Chamber, the Elizabethan and Stuart Lords Chamberlain presided over a very large number of administrative departments, some of which seem to have little to do with personal attendance on the monarch. Certain of these departments or offices had grown so large, and had such enormous responsibilities, that they had moved 'out of court', having their centres of operation either in other buildings under royal control–the Wardrobe and the Revels in Blackfriars (a confiscated conventual building), or, later, the Revels alone at St John's Priory, Clerkenwell (another such property)–or at a series of dispersed locations–the Works with a depot at the Tower of London, a storehouse in Scotland Yard, and workmen and equipment constantly on the move from place to place. 'The Chamber' is further complicated by the distinction which had gradually developed in topographical subdivisions of the royal living space, in the terms of which the Privy Chamber, to which access was restricted to the monarch's immediate attendants and intimates, was distinguished from the more public rooms in the royal suite, the first and largest of which was known either as the Great, or the Guard, Chamber. Under a female monarch, the attendants of the Privy Chamber were women, so that the honorific titles of the traditionally male attendants of the medieval kings were further ritualised. Recent historians of the court have argued that the intimacy and influence which admission to the Privy Chamber carried with it were important factors in the political life of the court, and political life certainly was one of the chief characteristics of the court as an institution; more will be said in a subsequent chapter on how this influenced entertainment.

Although access to the monarch's personal rooms might carry with it status and power, as it certainly did under James,[3] the official centre of administrative power under the king or queen was the Privy Council. In English palaces the Council Chamber was usually contiguous to the suite of the royal residence and audience chambers; chief officers of the royal administration and high-ranking intimates of the monarch made up the group that met there.

The Lords Chamberlain therefore had jurisdiction over chambers which were remarkably concentrated centres of power. The various royal palaces contained very little space in which the monarch could be absolutely private, which is perhaps one reason why James was given to retreating to rural hunting lodges. The complex enterprise of Tudor and Stuart government involved constant comings and goings of important people through the rooms and connecting corridors of the royal suite. The organisation and regulation of this traffic was the responsibility of the Lord Chamberlain, but he evidently relied on deputies: on the Master of the Guard, on his peers as hosts and guides of important foreign guests, and in the Stuart years on the Master of Ceremonies, a post established by James.

The ceremonial aspects of many royal events were also the business of the Heralds, who ensured that the pageantry and punctilio were suitably impressive, and in line with ancient precedent. The various ceremonial processions of the annual royal calendar—on St George's Day, or Maundy Thursday, for example—fell within their area of supervision, as did occasional events: the funerals of royalty and important nobility, marriages, christenings, and coronations. Even when such royal ceremonies did not move through the public streets, as they frequently did when King Street itself—modern Whitehall, which ran through the heart of the principal English palace—was a public thoroughfare, their function within the confines of the palace buildings was also to show off the king's or queen's magnificence and power, and they were watched by privileged selected observers who formed an audience.

Display and observation were constant features of court life, and they equally governed royal entertainments, to which monarchs came to watch a display or exhibition of some kind: war games, bearbaiting, or a play. Dramatic entertainment evidently varied in the degree to which it was public, and hence to which it was a formal occasion at which the etiquette of seating by rank and favour was of particular importance. From fairly early in the Jacobean period, players performed not only before the king in halls and great chambers at the traditionally important feasts of Christmas and Shrovetide, but also in smaller places to more select groups—the entourage and guests of the royal children, for example. As we shall see, by the 1630s there was a considerable variation in the size of the various places in which court dramatic entertainments were presented, and hence a corresponding range in their formality.

The court officer originally charged with the management of plays and similar shows was the Master of the Revels. The post had been created by Henry VIII, and, although the responsibilities of the job changed over the following hundred years or so, the Master remained a deputy of and responsible to the Lord Chamberlain, who therefore had some say in the appointment when it changed hands. During the rather less than a century between the accession of Queen Elizabeth and the Civil War, the post actually changed hands very little. The two principal incumbents of the mastership during the queen's reign were Sir Thomas Benger and Edmund Tilney, and the chief appointments by the Stuarts were those of Sir George Buc and Sir Henry Herbert.[4]

The substantial change in the post was from what one might call in modern terms a production co-ordinator to a licenser and censor of acted and published dramatic texts, with a consequent shift in the focus of the job from being principally within the court to principally outside it. The change, it has been argued, grew out of the success of the Office in promoting production standards: stimulated by court patronage, the London acting companies grew in size and sophistication, while a freeze on the extravagances of the court's budget correspondingly required the Master to look to the actors themselves for suitable costumes and settings, which in the earlier period had been provided either from the Revels store or by building them specially for a given occasion.[5] The surviving documents from the Revels Office show that the Master and his hired workmen were heavily involved in 'theatre business' only until the time that we have traditionally thought of as the beginning of the London professional theatre: the decade between the mid 1570s and the mid 1580s.

The success of commercial theatrical enterprise in those years, under the patronage of leading court nobles and, after 1583, of the queen herself, entailed the fading away of the Revels Office as an artistic centre. Such a story is certainly borne out by the records of expenditure, which are both more extensive and more carefully and intriguingly described in the years before the 1580s; certainly the Office appears to have stopped producing costumes, properties, and settings thereafter. Yet the production functions did not altogether disappear, and the costume store appears to have been maintained for some time. The Revels Office remained responsible for the selection and approval of plays for court performance, and retained primary responsibility for lighting at court shows, for example, as well as for some other aspects of the physical mounting of plays; and chiefly of plays, since the famous Stuart masques were from the start such expensive enterprises that they were not handled through the Revels budget.

These changes affected the physical accommodation the Revels Office enjoyed. The centre of the operation always remained in or near the city of London, rather than in any of the palace precincts. Hence one constant budget item in the accounts was for the cost of transport, by waggon and barge, of the 'Revels Stuff', as it was commonly called, to the palaces where it was needed. To move a large boatful of theatrical gear to Greenwich, for example, would probably have involved transporting it first by waggonloads through the London streets to the wharf at the Tower, downstream of London Bridge, which was a particular obstacle, especially on an ebbing tide, to any but small craft. From there the loaded boat would be sailed or rowed to the wharf at Greenwich palace, to be unpacked there and carried to where it was to be set up for the play. To move equipment in the opposite direction, to Hampton Court, either by road or water, would have involved a lengthy journey. The constant handling the Revels gear sustained would have had consequences for its durability, so that even in the later more quiescent years the Office would have had to employ workmen to repair or replace its equipment.

Apart from the Master's own living space–an element of his income and therefore to be jealously defended–the Office in its most expansive phase of operations needed a considerable area for the making and storing of costumes, properties, and scenery. Various kinds of scenic elements of the larger kind were finished and painted in the place where they were to be used, but they were planned and framed up in the Revels workrooms, and moved from there as described above. Once the production functions of the Office were reduced, it had a less pressing claim on space, although the Master retained the important function of reviewing plays for court performance, and he did so by summoning the actors to present their work before him, rather than visiting the playhouses himself. King Claudius asks Polonius if he has 'heard the argument' of the play presented in act 3 of *Hamlet*; the Lord Chamberlain's deputy was responsible for avoiding scurrility and political embarrassment in the English court. Since, from 1581 onwards, one of the Master's tasks had become to read and license all new plays for performance, when the actors visited him to show their suggested plays for the court he would not have been interested so much in hearing the play as in seeing it. The actors are more likely to have given a full performance with costumes and properties than a seated reading. The Revels Office property was also a rehearsal hall, then, large enough to approximate to the stage space either of the theatres or of the temporary stages in court rooms.

At the very beginning of Queen Elizabeth's reign the Revels Office was based in the Blackfriars, the complex of former conventual buildings which also accommodated two distinct theatres between 1576 and 1642, but it was moved in 1560 to a similar property on the north-west edge of the city of London, in Clerkenwell, north of Smithfield: the Priory of St John of Jerusalem, the gatehouse to which still stands. The Office remained here until the early Jacobean period, for a period of almost fifty years. After 1608 the physical facilities of the Office were never settled for so long in one space, nor perhaps with such convenience as they had enjoyed at St John's. There are very few references to the later premises having been used for the traditional functions of storage, workshops, and rehearsal rooms. Briefly, the Office was located in Whitefriars, south of Fleet Street (another theatre district), then once more in the city, between St Paul's and the river, and it made at least one more move within the city, into Cheapside ward, before the 1640s.

For the entirety of the three reigns the Office was consistently within easy reach of Whitehall and St James's palaces, but also of central London, never being sited more than three-quarters of a mile from St Paul's, and never located with the Office of the Works in either the Tower or Scotland Yard. The reasons for this metropolitan focus undoubtedly varied over time, but the central rationale must have been the need to communicate with the actors. Although the Revels staff had to travel and transport equipment to stage royal shows at Greenwich, Richmond, Windsor, Hampton Court, and other places, the central business of the office was evidently seen as being connected to the professional theatre, based in London. St John's lay close to the playhouses on the northern side of the city – the Theatre, the Curtain, and eventually the Fortune – while the subsequent sites of the Office lay at the centre of the circle formed by the seventeenth-century playhouses. As the Master became licenser of plays for publication, as well as for performance, his accessibility to Stuart publishers, most of whom worked within the city limits, also became a matter of importance.

Originally, however, the Revels Office must have located itself within the city precincts for the same reasons as did the royal Wardrobe: direct access to suppliers of cloth and other primary materials, and also to a pool of skilled labour–tailors, basket-weavers, painters, carvers, workers in wood and metal, and a host of other trades relevant to the preparation of costumes, scenery, and properties. As a patron of the furnishing and decorative trades, the Revels Office lapsed in importance after the 1570s, but its year-round business remained part of the cultural life of London rather than of Whitehall. Its officers and representatives travelled from the city as and when they were required. The Revels supervised and managed touring shows, in modern terms, and like a modern management they were based in the centre of theatrical activity. To take the modern analogy a little farther, while the Revels was a government department, some of its employees were involved in private theatrical ventures. The chief example is Edward Kirkham, Yeoman of the Revels between the 1580s and 1616, and entrepreneur of the children's companies at Blackfriars and at St Paul's in the early seventeenth century.[6] Equally, certain theatre people aspired to the security of the royal payroll, John Lyly and Ben Jonson chief amongst them.

Such a metropolitan focus for the Office rendered local arrangements, when a play was to be performed for the monarch at Greenwich or Richmond, of particular importance. The Revels Office staff arrived immediately before the show, to set up scenery, tiring house, and lighting, but they did not ever, even in their most expansive phase of existence, carry out all the physical preparation required. 'Making ready', as it is frequently called in contemporary documents, was carried out by the staff of the Chamber, with their ranks of ushers, grooms, and porters, who prepared royal apartments for any use. Cleaning and airing, and heating in the winter months, were presumably an important part of any 'making ready'; 'apparelling', the other recurrent word connected with preparations for plays, involved the decorating of the room in question with wall hangings, carpets, and upholstered seats, all of which were kept in storage when rooms were not in regular use. Since certain of these materials may have been under the official custody of the Wardrobe, yet another administrative area of the royal household would have been involved in the collaborative operation.

From early in the career of the Revels Office, however, a good deal of the labour and building required for mounting plays and similar entertainment was provided by the Office of the Works.[7] The actual division of labour, very roughly, appears to have been that the Works built auditorium seating and the basic stage structure, and, apart from their responsibilities for costuming, the Revels hung lights, built stage decorations, tiring houses, and music houses, and looked after backstage requirements. There evidently were many grey, overlapping areas in such preparation, however; certain specialised workmen turn up on the payroll of different royal departments, for example. Equally there would have been a compelling need for one managerial co-ordinator to oversee the whole job. The work of straining overhead wires and hanging chandeliers, for example, the habitual manner of providing lighting in court chambers for plays, should evidently have been done before expensive tapestries were hung in the room below, but we do not know who may have supervised the sequence of work.

The Office of the Works was a large department with a broad range of responsibilities, from the design and building of new structures, through running repairs to roofs and plumbing, to decorative art.[8] It was headed by a Surveyor, rather than a Master, and from 1615 the incumbent was Inigo Jones, the great neoclassical architect and chief designer for the Stuart court masques. The Works had depots and storage yards in the central metropolitan area, a regular staff of supervisors of all its operations, some of whom were resident at the more removed palaces, and, like the Revels Office of the mid sixteenth century, a large group of journeyman workmen hired for specific jobs. Among these, the carpenters were central to preparations for entertainments. The major task, whenever plays were performed in larger chambers, was to build rising ranks of seating around the perimeter; a framework of heavy timber scaffolding, braced against the walls, supported planks for steps and benches, and the assembly and subsequent demolition of these structures required many days of work from a team of carpenters. To build a stage for the actors must have been a relatively simple operation when compared to the heavy work of assembling the 'degrees', which had to be capable of withstanding both a good deal of dead weight, in the form of a seated audience, and the stress of movement as that audience assembled and dispersed, and hence would have to have been correspondingly massive and firmly built. Similar structures today, in studio theatres and gymnasia, are supported on metal frames; their Tudor and Stuart ancestors, built only of wood, would have been heavier in weight and appearance.

Decoration of temporary 'theatres' of this kind would largely have been done in a temporary fashion–that is, with hangings and tapestries–but a certain amount of painting would also have been undertaken. The Sergeant Painter and his staff of assistants were paid by the Works for decorative jobs of various kinds, but in the earlier years they were also paid by the Revels, for work in preparation for plays and entertainments. The sparser accounts of the Revels Office in the Stuart years need not suggest that painted decorations–of the stage and tiring house in particular–were no longer carried out, but simply that the responsibility for such work had been taken over by the Office of the Works. Compared with their immediate Tudor predecessor, both Stuart kings spent fairly freely on building operations and on art patronage, and it seems unlikely that the decoration of court theatres would have been skimped, in either effect or expense.

In the larger court hierarchy, the Master of the Revels was not a particularly significant figure, and after the 1580s the Office itself had a relatively modest turnover, and a small number of regular employees.[9] Those leading nobles who patronised the Elizabethan theatre companies and hence, in the case of the two best-known groups of players, gave their court titles to the Lord Chamberlain's Men and the Lord Admiral's Men, were, by contrast, of the very highest élite, both by birth and by appointment to the Privy Council. All sixteenth- and seventeenth-century court functionaries expected to derive income from their positions, but there was a considerable difference in personal wealth between those holding the very highest and the lowest posts, and hence a difference in expectation about the support which might be offered by a given job. The two dramatists who aspired to the Mastership of the Revels, John Lyly and Ben Jonson, no doubt expected the post to provide both money and status; if someone of origins as humble as those of Inigo Jones could rise to be Surveyor of the Works, Jonson is likely to have reasoned, his own fame as a writer and his favour with the royal family would fit him to head the Revels Office. In fact, the post was always held by members of the minor nobility or gentry, a characteristic which was perhaps enhanced by the general movement away from the Office's responsibilities for theatrical production and a considerable expansion of the Master's role in licensing and censorship, where social rank might reinforce authority.

The chief part of the income that might have been expected by a Master of the Revels in later Elizabethan years came from fees paid by the actors for licensing plays–a proportionate tax on the entertainment industry, but which was entirely at the Master's disposal. Otherwise the Master's annual fee from the crown was a derisory £10–exactly that of a lowly Page of the Bedchamber–although he also drew an allowance for housing and living costs, and was paid for each day of attendance at court.[10] Shrewd Masters, therefore, would soon have realised that their bread was buttered on both sides: part of their job was to control and administer theatrical activity, but they would prosper in direct proportion to the success of the players. Over the period between Queen Elizabeth's accession and King Charles's suspension of his London court the Master's original function, as chief organiser of court entertainment, dwindled to become a lesser part of his responsibilities, while the greater part of his time came to be given over to the tasks that generated the greater part of his revenue: the reading and licensing of plays for performance.[11]

By the end of the period we are considering, then, major parts of the Master's function went on outside the court, and had no essential connection with the rest of the Revels operation, and to that extent, despite his title, the Master of the Revels became rather tangential to the activity surveyed in this book. Much recent scholarly and critical attention has been focussed on the Master's activity—and on his power—as a licenser of the stage, and I am not going to rehearse that here. The staff of the Revels Office itself, however, continued to fulfil their long-established function as a production unit, although, by 1640, evidently far reduced in the extent of their operations, compared to their activity in 1558.[12] The very survival of the Revels Office is something of an anomaly, since its function after the 1580s could easily have been absorbed by the Works and the Wardrobe, offices which were otherwise involved in preparations for court entertainments; however, since the radical step of elimination was not taken at the time when the Elizabethan Lord Treasurer, Burghley, undertook serious cost-cutting and reform in the departments of the crown, the Revels Office survived on the basis of precedence and bureaucratic self-defence thereafter. Although the Master's duties now lay largely outside their origins in the ordering of court revels, the staff of the Office itself undoubtedly regarded him as their chief advocate and defender, and, in his access to influential people, a guarantor of their otherwise irrational survival. In this respect it was important that he be a courtier, and hence of a certain social rank. The Master also continued to be involved in his traditional job of selecting and preparing plays for court performance, present at 'Rehersalls, and making choice of playes, and Comodyes, and reforminge them' as an account of 1627 has it,[13] then attending to oversee matters on performance nights.

Although court revels could no doubt have gone on quite efficiently without a Revels Office therefore, as matters were organised during the period considered here the character and talents of individual Masters could have important consequences for the conduct of the Office as a whole. At the start of Queen Elizabeth's reign the incumbent Master was Sir Thomas Cawarden, who began the job in 1545, and therefore served four monarchs. As the last Master of the Revels of King Henry VIII (and the first to be issued with a patent for the post), Cawarden presided over an organisation which maintained close ties with the Office of the Tents, a Revels responsibility that was never wholly abandoned.

The early Tudor Office had wide-ranging duties in supervising and mounting all kinds of celebration and festival–not simply drama–within the court and outside it, particularly in connection with tournaments and military expeditions. The Revels inventories of this earlier period include not only the theatrical costumes which continued to be made and reworked for plays and masks well into the Elizabethan years, but also trappings for horses, for example. The buying, cutting, and sewing of fabric formed the major business of the Revels operation, and the early Tudor Yeoman of the Revels–the chief foreman and supervisor of artisans–tended accordingly to be a master tailor. The development of the Revels Office, it might be said, was historically connected to its function as a producer and a wardrobe store of costumes. Long after its production responsibilities ceased in this respect, the accounts still record the annual cleaning and airing of the costume store, a ritual event without, it seems, much practical application to what the later Tudor and Stuart Office was expected to do in preparing for court shows.

The pragmatic business of cutting out and sewing, supervised by the Yeoman, can hardly have involved the Master, whose rank and status gave him a dignified distance from manual work. Cawarden himself, however, was not so far removed in social rank that he would not have been able to tell good work from bad in the working of cloth. The son of a fuller, he was apprenticed as a mercer, but rose and prospered at Henry VIII's court, apparently as a protégé of Thomas Cromwell.[14] His Mastership of the Revels was one of a number of preferments and rewards he received in the 1540s, and it is unlikely that he was given the job because of his background in the cloth trade, but rather as a sign of favour and as a source of patronage income. The question behind Cawarden's appointment, as well as the appointment of subsequent Masters, is what special qualities the post demanded, since it was clearly not a sinecure. The Master was, in effect, a deputy of the Lord Chamberlain, was responsible for a fairly large budget (in the most expansive years of Revels productions), and his activities advertised the taste and status of his monarch.

Moreover, if the Yeoman was the practical engine of Revels operations, it is fairly clear that the Master was expected to be the theorist. Designs for costumes were produced 'after the Master's device', as accounts frequently put it. In the case of plays, the Master's role was one of selection and approval: he vetted the work of others, and, in the days when the Revels Office supplied acting troupes with costumes for plays at court, the particular demands of a play–its period, setting, genre, characters, and so forth–would have dictated what the costumiers made. The 'masks' however–seasonal costumed processions and dances–were expected to have a theme, and preferably a novel and entertaining one, possibly involving special properties, scenery, and surprising effects. In what sense might we regard the Master of the Revels as a supervising designer, as the Surveyor of the King's Works clearly was? Masters themselves might not be expected to have a detailed expertise in visual design, but they were certainly expected to supervise those that did, and to judge the best work, as they did with plays. To what extent such judgement was unusual, or whether it was regarded as knowledge that any man of a certain social rank might be expected to have or be able to acquire, are questions to which answers cannot easily be returned.

Whatever his artistic attainments, Cawarden set his seal on the Office as an efficient manager, and it was his practices that were extolled in Elizabethan memoranda from the 1570s. He also presided over an active period of Revels Office operations, for which we possess relatively detailed information in the form of account books retained by Cawarden and preserved by his executors.[15] These reveal – in addition to the habitual preparation of costumes – extensive work on scenic devices and spectacular effects. Cawarden presided over a production team which included skilled and sophisticated craftsmen and artists, with whom he was evidently able to communicate in an informed and knowledgeable manner. He was regarded by other members of the court–his peers and superiors–as an expert in translating conceptual outlines into theatrical reality, as he did with a show of Venus, Cupid, and Mars in 1553.[16] Despite some political trouble in Queen Mary's reign, Cawarden seems to have efficiently carried out the task of supervisor of the royal shows, the chief function of the Master of the Revels up to the time of his death. As a man of some social standing and a member of the court he provided the link between commissions for royal entertainments (from the Privy Council, the Lord Chamberlain, and so on), with their explicit or implicit expectations about taste and tone, and the practicalities of sets, properties, and costumes as they could be produced by the Revels Office staff, and by hired and seconded workmen and artists.

He survived to serve Queen Elizabeth for only two years of her long reign, but his influence lingered through his devoted servant Thomas Blagrave, who continued as Clerk of the Revels, and who later acted as Master, in the absence of any official appointment, from 1573 to 1578. Between 1560 and 1572 the Master was Sir Thomas Benger, a former member of Elizabeth's household at Hatfield before her accession, where he was an auditor; hence he was promoted both as a protégé and as a financial manager.[17] We know little about Benger's familiarity with the practices of theatrical production, but he was not successful in restraining the Revels budget, and after his death some hard thought was given to the management of the Revels Office–perhaps to the very need for a Revels Office–in the face of a continuing crisis over royal expenditure. During the middle 1570s–well before the period we usually recognise as the heyday of Elizabethan drama and theatrical activity–Blagrave managed the Office, and produced at least one of three surviving memoranda for the use of the Privy Council in considering its reorganisation.[18]

All these documents probably originated from within the Revels Office itself, and, informed by self-interest, do not make any particularly radical suggestions for improvement: traditional practice governed by wise and thrifty management is the right course to follow, they collectively suggest; the Yeoman's report even calls for more capital investment in repairs to the Revels Office storage and work spaces, which are described as decrepit and cramped. One chief problem, which can hardly have been unique to the Revels, was the practice of long deferrals in the payment of bills and wages, since disbursements by the Exchequer were made only after an annual account had been audited and approved, and the Revels carried an insufficient pool of cash to cover its expenses for the year. The results were artificially inflated prices (anticipated interest charges, as it were) and personal disaffection on the part of creditors and employees alike. As briefs in response to an enquiry the memoranda certainly succeeded in so far as no major organisational change was undertaken in the running of the Revels, but in other ways the concerted reduction of royal expenditure, managed by the new Lord Treasurer, Lord Burghley, gradually shrank the budget and hence the range of activities of the Office, although the full effect of these reductions was not felt until about a decade after the original enquiry.

In 1579 the post of Master of the Revels was conferred on Edmund Tilney, who remained until 1610, becoming the longest-serving Master, presiding over a period of central importance in English theatrical and dramatic history. His tenure saw the reduction in activity of the Office referred to above and a corresponding expansion in the authority of the Master over theatrical activity outside the court, in the course of which he became a deputy as much of the Privy Council as a whole as of the Lord Chamberlain. Tilney's personal background certainly assisted in his appointment–he was related to the Howard family, prominent in Elizabeth's Privy Council–but he was also a serious author, and a man of some learning.[19]

Tilney was presumably informed about the intentions of the central court authorities concerning the financing of royal entertainments; he may indeed have been given some early hint in 1579 about the expanded responsibilities he was to assume in 1581. That new role, however, was to do with the control of public entertainment, and can be said to be the court's response to pressure from magistrates at the local level, especially in London, over the problems of administering players and their business, especially when they could plead that their business was, after a fashion, royal business. The general plan for royal revels themselves was drastically to reduce the budget for production, and consequently to influence the kinds of performance or show that might be presented to the queen. Concurrently it reduced the number of skilled artisans hired by the Revels operation in the making of costumes, properties, and scenery, and some of them perhaps then sold their labour to the growing theatrical market in London.

The chief victim of the new court austerity was the 'mask', a traditional royal entertainment which became prominent, if it did not actually begin, during the reign of King Henry VIII at the start of the century, and which persisted thereafter. Like the more famous Stuart masques, it featured elaborately costumed and disguised amateur participants, music, dancing, and 'entries'–processions which sometimes featured floats or waggons with elaborate spectacular effects. Rich costumes were made in multiple copies, since the maskers were dressed in similar exotic or amusing style, exactly as the 'Muscovites' are in *Love's Labour's Lost*. The making, reworking, and storing of the costumes for the annual masks of Christmas and Shrovetide had been one traditional activity of the Revels Office for three-quarters of the sixteenth century. The rich fabrics used in the costumes and the hours of skilled work spent in their manufacture consumed a large proportion of the Revels expenditure; their storage and cleaning was a persistent concern of the Revels staff.

Whether the choice was taken simply on the basis of economy or whether it was felt that the old form of revel was rather *passé* and stale (as Benvolio in *Romeo and Juliet* feels about the tired old motifs of masked entries (1.4.1–10)), the production of masks disappears from the activity of the Revels after the 1570s, and as they abandoned the production of costumes for masks so they seem to have given up their older practice of providing or supplementing costumes for professional players performing at court.

The first consequence of the new dispensation over which Tilney presided, then, was a new reliance on plays as the chief source of royal entertainment. Masks seem to have been largely 'in-house' creations, as the Stuart masques were; the leading performers were members of the court, whose appearance in elaborate disguise contributed part of the fun of the occasion. Plays, however, were increasingly the business of professionals from outside the court entirely. A good proportion of court plays in earlier periods, that is to say, were staged by members of the royal household–the children or men retained as singers and instrumental musicians in the Chapel Royal, for example–or by amateur performers from schools or the inns of court, but as commercial theatre expanded after the middle of the sixteenth century the actors seen at court, though 'servants' of the chief lords of the realm, were likely to be men who made their living by performing plays to paying audiences in London and the provinces. Although such commercial playing was far more widespread at an earlier date than older historians of the English theatre would have one think,[20] the nature of both the typical play and the typical playing company changed considerably between 1550 and 1600: by the end of this period, larger groups of actors performed longer plays of increased technical and literary complexity.

Accounts of the history of the Revels Office have usually assumed that economies in production expenses were more easily achieved because the production standards of professional troupes had improved; actors in the playhouses spent considerable sums on costuming and otherwise producing the physical requirements of their plays as a matter of course, and hence were well prepared to present a performance before the monarch. However true this may be of the 1570s, it is certainly apparent from the inventories of Philip Henslowe, the prominent Elizabethan theatrical entrepreneur, that, by the end of the century, the leading acting troupes were spending large amounts on both acquiring costumes and retaining extensive stores of costumes, properties, and scenery. If the Revels Office had been established partly to furnish players with suitable gear, it had been superseded by the professional practice of the new Elizabethan theatre.

The increased reliance of the court on entertainment provided by 'common' players is also marked by two public signals of the special relationship between the theatre and the monarch's rule. The first chronologically was the extension of the Master's power in a commission of 1581, which gave him authority 'to order and reforme, autorise and put downe' all plays, players, and playing spaces throughout the realm as he saw fit.[21] All theatrical licensing, in theory, was therefore now in the hands of the crown, and the commission announced to actors and to local authorities alike that their interests could be pursued only with royal assent. The inflammatory and unruly tendencies of theatrical activity certainly required control, but the special status actors enjoyed as purveyors of revels and pastime also required protection against prohibitions and restrictions put in their way by lower levels of authority in the cities, towns, and counties where they worked.

In 1583, as a further sign of the connection between the crown and the theatre, Tilney was charged with establishing a new troupe of players which bore the monarch's name: the Queen's Men. In doing so he chose an 'all star' group of the leading actors of the day, including the famous clown Richard Tarlton and the tragedian John Bentley. Favoured as performers at court for the next decade, the Queen's Men were also something of an arm of propaganda in their performances in London and the provinces, announcing the alliance between royal munificence and theatrical skill, and prominently advertising official approval of players and playing, which the widespread popular affection for Tarlton no doubt helped advance.

A second consequence of a 'thinned-down' operation in the Revels Office was that extraordinary costs which might be incurred on an *ad hoc* basis had to be dealt with by special payments. Particular occasions that the Revels might once have dealt with as a matter of course were paid for increasingly through the budgets of the Works or the Wardrobe, or approval might be given for one-time extensions to Revels budgets. So the entertainments connected with negotiations over a proposed French marriage for Elizabeth in the early 1580s involved the Revels Office in a number of unusually large expenditures, after which the annual budget for the remainder of Tilney's mastership averaged a modest £300. That the Revels were never extensively involved in creating costumes and scenery for the Jacobean masques might be explained partly by the Elizabethan tradition of restricting the Revels budget and of paying for extravagant special occasions through other funds.

Yet the 1581 commission which gave Tilney power to license plays and players also extended his authority to requisition for the Revels both raw materials and workers, of an impressive variety: 'painters, imbroderers, taylors, cappers, haberdashers, joyners, carders, glasiers, armorers, basketmakers, skinners, sadlers, waggon makers, plaisterers, fethermakers, as all other propertie makers and conninge artificers and laborers whatsoever'.[22] A barebones operation would have had no need of such people, and production preparations on some lesser scale evidently continued. In the absence of fuller, more informative accounts from the later Elizabethan period we can only guess at what these preparations may have been, but the accounts for Tilney's Jacobean years (1603–10) probably give a fair guide.

The Christmas and Shrovetide court seasons during those years were preceded by a period of rehearsals and auditions at the Revels Office premises in St John's (until the move in 1607). Acting companies would have taken their plays there to perform before Tilney himself, and some agreement would have been reached about the play or plays to be performed. At that point the actors and the Revels staff would have discussed the requirements of the play, and agreed upon what the actors themselves were to provide and what, if anything, needed to be brought or made by the Revels. The St John's property included a 'great hall' for rehearsals, and the actors probably gave their plays there in conditions generally similar to those at court, the features of which I discuss in more detail in subsequent chapters. In 1604 the Office refurbished its own 'Tiering house' with canvas, and the plays were performed at St John's by torchlight and candlelight.[23]

'Robes, garments, and other stuff' were still being stored in the Revels wardrobe, and it seems quite likely that actors may have received help with costuming when they needed it, although there are no specific indications of this practice. Painted decoration for the stage was still being produced to some extent, as it had been in the early Elizabethan period, but the chief effort of the Revels staff during the production period, it seems, was directed partly to the actors' needs in the form of backstage security, heat, and sanitation (chamber pots for the players appear in more than one account list), and chiefly to the special lighting, which appears to have devolved on the Revels Office, for no very compelling reason, as a chief responsibility. Elaborate lighting of the court halls for festive occasions had been undertaken by the Revels in the years of its widest sphere of operation, and it seems that the Office of the Works, which took over many of the Revels' responsibilities after the 1570s, never assumed that of lighting, as it might easily have done. So account after account for the Revels in the Stuart period is filled with details of payments for hanging chandeliers, fixing wall brackets, and for the wire, spikes, and strainers required to secure them. One group of workmen who were never dropped from the Revels payroll were wire-drawers: specialists in bracing, hanging, and repairing the many candle-holders which lit royal chambers for the plays.

The vulnerability of the Revels Office as a rather marginal department of the household is demonstrated by its uprooting from its long-held premises in 1607. King James granted the part of St John's Priory in which the Revels Office was housed to his cousin Esmé Stuart for his own use as a residence, and he is unlikely to have done so if the Lord Chamberlain had intervened to suggest that such a move would be seriously inconveniencing royal entertainments; nor did the court authorities themselves provide an alternative property: it was the Master's responsibility to find suitable lodgings, stores, and workplaces for the Revels staff. Subsequent premises in which the Revels Office was lodged are unlikely to have been as extensive or commodious as those at St John's; we know little about them, but presumably they were required to serve the same functions of rehearsal space, storage, and workrooms. The Office moved first, early in 1608, to somewhere in Whitefriars, the old conventual complex west of Fleet Ditch and south of Fleet

Street, but by 1612 it had moved again within the city of London, to a site on St Peter's Hill, near St Paul's. The London address, though further away from Whitehall, was certainly central to the theatres which ringed it, and quite close to the Blackfriars theatre; communication between the Master and the players over licensing matters was thus as physically convenient as it could be. It was also near the major centre of publishing in St Paul's churchyard, and equally convenient for the expanded licensing responsibilities of the Master over printed plays.

At Edmund Tilney's death in 1610 the Mastership passed to Sir George Buck, or Buc, who had held the reversion to the post as officially sanctioned successor for a number of years, and he served in it until 1621. Buck was, like Tilney, a protégé of the Howard family, and similarly an author of historical works, and a poet. His surviving annotated commentary in the manuscript plays *The Second Maiden's Tragedy* and *Sir John Van Olden Barnavelt* has most interested modern scholars as evidence of the kinds of censorship which Masters of the Revels imposed on the professional theatre, but he also wrote a commentary on the Revels Office itself, which no longer survives. He took an exalted and idealistic view of the 'Art of Revels', which brought together skills in 'Grammar, Rhetoric, Logic, Philosophy, History, Music, Mathematics' (the seven traditional liberal arts), as well as in other arts, but it seems unlikely, given the generally low annual budget of the Office, that in practice he presided over the creation of ambitious *gesamtkunstwerke*.[24] The most remarkable theatrical shows produced entirely within the court during the Jacobean years were the extravagant masques, but the Office of the Works had far more to do with the planning and execution of these than did the Revels. One may speculate whether the literary bent of successive Masters and their increasing involvement with the vetting of dramatic texts contributed to the gradual decline of the Revels from a centre of theatrical creativity to a rather dull service department of the court.

The ambitions of Stuart Masters, in other words, were not to make an impact on court culture, as Inigo Jones quite consciously did, but to oversee the world of the commercial theatre, principally in London. In doing this they were fulfilling what the Lord Chamberlain and Privy Council expected of them; we have no indication of complaints that Masters were neglecting their proper business. Such a role was partly entrepreneurial—an active Master would see to it that his privileges were respected by actors and publishers, and that all his fees were duly collected—but the supervisory function was central. The other officers of the Revels—Clerk, Clerk-Comptroller, Yeoman, Groom, and Porter—had no involvement in these licensing activities, and the Master, though he may have been busier throughout the year than his early Tudor predecessors, might have become more remote from the traditional common business of preparing and producing shows. On the other hand, residence in London and a constant contact with plays submitted for new production in the theatres would have rendered the Master entirely *au courant* with theatrical taste and fashion, and the ritual auditions and selection of plays for court performance were probably made rather easier. Stuart Masters of the Revels knew the theatre world intimately, and could present its best achievements to the court. Actors for their part would have known that the Master of the Revels was a broker for prestigious and profitable court performances, and therefore would have attempted to keep their relationship with him as a licenser as smooth and untroubled as they could.

In old age, Sir George Buck became incompetent to manage the Mastership, and he was succeeded by Sir John Astley, or Ashley, in 1622. Astley officially remained the Master until his death in 1640, but in 1623 he deputised Sir Henry Herbert to take his place; Herbert paid him an annual fee to exercise the authority of acting Master. Herbert therefore served for the final two years of King James's reign, and for the entire length of King Charles I's until the cessation of court activity in the early 1640s. Herbert is probably the best known of all the Masters of the Revels in that his personality and sensibility emerge the most clearly from surviving documents. Astley, by contrast, is a shadowy figure, although he is the only Master known to have been a performer in court revels: he was a masquer in *Hymenaei* in 1606.[25] Why Astley gave up the Mastership is not known; it has been suggested that he lacked a strong patron among the powerful nobles at the centre of the court. Herbert, however, was related to the serving Lord Chamberlain at the time of his assumption of the Mastership: William Herbert, third Earl of Pembroke.[26] Early in his career as acting Master, Herbert was involved in the scandal surrounding Thomas Middleton's play *A Game at Chess*. He issued a licence for the play's performance at the Globe, which continued until it was stopped by the protests of the Spanish ambassador, and in the ensuing enquiry Herbert probably benefitted from his connections to those with more power.

Many of the surviving records kept by Herbert–known to modern scholars through transcriptions of a manuscript which has now been lost–are to do with his dealings with actors over the licensing of plays, and with registering his fees and payments for those transactions.[27] His court responsibilities must also have kept him well occupied, however, given the constant theatrical activity of all kinds in the Caroline court, up to about 1640.

All four Masters who served the Stuart kings, however, were in a rather paradoxical position when compared to their earlier Tudor counterparts. Revels under James and Charles expanded enormously. The court-produced entertainment was reborn in the magnificent masques, staged with great spectacle, consciously copying fashionable European style, but the importance of the Revels Office as a centre of theatrical production was not reborn with it. The season during which entertainments were presented was lengthened, the number of plays presented each year was increased considerably over those seen at court in the later years of Queen Elizabeth, while the dispersion of the royal family over a number of London palaces–chiefly St James's, and Somerset or Denmark House, as well as Whitehall–increased the patrons and the venues for the performance of plays. The princes Henry and Charles and the queens Anne and Henrietta Maria were all independent sponsors of theatrical performances. King Charles's conversion of the old cockpit at Whitehall into a permanent theatre is one prominent sign of the importance of theatrical entertainment at his court.

This greatly expanded activity was not matched by an expansion in the size or the budget of the Revels Office, so that inevitably the Revels could have supervised and controlled only *some* court theatre; unlike the Office of the early Tudor monarchs it was not the animating centre of theatrical activity at court. Frozen by Elizabethan austerity and, whether deliberately or accidentally, never reorganised by subsequent court authorities, it remained in a rather awkward organisational position, at least to modern managerial eyes, in relation to the entire range of theatre at the Stuart court. It was emphatically *not* in complete charge of theatrical events, and therefore the Master's position was partly a ceremonial one. The Revels mounted a certain number of plays each year, and provided services–chiefly lighting–for some other events, including masques, but other play and masque productions were mounted and financed by other departments of the household. In considering the staging of plays at court, therefore, probably from the 1580s onwards but certainly in the Stuart years, an enquiry into the practices of the Revels Office will not be sufficient. The Revels staff did not carry out all the work in creating court theatre spaces, and many plays were staged entirely without their participation.

Equally, despite my claim that the Master was a broker for court performance, actors performed at court without the Master's official involvement. Stuart acting companies carried the names of the royal family as patrons–the King's Men, the Queen's Men, the Prince's Men, and so on–and Prince Henry, for example, kept his own court, with his own budget and his own household staff and officers, through whom he might commission play performances without any participation from the Revels Office. The size and complexity of the Stuart court, or courts, to take the point made above, meant that a department as small and as poor as the Revels had become was simply unable to administer and help produce all the theatrical entertainment shown there. No reorganisation was ever undertaken to extend the Revels' mandate to match the prevailing court theatrical entertainment, and until the Civil War it remained something of a residual limb, an ineffective relic of a previous system of operation.

It has often been said that the earlier vigour of the Revels Office, in the first three-quarters of the sixteenth century, was a principal stimulus for the nascent professional theatre of London. Not only did it offer a prestigious show-place for actors, but the costumes in its store were available for hire and sale to players, a practice that elicited a complaint in 1571.[28] The close relationship between the Revels Office and the professional players certainly continued, but the partnership became reversed in terms of dependency. The large, successful London companies of the 1630s, led by the King's Men, were far better equipped to mount plays than was the Revels Office. With two active theatres and a continuing schedule of touring, the actors of the King's Men knew very well how to adapt their plays to different venues, and to set up for a show. Moreover, the vigour of the commercial theatre sustained the Master in his changed role as licenser of the stage, from which he drew much of his power and profit. Within the ambit of the court the Office of the Revels no longer was a particularly significant presence, and to understand theatre at court in the later period we must look beyond it.

The Revels ceased to be a major employer and buyer of supplies during the 1580s, and the elaborate scenic effects of earlier court plays and masks–rocks, clouds, towers, and so forth–and even the simpler curtains, painted cloths, and 'houses' either disappear entirely from the accounts or receive mention only occasionally. As far as we can judge from written records it seems that no particular attention was being given to stage decoration in the later periods of the Revels operations. One might explain this by the increased reliance on plays over masks, and on the increased literary vitality of plays, which needed less painted show to support their weaknesses. Most plays from the period between 1580 and 1640, modern theatre scholars have amply demonstrated, actually require very little in terms of stage space and equipment beyond an acting area and a contiguous place from, and to, which to enter and exit (a 'tiring house' in contemporary theatrical terminology); costumes and stage properties formed the other chief elements of the physical language of the Elizabethan and Stuart theatre. The minimalism of modern workshop productions would, however, have been far from appropriate to holiday occasions at court, in addition to which there are numerous indications from both the stage directions of contemporary plays and Philip Henslowe's theatrical inventories that play production may not have been as austere and simple as the bare requirements of play texts might now suggest.

The furnishing of stages for court plays, although it may have remained entirely within the Revels' sphere of responsibility in official terms, seems likely, for the reasons given above, to have been shared with the other two departments of the household with which the Revels had collaborated throughout its history: the Works and the Wardrobe. As far as theatrical preparations are concerned, the Works dealt in lumber and hardware, and the Wardrobe in fabrics and upholstery. The particular requirements for a given play or series of plays may have been determined by the Revels, while much of the required workmanship and material was provided and paid for through the budgets of the other two Offices. Thus we need not assume that the cost of mounting plays went down after the Revels finances were restricted, other than by the economy of using large departments that were engaged in a great deal of other work.

Of the two departments, the Works was the larger, more complex, and the more involved in creative work of various kinds. Many employees of the Wardrobe were engaged in the simple storage and maintenance of manufactured cloth, from the clothes of the monarch and his or her immediate entourage to the carpets, hangings, canopies, and cushions used to decorate and furnish court chambers on formal occasions. The 'state', for example, the monarch's seat at events of any official importance, was elaborately decorated with a hanging embroidered backcloth and a suspended upholstered canopy, and it was set up and taken down as need dictated. The 'making ready' and 'apparelling' of court rooms, which were paid for through the account of the Treasurer of the Chamber, frequently involved employees of the Wardrobe, who would have taken curtains and hangings from storage and decorated the given room with them. Such preparations for plays could easily have included, as a matter of course, the provision of rich cloth or arras to decorate the front of a stage platform, or a tiring house. One version of the court theatre, then, may well have been a timber framework hung with expensive drapery, its magnificence matching the decoration of the temporary auditorium around it. We will return to this question in a subsequent chapter.

The Office of the Works would have been the natural inheritor of any necessary work on physical material which the cutbacks in the budget rendered no longer possible for the Revels. The Works covered an impressive array of operations, from original building in stone, brick, and wood to repairs of all kinds to the decaying fabric of numerous palaces and other royal buildings, and its employees and contracted workers ranged from the lowest rank of building labourer to architects, visual artists, and fine craftsmen. It maintained its own storeyards of building materials, scaffolding, and tools. The budget of the Office was counted in thousands rather than hundreds of pounds, and its expenditure was never called into question, as was that of the Revels. In times of royal expansiveness the construction operations of the Works evidently cost more money, but its necessary function in providing upkeep–repairs and modifications to living quarters and state chambers alike–meant that it needed no justification before the accountants. Its impressively large work-force, its stores of raw material, and its managerial structure meant that it could take on extraordinary tasks relatively economically. The Surveyor, who headed the Office, had probably been a practising designer and architect even before the most famous incumbent, Inigo Jones, assumed the post in 1615, and hence he had a practical creative connection with the department he supervised, which the later Masters of the Revels, by contrast, did not.

The Surveyors designed and oversaw the building of performance spaces as part of their brief to create and maintain royal structures. One particularly 'theatrical' class of building included the banqueting houses and garden houses which were popular from the early Tudor period onwards. Intended for temporary ceremonial or festive use, in palace grounds and on progresses, they were lightly built of timber framing covered with painted cloth or thin boards, and thus not dissimilar from the large tents which the Revels Office, in its old association with the Office of the Tents, maintained and decorated in the reign of King Henry VIII.[29] The finish of such buildings was consciously extravagant, with elaborate painted surfaces (especially with 'faux' effects to imitate more solid materials), and much use of 'pastoral' adornments in the shape of real or artificial flowers, leaves, and branches. Larger versions of such buildings could be employed for more than alfresco feasting. One such was the banqueting house built at Whitehall for the French ambassadorial visit in 1572, inside which a mask and military games were presented to an audience. At this date the collaboration between the Works and the Revels is clear enough; both Offices recorded expenditure on the building, with the Works probably performing the heavy labour of framing and erection, and the Revels the decorative finishing, or at least some of it. The collaboration also makes clear how such buildings were regarded: as places for recreation and entertainment in the warmer months of the year.

The banqueting house erected for a further French visit in 1581 was a rather more ambitious version of such festive buildings; it lasted until 1606, and was succeeded on the same site (alongside King Street, the modern Whitehall) by two Jacobean buildings of more substantial material – the second, following the destruction of the first by fire in 1619, designed by Inigo Jones, and still standing. The size and layout of the surviving stone building probably gives some guide to its predecessors; the 1581 building was also rectangular in plan, and designed from the start to accommodate an observing audience, with 'ten heights of degrees for people to stand upon' along its sides.[30] It can therefore be regarded as something of a model for the buildings which came after it, and in which both plays and the Stuart masques were performed. Jones's 1622 Banqueting House was so expensively decorated by King Charles I that the black carbon deposits created by the torches and candles used to light theatrical occasions could not be allowed to damage it, and a cheaper lumber structure to house the masques was put up directly beside it. The larger banqueting houses, such 'masquing houses' as that commissioned by Charles, and the temporary theatre Jones put up at Somerset House in 1632–33 were, however, all of the same general plan and interior layout, although their decoration and finish certainly reflected the changing taste of the successive courts between 1581 and the 1630s.

If the earlier Revels Office can be thought of as providing some stimulus for the costuming and mounting of plays in the professional theatre during its early development, one might also consider that the court tradition of festival buildings—made of framed lumber, elaborately decorated with relatively cheap finishes, and provided with ranked seating for a large audience—might have had some influence on the London playhouses, which began to be built in the 1560s. The connection between court playing spaces and those of the commercial theatre, it has been argued, continued in the work of Inigo Jones.[31] The Office of the Works may also be regarded as having some importance for English theatrical history.

Certainly Jones designed the conversion of the Whitehall Cockpit in 1629–30 into a permanent theatre for the acting of plays, the first court theatre in England, if by that phrase one understands a building devoted to no other purpose but the performing and watching of dramatic entertainment. Its relatively modest size suggests that it was intended for the royal family and immediate court to use throughout the year, rather than for the large gatherings at plays during the traditional festivals. The rather surprising plan of its stage—five entrance doors and a curving tiring-house façade—was dictated partly by Jones's classical or Palladian architectural models, and partly by the exigencies of a rather 'theatrical' (or cheap) translation of a late-Gothic building with a singular plan into a functioning theatre. Otherwise, however, its purpose was to serve visiting troupes of professional actors, who used it during the remaining decade of Charles's London court. The history of the English court theatre reached a symbolic peak in this building and the patronage it represented. Charles I was the most generous and consistent supporter of the professional stage in the entire career of the English monarchy. His son briefly revived the practice of keeping a theatre within the court, but thereafter the relationship between the stage and the court was never a close one, and the English court, compared with many European courts of the eighteenth century, for example, became culturally inert and impoverished.

More regularly than creating new buildings for theatrical performances, the Works was charged with converting palace chambers into temporary theatres. I have outlined this practice above; we should remember that the workmen who carried out such jobs probably did not distinguish between theatrical spaces and those used for any other large gathering for which they were required to provide seating, the safe assembly of which must have taken most of the time of the entire procedure. There are many contemporary illustrations which show the kind of audience accommodation–for trials and executions, for state weddings and funerals, for tournaments, races, and games–provided for plays and other shows. Pictures of medieval entertainments reveal that such structures had been built for hundreds of years; the weight and stress they had to withstand, and hence their structural engineering, were well understood.

Banks of seating were built from stock material from the Works storeyards. The framework which held them up was simply scaffolding, put together in the same way as it was elsewhere, using the same long, stout, timber poles as were used to erect scaffolds for building and for repairs to high walls and roofs. Lashed and nailed together, with uprights, horizontals, and diagonal bracing pieces, the scaffold supported steps, seats, and walkways, all constructed from planking, and with safety rails at appropriate places. Large structures of this kind built within court chambers were supported against the walls at the rear; probably supporting beams were let into the stonework, as was the practice in erecting exterior scaffolding. The provision of such temporary seating was a habitual task of the Office from the earliest Tudor period onwards, and such jobs were undoubtedly regarded pragmatically: the technique and materials could be applied to any occasion, and adapted to suit the venue and the size of the expected audience.

Less mention is made in the annual accounts of the Works of the building of stages for the actors, although they were probably regularly made by the Works carpenters, and were not singled out for special mention because they were, once again, the kind of structure which was a standard repeated unit, with variant versions constructed in many sizes, heights, and degrees of finish. Platforms to hold a seat or a throne (one possible meaning of the word 'state'), observation stands, large steps, daises, and so forth, were constantly required for court business, and they were made by the Office of the Works. A stage for actors was simply one more example of such a structure, with a boarded surface supported on a framework or some temporary expedient, of a certain extent and height. Should the actors have required a trap in their stage, then to set in a hinged door flap was another entirely standard job of work for experienced carpenters. Compared with the heavy, laborious job of erecting the seating, the building of a stage and its accompanying tiring house must have been regarded as a simple matter.

This is not to say that the Office of the Works was entirely without theoretical pretensions. The ambitious conversion of the medieval hall at Christ Church, Oxford, into a temporary theatre for performances before the visiting King James in 1605 was undertaken by the staff of the Works; that they were given responsibility for the occasion is a sign that they were regarded as expert in theatrical structures.[32] The theatre itself, however, was rather more ambitious and culturally fashionable than the traditional temporary theatrical spaces within a court hall, and it was not made with a view to the requirements of professional actors and their repertory of plays. The surviving plan for the auditorium and the manuscript notes which accompany it show the clear influence of Sebastiano Serlio's attempt to unite a version of classical theatre architecture with the Italian court fashion for theatrical scenery composed in linear perspective. Although he had no official connection with the Office at this date, Inigo Jones was responsible for the arrangements of the stage at Oxford, while Simon Basil, Comptroller and the next Surveyor of the Works, oversaw the building of the auditorium. That more than mere carpentry was at stake is revealed by the final note written on the plan: 'In anny case remember that a slight Portico bee made . . . of hoopes and firrpooles. wherupon many lights or lamps of seueral coulers may bee placed. This portico giues a great grace to all the Theater, & without it, the Architectur is false.'[33]

While the portico itself may sound rather factitious to modern taste, the concern for the architectural effect, for the dignity and unity of even temporary structures, evidently would have informed occasions at court quite as much as it did the Oxford theatre. We have in the phrasing of the note a clear sign of the supervising spirit which informed the raw operations of the carpenters and other artificers employed by the Works. Although the Christ Church conversion must be regarded as a particular and individual creation, the grace of the theatre would also have been looked to at court when the Office of the Works created spaces for actors and audiences. Throughout the period of the most intense activity in the English theatre in the late sixteenth and early seventeenth centuries, it was the Works rather than the Revels which gave physical form to the theatre at court. Even before he became Surveyor, Inigo Jones was evidently influential in changing that form in the direction of Italian style. He could not re-invent English theatrical practice, however, and while court entertainment depended so largely on plays from the commercial companies then actors' traditional treatment of stage space dictated the form of the stages on which they worked; nor could Jones change the century-old palaces in which he built his performance spaces, although the conversion of the Cockpit theatre was one attempt, and Charles would gladly have transformed Whitehall in the general fashion of the elegant new Banqueting House, had he had the money to do so. The style of the English court as expressed in its buildings, however, had been largely determined by King Henry VIII.

2 Royal places

St. James's. Why, *Richmond, Richmond,* why art so heavy?
Richmond. I have reason enough for that, good-sainted sister. Am I not built
with stone, fair, large, and free-stone, some part cover'd with lead too?
Thomas Middleton and William Rowley, Induction, *The World Tossed at
Tennis* (London, 1620)

Inigo Jones was not the first to introduce continental European visual style to
the English court. The first two Tudor kings patronised foreign artists and
workmen extensively, particularly in the decoration of their palaces, the style
of which had a dominating effect on the courts of their successors. The reigns
of Henry VII and his son also saw the building or rebuilding of the palaces
principally inhabited by Queen Elizabeth, King James, King Charles, and their
families, and the prevailing architectural style of the early sixteenth century in
England was relatively conservative, a version of the late Gothic, predominantly in brick, with stone details around windows and doors and as accents
on walls. Whitehall Palace, despite its name, was overwhelmingly a redbrick
institution, as is the surviving Tudor part of Hampton Court Palace. The
earliest of the Tudor building projects, Richmond Palace, the chief building
enterprise of Henry VII, has some claim to having been the most ambitious
and architecturally successful, as well as having shown most clearly the influence of European taste. The design featured a massive central block directly
fronting the river, ornamented by many towers and turrets which appear to
have beeen inspired by contemporary French and Burgundian design.[1] The
effect was less sprawling than that of Whitehall, Greenwich, or Hampton
Court, and as far as one can judge from pictures–the palace was demolished in
the seventeenth century–the entire building had more grace and presence than
the other large royal residences, which tended to look like small towns made

35

up of contiguous structures rather than conforming to one unified architectural idea.

The Renaissance idea of the palace, a centre for the exercise of power largely through verbal and symbolic means, was rather different from its ancestor the castle, in which the king was at the centre of a fortified camp. The Italian *palazzo* slowly changed its aspect from that of a stronghold to a building open to the light and the outside world, but English palace architecture of the early sixteenth century was still strongly influenced by concepts of fortification. Massive gatehouses with narrow entrances, relatively small windows on exterior walls, battlements, and observation towers all characterise Tudor palaces. The typical plan of a series of connecting courtyards, from a large, open, more public yard (the base court) to smaller, more private areas, also reflects that of the castle, with its rings of defensive walls surrounding an inner final redoubt, the keep. Correspondingly, massiveness of masonry and rather cramped, dark, interior space mark Tudor buildings. Two of the royal residences, although they were not frequently used as such by the sixteenth century, actually were medieval forts: the Tower of London and Windsor Castle.[2]

Tudor palaces, however, were not organised on serious defensive principles, which had in any case been transformed with the development of artillery, and many of the chambers and special spaces that had, in earlier times, been contained within one fortified unit more typically formed part of a more dispersed and expansive complex by the late fifteenth century. Principal large units of this complex, still to be seen at Hampton Court, were the hall, usually the largest indoor gathering place of any palace, and the chapel, used for daily services supported by the choristers and musicians of the Chapel Royal. Both of these structures had firm medieval roots. The most impressive royal hall ever built, that in Westminster Palace, the medieval predecessor of Whitehall as the chief royal residence in the immediate vicinity of the city of London, dates from the reign of Richard II. It has stone walls and a very large timber-framed roof; the hall at Hampton Court is visibly in the same tradition of building. Tudor halls are important places in the history of the theatre; many performances of plays were given in temporary theatre spaces built within their walls. As gathering spaces for large numbers of people they functioned crucially in court culture, although their functions were considerably different in 1600 from what they had been when Henry VII became king.

Architecturally the Tudor hall gave scope to a less constricted treatment of volume and space. As the loftiest, largest, free-standing chamber it made more extensive use of light, through larger windows. The hall at Hampton Court, in addition to high windows along the side walls, has a large bay window at the dais or high end which creates considerable illumination. The predominant effect of such halls, however, is of a medieval building, both solemn and massive. The dark, heavy, elaborate roof at Hampton Court tends to counteract the increased brightness of the window space. The urge to construct rather frivolous banqueting houses may have arisen in reaction to the somewhat oppressive effect of the typical hall. For all its architectural prominence, however, the hall had become something of an anomaly by the Elizabethan years, since, apart from infrequent festive occasions in regular court life, it was no longer used as a communal gathering space.[3] Originally the entire community had met there to eat, as college communities still do in medieval halls at Oxford and Cambridge, and in imitations of such buildings throughout the world. As the court grew in size and as notions of privacy increasingly influenced the domestic life of the monarch, the practice of 'commoning'–the king or queen eating a meal together with his or her assembled court–became less and less frequent, and thus the hall became a place with a largely ceremonial purpose, not much used in day-to-day court life in the older fashion, although it may have continued to serve as a refectory for the large numbers of people employed in the household in the lower ranks of service. Such a function was expendable when the hall was required as a theatrical space; particularly at the feasts of Christmas and Shrove it was called on frequently to house all kinds of festive events.

By the time Queen Elizabeth came to the throne, then, the hall was not an essential location in the day-to-day life of the monarch. The smaller palaces – like St James's, where Queen Mary had spent considerable time during her short reign, and the rural Oatlands and Nonsuch – did not have halls at all, and while at Whitehall and Hampton Court the halls were closely connected with other chambers, at Greenwich and at Richmond they were not. (The 'typical' palace, it should be said, did not exist; each one had some elements in common with others and also many individual and unique features, so that it will be necessary to consider each place individually, following this survey of general characteristics.) Where halls were available they were used to stage plays, exactly as similar halls were elsewhere: in aristocratic houses, in colleges and inns of court, and in guildhalls and market halls throughout the country. Setting up a stage and playing before an audience gathered indoors within a hall was not specific to the court; the professional players performed under these conditions for both private patrons and paying audiences from an early date, and Shakespeare and his fellow actors continued to do so on annual provincial tours, as well as on occasional commissioned performances in London, like that of *Twelfth Night* for the legal community of the Middle Temple within their hall in 1602.[4] Staging a play inside a hall was a practice the actors carried out for royal patrons under the lavish conditions at court, but also for demotic paying audiences in towns throughout the country. To that extent, court performances were directly related to the actors' experience and practice during the rest of the working year. Quite what the practice may have involved will be considered in more detail below.

If the hall was a survival of a medieval original, so was the habitual plan of a suite of rooms leading to the sovereign's bedchamber, the most intimate and private space he or she enjoyed within the palace. Like the architectural plan of connecting courtyards, the group of rooms progressed from larger, more public spaces to smaller, private, and increasingly secure and inaccessible chambers; the scheme was once again defensive in origin.[5] The first and largest room in the series was known as either the guard chamber or the great chamber; sometimes the room was referred to indifferently by both titles. After the hall it was typically the largest indoor space which might be used for secular ceremonies in a palace, and plays were frequently staged in the Great Chamber at both Whitehall and Richmond, for example. Its characteristics were not dissimilar from the hall, although it was provided with a flat plaster ceiling – decorated in early Tudor style with ribs and embossed ornaments, like those of most interior chambers within the central block of the palace – rather than the pitched open timber roof of a hall.

We can give a fairly confident account of the Great Chamber at Whitehall since the cellar which lay below it still survives, and hence defines its dimensions.[6] It was a rectangular room on the second storey of the palace, sixty feet long by thirty feet wide. One entered it by way of a stair from the courtyard below, and if allowed to do so passed out of it to the next chamber by way of the only other door, at the western end of the southern wall.[7] It was probably a bright room, since it had a large bay window, facing north and looking towards the successive banqueting houses at the opposite side of the courtyard; other windows were probably set in this wall also. It was occupied partly by members of the royal guard, armed, and dressed in a fashion similar to their modern descendants, the Yeomen of the Guard. They were a ceremonial reminder of the monarch's power, they marked the boundary of a restricted and privileged area, and they were an entirely practical measure of security, like the police at a modern parliament or legislature building.

Although the monarch certainly appeared at events in the great chamber, plays included, more typically the room was used as a lobby of assembly, where one waited for an audience in the smaller room which lay beyond it, the presence chamber. When the monarch was in residence, this room was set up with a throne and state—the dais, canopy, and heraldic backcloth—where the king or queen would give a hearing to petitions and communications of one kind or another. Although marked by the formal circumstances of its purpose, it was not required to be a particularly large space, and was not used for large assemblies. Beyond it lay, in differing arrangements at different places, the privy chamber and the bedchamber, sometimes with supplementary lobbies and smaller rooms connecting them, and forming a suite into which the monarch could retreat from official business and public view. None of these rooms was large, and hence not used for festive assemblies. Depending on the formality of one's business, and one's status and trustworthiness, one might also be admitted to an interview with the ruler on his or her own ground, as it were, in one of the rooms beyond the presence chamber. A rather fantasticated version of a visit to Whitehall, and of progress through the various areas and chambers of the palace, is given in Richard Brome's comedy, *The City Wit*: Sneakup is being instructed by his dominant wife, Pyannet, how to bear himself in a scheme to sell some jewels to the king.

> Now mark. I will instruct you: When you come at the Court gate, you may neither knocke nor pisse. Do you mark? You go through the Hall cover'd; through the great Chamber cover'd; through the Presence bare; through the Lobby cover'd; through the Privy Chamber bare; through the Privy Lobby cover'd; to the Prince bare.[8]

That such a booby as Sneakup would be allowed to proceed unchallenged through such a restricted area is part of Brome's joke, but two scenes later the gulls who are victims of an elaborate scam have penetrated the palace precincts: Sarpego begins the scene by announcing 'This is the Presence.'

The titles and the functions of rooms in a palace tended to change somewhat to reflect the changing demands on them made by the various resident courts, over the eventful 84-year period covered in this book. A large household centred on a married monarch with children (those of Henry VIII, James I, and Charles I) made more extensive use of court chambers than that of an unmarried ruler (Edward VI, Elizabeth I, and, for all practical purposes, Mary I). Medieval tradition had recognised a 'king's side' and a 'queen's side' to the central block of the royal residence, and this nomenclature survived, at Whitehall and elsewhere, even when the consort lived in an entirely separate building, as Queen Anne, James's wife, did at the palace variously known as Somerset or Denmark House, for example. The division of the palace into 'sides' gave the king and queen each a distinct suite of rooms, so that there could be duplicate great chambers, presence chambers, and privy chambers within one palace. Moreover, as functions changed, the same room might take on a different title, and hence one must be quite clear about the particular contemporary context when one reads that in a certain year the queen saw a play at Shrovetide in her great chamber, for example.

In plain terms, then, the hall and the great chamber were the two court rooms most frequently used for plays, while the Whitehall banqueting houses were increasingly used as additional venues in the seventeenth century. The physical relationship between the hall and the great chamber varied from place to place. At Hampton Court they are contiguous, so that in effect the hall was yet another large addition to the successive series of rooms approaching the private space of the monarch. More usually they were entirely distinct; at Whitehall, Richmond, and Greenwich the great chamber was situated on a second storey, while the hall was at ground level, and in a different part of the complex of buildings. Halls, being larger, were better suited to the large audiences which might be expected at the two feast seasons. For reasons suggested above, to set up the hall as a temporary theatre was probably less inconvenient than to do so in the great chamber, which was in effect a major artery in the day-to-day flow of court traffic on all kinds of business. Nevertheless, plays were frequently given in the great chamber, and any consequent disturbance to the functioning of the court was evidently absorbed. In the large palaces there were usually other routes to be taken to arrive at a particular destination. Sir John Finet, Master of Ceremonies to Charles I, has left amusing accounts in his notebooks of leading one set of departing foreign ambassadors through more obscure passageways to avoid meeting an arriving ambassadorial party from a hostile state.[9] The physical disturbances introduced by the Works carpenters in converting large chambers into theatrical auditoriums would have made similar diversions necessary.

So far I have largely characterised court rooms in general terms, but the effect of a particular theatrical occasion at court was determined as much by the special ethos of the place where it was held as by the kind of show or play performed, the skill of the actors, and the composition of the audience. We must therefore look in more detail at the architectural character of individual palaces, beginning with the most important.

Whitehall

Whitehall Palace was based on the nucleus of York Place, which had belonged to Cardinal Wolsey and was appropriated by Henry VIII, who extended it.[10] It continued to be extended and adapted until a severe fire destroyed large parts of it at the end of the seventeenth century. Nearby Westminster Palace had been one of the principal London residences of medieval kings, but its damage by fire in 1512, and again in 1549, had rendered it less convenient.[11] While its surviving buildings functioned for legislative purposes–for parliament and law courts–the neighbouring site of Whitehall was no doubt regarded as suitably and symbolically near to a historic centre of English monarchical power. Whitehall, like the other large palaces, lay on the river, which gave it one reliable means of communication, by boat. It was not exactly planned to present an architectural frontage to the river, as the palaces at both Richmond and Greenwich did, although a range of rooms with a river view was eventually built along the bank. The palace extended in an elongated strip between Westminster and Charing Cross, and it was largely though not entirely bounded on the western side by a public road, King Street, the line of which is followed by the modern road called Whitehall. Two gatehouses in the fortified style spanned the street, and reminded travellers that they were passing through a special space; if the highway could not be closed off, it could be dominated. Whitehall was the chief residence of English monarchs from the 1530s until the 1690s; Oliver Cromwell also lived partly there and partly at Hampton Court during the interregnum.

I have already said something about the changes to the style of the palace over the century and a half of its active history. Most of the reliable and more evocative views of it, in paintings, drawings, and prints, were made towards the end of this period, and they give prominent attention to Inigo Jones's elegant Banqueting House, standing out in white stone against the warm brick of the Tudor buildings. A good impression of the character of the palace in the reign of Charles II is given by Hendrick Danckerts's long view of the buildings as seen from St James's Park, composed from an observation point somewhere opposite the modern Horse Guards (Plate 1). This painting incidentally gives the best view we have of the Cockpit, and shows that the exterior character of the building was largely untouched by Inigo Jones when he turned it into a theatre in 1629: it stands foursquare in Tudor brick, with stone mullioned windows on two storeys. Danckerts gives pictorial prominence, however, to the major mark Jones made on the exterior character of Whitehall, and the Banqueting House continued to be a central feature of views of the surviving parts of the old palace throughout the eighteenth century. Since it was built directly facing on to King Street (and remains fronting Whitehall), abutting the principal entrance to the palace precincts, its visual prominence was inescapable; in the seventeenth century its distinctive character was enhanced by contrast with what lay around it.

WHITEHALL, S.ᵗ JAMES PARK, TIME OF CHARLES 2ᵈ BY DANCKERT.

677

1 Hendrick Danckerts, painting of Whitehall from St James's Park in the 1670s. The Banqueting House is at the left of the picture, and the Cockpit on the right.

Once inside the palace, however, even at the time Danckerts painted his picture, one's impressions would have been dominated by architectural and decorative display as it was understood by Cardinal Wolsey and King Henry VIII. Most of the major court rooms had been built by them, and the interior decorations had been retained, having been repaired and repainted over the intervening years. The effect of such a style can be observed today at Hampton Court, or in the Tudor chapel at St James's Palace. In contrast with the rather conservative effect of early Tudor architecture, interior decoration was both lavish and eclectic. Sculpted, relief, and painted details decorated many surfaces; bright reds, blues, and gilded details create extremely lively visual effects, dynamic and exciting when they succeed, garish and distracting when they do not. Early Tudor interior decoration is quite unafraid of vulgarity. The palaces of the Tudor kings were not characterised by restraint and subtlety in their visual environment, but rather by a somewhat hectic richness. Some of the techniques of decoration were inherited directly from medieval style. Geometrically ribbed and compartmentalised ceilings and walls, carved bosses and finials, floral decoration and heraldic motifs were all employed throughout the career of so-called Gothic architecture, and they remained part of the vocabulary of the early-sixteenth-century masons, carpenters, and painters who worked on the Henrician palaces. Newer ideas were mixed in with the older ones, however, and styles which we connect with the Italian Renaissance were also to be found at Whitehall, and elsewhere.[12]

One characteristic form of decoration of interior surfaces was so-called antic or grotesque work, a lively design using interlacing plant forms, human and animal figures, conceived in Italy as an adaptation of classical Roman mural painting. This kind of decoration was used in Tudor palaces in various media: mural painting, carved detailing on plaster or woodwork, and in fabrics. Neoclassical style was also increasingly apparent in English interiors in the opening decades of the sixteenth century in the form of round-headed arches, niches, and columns in various interpretations of the traditional orders. The mixed effect created by the bringing together of these varied decorative traditions can be appreciated in the painting of *Henry VIII and his children*, which is set in an interior at Whitehall, with views of the exterior of the palace visible through the open doorways.[13] The small throne room at the centre, though it might be a generalised pictorial scheme rather than a representation of an actual chamber in the palace, gives an impression of dignity and richness; the colours are rather muted, while the lively and delicate antic detail is picked out in gold. The ceiling is panelled, coffered, and painted. The views of the outside give some glimpses of the less restrained side of early Tudor taste, with chequered black and white rails decorating the garden, gilded heraldic beasts holding bannerets, and painted designs on the exterior of one of the buildings on the left (Plate 2).

If spending on the decoration of buildings had remained as high as it was under Henry VIII the character of Whitehall and other palaces would have changed more than they did. As it was, austerity affected not only the Revels Office, but also largely restricted subsequent monarchs to the upkeep and restoration of what Henry had built. The Works accounts for the Elizabethan and Stuart periods show that the early Tudor decoration was looked after through repairs and repainting; even when the fashionable Palladian conversion of the Cockpit was undertaken, the old ribs and bosses of the Tudor roof were simply given a new coat of paint. Charles I, as the leading connoisseur among the successors of Henry VIII, probably chafed most under the legacy of this unfashionable past, although it was his father, in commissioning the two successive banqueting houses in the classical style, who made more architectural impact on the atmosphere of Whitehall. These new buildings were also of great significance to dramatic activities, and we must return to them, but we will begin with the older chambers which accommodated dramatic activity.

The Hall at Whitehall was very similar to the surviving Hall at Hampton Court in size and character. Part of the original palace as built by Cardinal Wolsey, it was a stone building, the pale colour of which later gave its name to the palace as a whole, and it had a high pitched roof with a lantern originally designed to exhaust smoke from the open fire below. Like other halls built in the medieval tradition it was rectangular in plan, with the long side walls built as six bays, buttressed on the outside, and with a window set in each bay. Larger windows lit each end, and as at Hampton Court a large, full-length bay window lit the dais end of the hall. The inside of the roof was probably a decorated timber hammer-beam construction like the elaborate roof of Hampton Court Hall. The Hall at Whitehall lay on a north–south line parallel with the river, and directly alongside the chapel. At the northern end it could be entered from either side, from a passageway which ran from Whitehall stairs – the public river landing – to the court gate on King Street. This entryway was separated from the hall proper, as at Hampton Court and elsewhere, by a timber screen, with two entries and a gallery overhead – apparently in size and character very like the surviving screen at Hampton Court.

No detailed measured plan of the Hall survives, but its overall length, including the screens passage, was approximately 90 feet, and its width 40 feet; the Hall at Hampton Court, by way of comparison, is 106 feet long overall, and 40 feet wide. The Hall at Whitehall is a building of principal importance in the history of

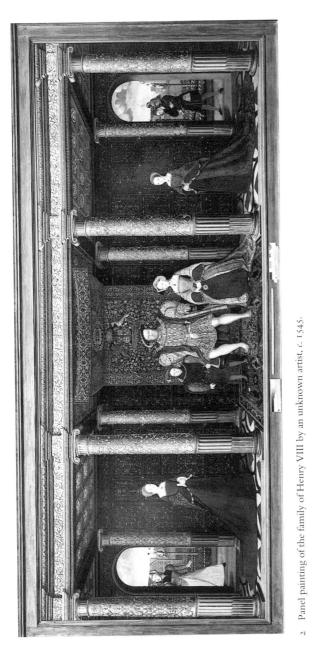

2   Panel painting of the family of Henry VIII by an unknown artist, c. 1545.

English court theatre, since it was probably used to mount festive dramatic events from the beginning of its existence in 1528, and for the last 40 years of its life it was converted into a permanent court playhouse, replacing the smaller Cockpit theatre, until it was destroyed by fire in 1698.[14] The history of this particular phase of the building, as a theatre set up to accommodate Restoration acting companies playing a mixture of new repertory and some of the plays of the pre-war playwrights, lies beyond the scope of this study. The Restoration court theatre, however, did not exactly represent a new idea. Although the conversion included a proscenium stage with scenery, similar to the new London playhouses of the Restoration but quite unlike the old stages and auditoriums at the Globe, the Fortune, and the Blackfriars, proscenium stages and 'scenes' had been built in the Hall before the Civil War. One of the most informative documents about the Hall is a plan of a temporary theatrical conversion in 1635, designed by Inigo Jones and drawn by his assistant, John Webb (Plate 3). This was made for the performance of a French pastoral play, *Florimène*, with scenery and some dancing, and in those respects more like the contemporary masques than plays from the commercial theatre. The performance was by amateurs, the queen's French maids of honour, but Jones's plans and related scene designs show that it was elaborately and lavishly produced.[15] The plan shows one model of staging a play within a hall, and we must return to it when considering the range of staging arrangements at court.

The 1635 theatre drawing clearly shows the architectural plan of the Hall. At the north end, on the extreme right, the two entries to the screens passage through the thick masonry walls may be seen; the screen, with its two entries into the hall itself, forms a backstage wall behind the scenes–a set of steps leads up from ground level through the western screen entry to the temporary raised wooden stage. At the opposite end of the Hall we may see on the eastern side the plan of the great bay window, and, opposite, a large doorway which connected with the royal suite and was the chief entry for the monarch. The state, with two steps up to the platform, may be seen at the centre of the Hall, facing the stage; this arrangement was traditional in any entertainment watched by royal patrons. Around the state are set up the raised wooden seats or degrees which accommodated the other observers; they are built up against the walls of the chamber, and follow its rectangular plan. Certain sections of the seating are railed or partitioned off as reserved private boxes, with notations marking their owners, and with stairs giving access to them.

Such wooden seating could be set up for festive and ceremonial events as the needs of the occasion required. The 1635 plan, even though it shows a type of

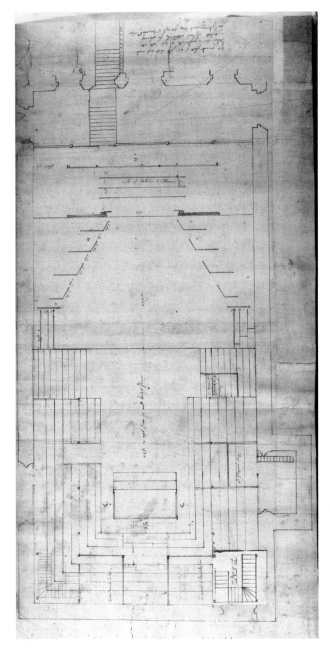

3 John Webb, plan of the stage and auditorium for *Florimène*, set within the Hall at Whitehall in December 1635. The places for the king and queen are shown at centre left, and may be compared with the royal seats shown in Plates 2, 4 and 5. The hall screen, with two entries, lies behind the stage, to the right of the plan.

stage unusual for its time, at least when compared with contemporary play-houses, is in no respect extraordinary in its auditorium. Similar seating was put up in halls not only for dramatic entertainment by the commercial players, but also for other ceremonies. When the monarch spent Easter at Whitehall, for example, the distribution of charity on Maundy Thursday, immediately preceding Good Friday, was held in the Hall, following service in the adjoining chapel. Once again the carpenters set up a state for the monarch, seating for the observing and participating poor subjects who received the royal charity, and, in 1634 at least, a gallery, where the chapel singers sang anthems through part of the ceremony.[16] In November 1616 the Hall saw the installation of Charles as Prince of Wales, a processional investiture arranged with a good deal of pomp and spectacle, and featuring the throned King James, the assembled nobility in heraldic robes, and seated observers ranked around the walls; following a feast, fighting at barriers—at which the armed combatants are separated by a waist-high rail—was held in the Banqueting House, which was also made ready by the Works with seats for the onlookers.

The probable physical arrangement of the Hall on this occasion is indicated by a surviving plan of the chamber used for the previous installation of Prince Henry in 1610 (Plate 4). This ceremony was held in the chamber used for the Court of Requests within the old Palace of Westminster, but the plan, of a rectangular room with the king seated on a state at one end, and with raked seats set against three walls, would fit the Hall at Whitehall equally well. The plan also shows that the floor of the hall was left largely free for the processions in and out of the room, and that, as for the 1635 play, a certain amount of the seating was reserved as boxes, raised above and separated from the general rows of benches. On the king's right is a box for 'The Queenes Matie and her Children', and on the opposite side is a similar structure reserved for 'Ambassado^rs'. Some indications of the structure of these areas are also given. There are rails along the bottom of the raked seats, to restrict access, and rails marking off a section of seating on each side at about half-way down the length of the room. The boxes are raised on timber legs, with various systems of bracing, both rectilinear and diagonal, supporting them. These structures would have been built by the Office of the Works, and they are typical of the kinds of seating which would also have been provided for a play.

Not a great deal is known about the permanent interior decoration of the Hall at Whitehall. It is assumed that the roof was similar to the surviving elaborate timber roof at Hampton Court, with painted, gilded, and carved decoration. Also as at Hampton Court, the windows of the hall were set relatively high in the

4   Plan of the chamber of the Court of Requests, Palace of Westminster, as prepared for the
investiture of Prince Henry as Prince of Wales in June 1610. The seating around the walls includes
the degrees, partitions, and rails frequently mentioned in the accounts of the Office of the Works.

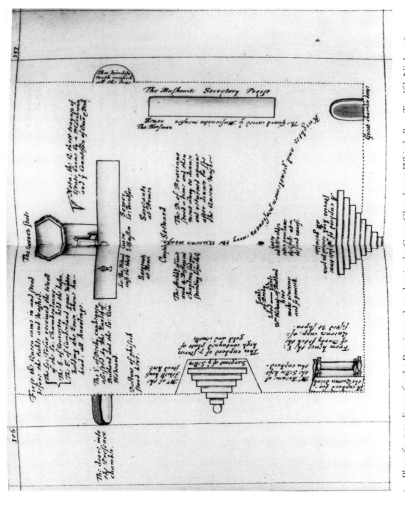

5 Plan of a state dinner for the Russian ambassadors in the Great Chamber at Whitehall on Twelfth Night, 1601. This schematic representation may be compared with Hollar's depiction of a ceremonial banquet in Plate 12.

wall, and the space below them was hung with tapestries, most usually in a connected narrative series, with both secular and religious subjects. The setting up of temporary seating, however, would have involved the removal of the valuable wall hangings, although other tapestries are likely to have been used – for example, to hang around the boxes shown in Plate 4, and similar temporary structures. The soft colours of tapestries and the rich effects of gold and silver thread and fringe undoubtedly formed part of the effect of temporary theatrical auditoriums at court. In large spaces like the halls at all the major palaces the effect of vertical surfaces hung with luxurious woven cloth and lit by bright candlelight must have been a memorable and impressive sight.

The Great Chamber at Whitehall lay close to the Hall, immediately to the south-east, but on a second storey reached by a staircase. It was a room in constant use when the court was in residence, and it was the first place to which visitors on formal business to the palace were conducted–hence the impression it gave was of some importance. Although we have very little information about its appointments it is likely to have been richly decorated in the early Tudor style, with decorated surfaces in painted and gilded finishes, and with coloured glass in the windows. It was a rectangular room roughly sixty feet long by thirty feet wide, hence with less than half the floor space of the Hall. Plays given in the Great Chamber, we may accordingly assume, were watched by smaller audiences. Its main physical features were the two points of entry shown in the Elizabethan plan of a state dinner in early 1601 (Plate 5), and a large bay window looking out to the west; other windows on the western wall probably also lit the room. The Chamber was probably quite high–at least twenty feet–without being as lofty as the Hall. The slightly pitched roof of the range lay immediately above it, and the ceiling of the room was probably flat, with geometrically segmented ribs and bosses, painted and gilded. The room was heated with a fireplace, in the centre of the eastern wall, and its floor was wooden, unlike the stone-paved floor of the Hall. Its walls were probably usually decorated with hanging tapestries.

Other chambers within the palace may occasionally have been used for entertainments during the Tudor years, but no surviving records indicate as much. The third major venue for dramatic entertainments at Whitehall was within the successive banqueting houses, until the Masquing House, set up to prevent smoke damage to the expensive Rubens ceiling paintings installed in the 1622 Banqueting House, was built in 1637. The banqueting houses, like other court chambers, were adaptable to a variety of uses, theatrical occasions among them. During the Elizabethan period it seems that the elaborately decorated building erected in 1581 was not used as a theatre, perhaps because at the regular

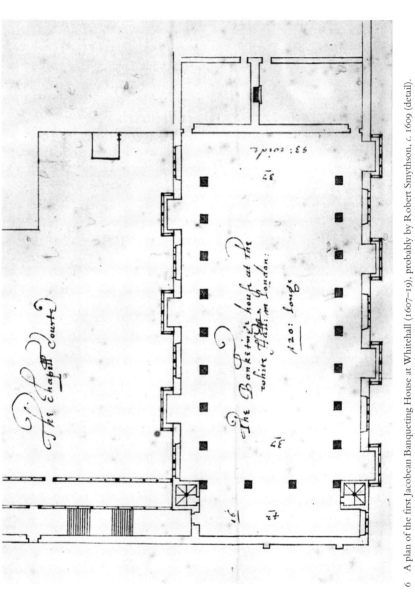

The Chapell Courte

The Banketing hous at the white Hall: in London:

120: longs

53: wide

37

37

42

19

37

6 A plan of the first Jacobean Banqueting House at Whitehall (1607–19), probably by Robert Smythson, c. 1609 (detail).

festival seasons it was a cold room, incapable of being adequately heated. The two Jacobean buildings which followed it on the same site, in 1607 and 1622, were more substantial.[17] The surviving Banqueting House, designed by Inigo Jones in an elegant Palladian style, is probably not entirely dissimilar from its wooden predecessor, destroyed by fire in 1619. This rectangular hall (120 feet by 53 feet) was surrounded on the interior by classical colonnades of two storeys; a plan by Robert Smythson survives (Plate 6). All three successive buildings on the site conformed to the spatial arrangement we can see in this drawing, with a large, flat open floor which might be set up for feasting, dancing, or entertainments of various kinds. Like the Hall, the banqueting houses had to be prepared with temporary seating for the staging of plays or masques, and the layout of such seating would have been the same. The banqueting houses were particularly favoured for the masques which became a feature of Stuart court life, no doubt because they offered plenty of space for the special demands of these entertainments, which called for a dancing-floor in front of a scenic stage which was commonly quite large. The banqueting-house site also lay off the regular track of court business traffic, and hence it was undoubtedly more convenient to use it for the prolonged rehearsals and stage preparations which the masques required.

The theatrical space at Whitehall about which we have the most detailed information is in many ways the most unusual and atypical, and it was used only in the final decade of court activity before the Civil War. The Cockpit Theatre of 1629 was, as I have said, a building permanently devoted to one purpose: the staging and watching of plays. Since the prevailing model of court theatre between 1558 and 1642 was temporary conversion with wooden seating and staging, the Cockpit marks a new recognition of the place of theatre in court culture. The building itself was also unusual, although it had been used for the presentation of plays in the familiar court manner since at least 1607.[18] The Cockpit was built by Henry VIII specifically to accommodate cock-fighting, with a central table on which the birds fought, and a ring of raked seats surrounding it. The plan of the outer walls was square, inside which lay an octagonal plan. The major architectural feature was a large lantern, or turreted window, surmounting the sloping central roof, which lay directly above the central cocking table and lit it from overhead. The roof was carried on eight large posts, the plan of which described an inner octagon around the central space, and which also supported a second-storey gallery.

In short, the building was focussed on a central point. As a special version of an animal-baiting ring, it may remind us of the connection between Elizabethan and Jacobean outdoor playhouses and the larger bull or bear rings,[19] but it was

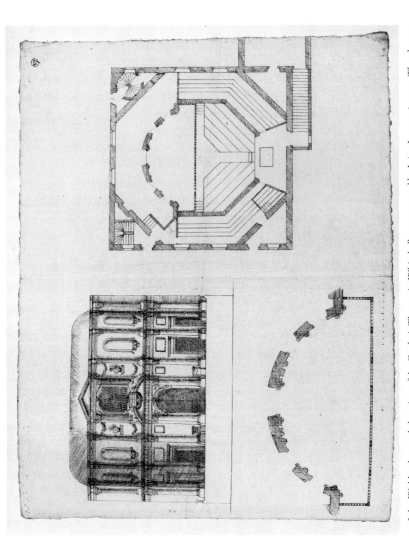

7   John Webb, plans and elevation of the Cockpit Theatre in Whitehall, as converted by Inigo Jones, 1629–30. The plan on the right shows the whole building at ground level, and on the left is a detailed plan of the stage, with above it an elevation of the façade, with five entries and a central balcony.

otherwise an unusual space in which to stage plays. As far as we have been able to observe so far the dominant model for temporary court theatres was a rectangular space in which seating was positioned to watch a performance at one (narrow) end of the area. The space within the Cockpit was quite differently arranged. On the analogy with the Rose or the Swan playhouses, we might imagine that temporary conversions of the Cockpit for plays before 1629 would have placed the stage and tiring house at one edge of the octagonal space; as we may see in the surviving plans of the converted building, Inigo Jones did not do so. The stage at the Cockpit theatre lay at the centre of the building, below the lighting from the lantern and over part of the space where Tudor courtiers had watched the cocks fight. The result is an auditorium which approximates to a neoclassical curved shape, but which is small. The resulting theatre may have had something of the character of the contemporary indoor playhouses of London, but it was quite different from the large playhouses like the Globe and the Fortune, and from the court conversions within the Hall, Great Chamber, and banqueting houses.

The Works accounts which describe the operations at the Cockpit in 1629–30, in some detail, have been widely quoted in histories of the theatre.[20] They tell of the turning of the wooden columns which we can see in the elevation of the *frons scenae*, or the scenic façade behind the stage platform, and of the making of statues out of plaster (Plate 7). Jones was copying the style of the *frons scenae* at Palladio's Teatro Olimpico in Vicenza, which he had seen and drawn during his visits to Italy. The accounts also give information about details we cannot see in the drawing: gilded candelabra and sconces for lighting, and a flying machine in a retractable cloth ceiling made to look like clouds and a starry sky. If the stage was richly decorated in a predominantly new style, however, Jones did not transform the Cockpit beyond recognition. In Danckerts's painting, the building from the outside looks much as it must have done a hundred years before, and the Works accounts to the painter Matthew Gooderick in 1629–30 make clear that the old structure of the Tudor interior was still visible, and was repainted in its traditional colours of white, blue, and gold. As they might in the converted Hall or Great Chamber, court audiences at the Cockpit could have noted the history of their surroundings through the mixture of styles on view.

Greenwich

The palace at Greenwich was the nearest to the city of the large royal buildings which lay outside the immediate London area (from Westminster to the Tower), and was situated on rising land on the south bank of the Thames, with an architectural frontage directly onto the water. The site today is occupied by the Royal Naval Hospital. The royal suite at Greenwich, unlike that at Whitehall, had uninterrupted river views. The choice of riverside sites for all the large palaces was partly governed by considerations of communication and supply (by barge and boat), partly by aesthetics, and not incidentally by the requirements of water supply and sanitation for a large group of people. The tidal Thames flushed the sewer vaults regularly.

Like Whitehall, the palace was built predominantly of brick, with stone dressings for windows and doorways. It was largely the creation of King Henry VIII, who extended the earlier medieval manor of Placentia or 'Plesaunce', and took over a nearby friary, the church of which remained standing, and which can be seen in various views of the palace.[21] Greenwich was heavily used by Henry and his Tudor successors; the Stuart kings held court there less frequently, and King James granted the palace to his queen, Anne. The remaining pre-Restoration building at Greenwich is the Queen's House, begun to Inigo Jones's design to the south of the old palace, on the edge of the park, in 1616, but not finished until twenty years later.

Henry VIII established Greenwich as a primary locus of royal display.[22] The palace was bounded by a park in which hunting could be carried on, and the tiltyard, which lay alongside the residential block on the south-eastern side, was flanked by fantastic castle-like structures which celebrated royal military prowess in a rather romantic fashion. A more down-to-earth feature was an operating armoury, which fashioned the helmets and body-armour the king and his courtiers wore in the tiltyard and on the battlefield. Greenwich was one of the two musical centres of the Chapel Royal (Windsor was the other), with a resident Master and both adult and boy choristers. From the beginning of Henry VIII's reign, chroniclers took notice of the elaborate entertainments held at Greenwich, frequently in the Hall. Dramatic activity from this time onwards was regularly performed in the Hall and the Great Chamber. In general terms they must have been similar to the rooms at Whitehall, with which they were contemporary, but we have rather less detailed information about them. The Hall is the better documented: part of the undercroft which lay below it survives under the north-western block of the Royal Naval Hospital, and hence shows its position, and something of its size.[23] It had a rectangular plan, approximately 68 feet long by 30 feet wide, and hence in total floor area only 57 per cent the size of the Hall at Whitehall. Its general character appears to have been similar, however—a large, high chamber with a pitched roof of timber, and a wooden screen.

In Elizabethan times, at least, both roof and screen were painted. It lay to the south of the main block of the palace, but at no great distance from the royal suite; in 1604–5 'a newe paire of staires' was built to connect the Hall to the Great Chamber.[24]

The Great Chamber itself, as at Whitehall, was a second-storey room, probably of the same general character as that at the central palace (a rectangular chamber of roughly 1,800 square feet in area) and certainly with the same function, as a large guarded antechamber to the royal suite. Its flooring was of wood; it had a ceiling of 'frett', or geometrical battens, and a fireplace–all details which emerge incidentally from the Works accounts for repairs to the palace.[25]

Preparations in the traditional manner were made for plays at Christmas and Shrove in both Hall and Great Chamber throughout the Elizabethan years. The similarity of the temporary seating which transformed these places into theatres to that provided at other gatherings of festive or solemn significance might be illustrated by two consecutive entries from the Office of the Works accounts. In 1587–88 the Works looked after 'makinge of a greate Scaffolde with degrees and pticons for a playe presented to the Queens mat^ie by the Gentlmen of Greyes Inne',[26] an occasion which is discussed at greater length below. Such an indoor 'scaffold'–a framework supporting rising ranks of seats, or bleachers, in modern North American terms–could just as easily be erected outdoors to create a viewing stand or temporary arena. Precisely the same word, which describes the same structure, is used in the account for the following year, when the Works carpenters made 'Scaffouldes in the Parke for the Ladies and gent' to stand one to see the Turkes plaie their feates of actiuitie'.[27] Court theatres were one variant of structures put up to allow large groups to watch special events.

After Queen Elizabeth's death, Greenwich seems not to have been used much for dramatic entertainment, although under Queen Anne at least one masque was mounted in the Hall and a play presented in the Great Chamber, Queen's Side–the first in the suite of rooms originally designed for Henry VIII's queen, which was probably similar in size and interior design to its partner.

Richmond

Richmond lay at some distance upriver from Whitehall, on the site of the earlier medieval palaces of Sheen.[28] Thoroughly rebuilt by King Henry VII following a fire late in 1497, the palace was perhaps the most impressive in its general aspect, and the most orderly in its planning of all the Tudor palaces. Most of the buildings were demolished during the Commonwealth period; today only the

The Livery Kitchen   The Privy Lodgings   Part of the

The Great Orchard   Gallery of the

Privy Garden

Richmond

Thames is fluving

Water hill

8   Wenceslaus Hollar, drawing of Richmond Palace from the river, 1630s.

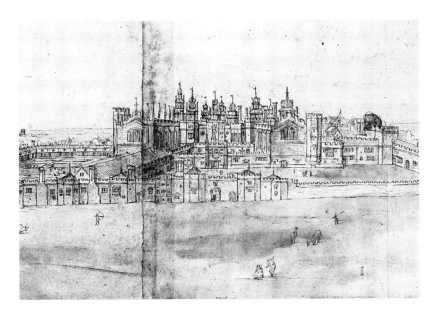

9 Anthony van den Wyngaerde, drawing of Richmond Palace from the north-east, *c.* 1558 (detail). The Hall may be seen on the right.

outer gatehouse and part of the Tudor walls of the Great Court can be seen. These are built in the familiar Tudor brickwork, but the main residential block of the palace, which lay on the river, was entirely faced with stone, and its vertical, sprightly effect, with many bays, towers, and cupolas, was a good deal less domestic and homely than that of any other contemporary English royal palace (Plate 8). This squarish three-storey block which faced the river contained the royal apartments; it had a small courtyard on the interior which gave light to rooms in the centre of the plan. The rest of the palace was arranged as two courtyards which lay behind and in line with this block. From the land side (modern Richmond Green) the palace displayed two matching gabled and turreted walls, each with a large late-Gothic window set high in the wall (Plate 9). These were the Chapel, on the left or eastern side, and the Hall, on the right. (The Hall can partly be seen from the opposite aspect, behind and to the left of the palace block, in the drawing by Hollar reproduced as Plate 8). Hall and Chapel defined two sides of the Fountain Court; a gallery ran between them, and they were connected to the palace block to the south by bridges over a small moat.

Once again the Hall and the Great Chamber are the two rooms we know to have been used for the performance of dramatic activity; once again at least one masque was performed in the Hall in the Stuart years. Unlike the disposition of rooms in the other major palaces, however, these two places were not contiguous. The Hall at Richmond was a free-standing building, connected to other parts of the palace by low galleries and covered walks. It was a major architectural feature of the palace and was the earliest of the great halls in the large Tudor palaces, having been built at the turn of the fifteenth century. A large rectangular space, 100 feet long by 40 feet wide, the Hall had buttressed stone walls built in bays, high windows, and an elaborate timber roof of steep pitch, crowned with a central lantern for ventilation. Richmond Palace Hall was probably the model for the halls subsequently built at Whitehall, Hampton Court, and Greenwich, which followed it in proportions and general style.

Like the central palace block the Hall was built of stone, and it was raised above ground level on an undercroft, with stone steps at its main entrance. It had, like the other halls, a wooden screen at the lower end, and a central hearth below the lantern in the roof. Early in its life it was described in the following terms by a herald recording the events connected with the marriage of Prince Arthur and Catherine of Aragon in 1501. One may hear the consistent note of professional wonder at the magnificence of the patron who sponsored its building.

> The pleasunt halle is uppon the right hand of this curtilage [the inner court]. XII or XVI greces of highte, pavyd with goodly tille; whoes rof is of tymber, not beamyd ne brasid, but proper knotts, craftly corven, joyned, and shet toguyders with mortes, and pynned, hangyng pendaunt from the sede roff into the grownde and flowre, after the moost new invencon and crafte of the prospctif of Gement; cast owt with wyndowes, glasid right lightsume and goodly. In the wallys and siddys of this halle, betwene the wyndowes, be the picturs of the noble Kings of this realme, in their harnes, and robes of goold; as Brute, Engest, King William Rufus, King Arthur, King Henry, and many others of that name; King Richard, King Edward, and of thoes names many noble waryours and Kings of this riall realme; with ther fachons and swords in ther hands; visaged and apperyng like bold and valiaunt knights, and so ther dedys and acts in the cronicles right evydently be shewen and declared. Emonge thes nombre of famous Kings, in the higher parte, upon the lefte hond, is the semely pictur and personage of our most excellent and highe Suffrayn now reigning upon us his liege people, Kyng Henry the VIIth, as worthy that rume and place with thoes glorious Princes as eny King that ever reigned in this lond; that with his great manhode and wisdom hath contynued nobly and victoreous unto this now the XVIIIth yer of his reigne. The wallis of this plesunt halle are hongid with riche clothes of Arras, ther werkys

representyng many noble batalls and seages, as of Jerusalem, Troye, Albe, and many other; that this hole apparement was most glorious and joyefull to consider and beholde.[29]

The Hall, then, was an architectural and artistic endorsement of the historical pattern which had led to the fortunate outcome of the Tudor dynasty. Impressive in its size, and decorated with attractive painting, carving, gilding, and coloured fabric, the Hall was simultaneously an aesthetic experience and a lesson in providential history. It was within this physical setting that dramatic entertainments were presented, from the very beginning of the building's use. Towards the end of its life, before it was broken up for building materials, the Hall was surveyed in 1649 by the colder eyes of the Parliamentary assessors who were charged with valuing the worth of the crown estates and possessions. In their account it is described as

> one fayer and large roome conteyning one hundred foote in lenght and fortie foote in breadth called the greate hall, this roome hath a skreene at the lower end thereof over which is a litle gallery and a faire foote pace [dais] in the higher end thereof. the pavement is square tile and it is very well lighted and seeled and adorned with eleven statues, in the sides thereof, in the midle of this roome there is placed a brick hearth for a charkoale fier having a large lanthorne in the roofe of the hall fitted for that purpose turreted and covered with lead.[30]

Henry VII's 'show of kings', a dominant decorative motif of the interior of the Hall, survived until the demolition of the building, and looked down on all the events that took place there for a century and a half of court activity.

Shows and pageants accompanied the elaborate celebrations of the royal wedding in 1501, perhaps initiating the use of the Hall as a chamber for dramatic revels, but it is not until the 1588–89 season that we hear of a second room at the palace being used for drama. This was the Great Chamber, which is described in records either under that name or as the Guard Chamber, a title favoured in the later history of the palace, and where plays continued to be staged until the Civil War. While views and verbal accounts give us a fairly clear impression of the Hall, the Great Chamber remains more obscure. No contemporary records give its dimensions. The Parliamentary commissioners described the central block of the palace in a fairly simple enumerative way, listing chambers as they walked around the building. On the ground level were the rooms of the household officers, and the royal suite lay on the second storey. What was probably a sequence of rooms is described in these terms: 'one roome called the Lobby arched over head and covered with Lead, in the middle of which roofe is a fayer lanthorne one other fayer chamber floored with board called the guard chamber; one other roome called the presence chamber . . . being all of them well lighted and seeled and matted upon the flowres'.[31]

To locate the Great Chamber, therefore, one might start with the Lobby. It is mentioned quite frequently in the Works accounts. Like the Hall it was paved with tiles, or at least 'the halfe pace [step, or landing] before the great Chamber dore' was so paved.[32] The Works accounts confirm what the Parliamentary survey suggests: that the Lobby rose to the full height of the building, with a roof over it. They also reveal that it contained 'greate stone steppes of Portland stone';[33] it was, in essence, a stair tower which led up to the higher storeys. I think that it was probably the tower at the north-western corner of the southern block, directly to the south of the Hall. Hollar's drawing shows a high window in the south-western face of this structure, equivalent in height to the two upper storeys of the entire building.

The Great Chamber must have been of a similar height; the Works accounts record several repairs to the roof over the Great Chamber. They also tell us that the room was heated by a fireplace, not an open hearth, and that the wooden floor mentioned by the commissioners was subject to occasional repair.[34] The 1501 account cited above, in its more general survey of the palace, describes the Great Chamber as lit with 'goodly bay wyndowes glasid set oute'.[35] I think that these windows, which were probably quite large, lay along the western wall of the palace, looking over the immediately adjoining Great Orchard. The interior of the Great Chamber at Richmond was light, lofty, and spacious. How large its floor area may have been is more difficult to estimate. The entire width of the architectural ranges at Richmond was approximately 50 feet, and a length of 70 feet overall seems to be the maximum possible dimension of the Great Chamber. The room was probably somewhat smaller than this hall-like scale, but it is likely to have been at least as large as the room of the same name at Whitehall.

The interior decorations at Richmond receive some attention in the 1501 description. At that date the Great and Presence chambers were hung with arras, and they had ceilings with a diapered design, and with golden roses and portcullis motifs set in the lozenges. The Works accounts show that this relief decoration in the Tudor style was repaired and repainted, and the arras is likely to have been similarly looked after by the Wardrobe. The general aspect of the décor was probably much the same in 1642 as it had been at the start of the sixteenth century.

The palace was less used by the Stuart monarchs than it was by the Tudors. Elizabeth kept court there often, and she died at Richmond, as did her grand-father before her. James assigned the palace to Prince Henry as his residence outside London; it was from Richmond that Henry travelled by barge to his installation as Prince of Wales in 1610. Had he survived, the palace probably would have seen a greater amount of dramatic activity, of which Henry was an enthusiastic patron. After his death in 1612 the palace passed to the use of Prince Charles, and although he had an interest in the theatre at least the equal of his brother's the surviving records oddly do not show any dramatic activity at the palace until 1636, when there is a sudden renaissance of the preparation of chambers for plays and entertainments. By then the heir to the throne resident at Richmond was the future Charles II, who even as a relatively young child kept a court at which theatrical entertainment was a favourite pastime.

Hampton Court

The palace at Hampton Court can still be visited. Large parts of the extensive Tudor buildings remain in a substantially unaltered state, including the magnificent Hall and Chapel, and to walk round the rooms, courtyards, and adjoining park and gardens gives the best impression one can have today of what the court, as a physical place, was like between 1558 and 1642. Its architecture and interior decorations give a vivid impression of the similar chambers at its now-vanished sister palaces, although it is not exactly a 'representative' palace in that many details of its plan and layout of rooms are unique. Equally, one must close one's eyes to the impressions created by those parts of the existing palace which were rebuilt after the Restoration to the designs of Sir Christopher Wren.[36]

Hampton Court did not lie at the farthest extreme from London of the Thames-side palaces–Windsor is still further upriver–but it was, and is, at a considerable remove from the metropolitan area, and was to that extent somewhat more of a retreat. When the monarch travelled on progress in the summer through the southern counties, and occasionally further afield, it was from Hampton Court that the court group commonly departed, and to which it returned. For all that, it was by no means a mere holiday villa, and it was planned on a scale which enabled all the activities of court life to be carried on; it remained in regular use throughout the period considered here.

The present structure may contain some fragments of the original manor which was very grandly extended and rebuilt by Cardinal Wolsey. The splendour of his palace excited the envy of the king, and the cardinal was persuaded, in one way or another, to grant it to his monarch in 1526. Henry VIII continued to extend and to alter the palace.[37] The buildings at Hampton Court stand back from the river, giving a rather different effect from the other three large palaces.

One approaches the royal apartments through two courtyards with gatehouses; the second is dominated on one side by the Hall. Yet again it was the Hall and the Great Chamber at Hampton Court which were converted for the staging of plays. The two rooms are in fact immediately contiguous, since the Great Chamber—unusually—is placed at ground level immediately behind the high end of the Hall. In effect this rendered the Hall the largest outer chamber of the royal suite, and the arrangement seems to be based on a rather older idea of domestic layout.

The Hall at Hampton Court is substantially preserved as it was in the days of King Henry VIII, and it looks today much as it did throughout the reigns of his successors before the Civil War. When we stand in Hampton Court Hall today, then, we can look around us at a space which was used as a theatre in Shakespeare's lifetime, and in which Shakespeare himself performed. His company, newly named the King's Men, played there during the first English Christmas court of King James in 1603. It is a large area: 106 feet long overall by 40 feet in width, and the room rises high above the observer on the ground into the dark recesses of the elaborate timber roof overhead; the highest point is 65 feet above the floor. Actors faced with performing there might feel intimidated by the acoustical challenges to the carrying power and clarity of their voices. At one end is the raised dais with a high bay window lighting it from the direction of the courtyard outside, and at the other end is a large, plain, dark wooden screen, with two doorway openings and a gallery over the top. The screen in Whitehall Hall as it is shown in the drawings and plans for *Florimène* in 1635 looks very similar to what we see in Hampton Court Hall. Performances of plays staged in the Hall at Hampton Court—and plays continued to be staged there until at least the later 1630s—could accommodate large audiences; with the exception of the Jacobean banqueting houses at Whitehall, both wider and rather longer, the Hall was the biggest court theatre space in England before the Restoration.

As great chambers were at all the other palaces, the Great Chamber, or King's Great Watching Chamber, is smaller, and would have been more suitable for entertainments which were not attended by the full court and large numbers of guests. At 55 feet in length and 27 in breadth, the floor area is comparable to that of the Great Chamber at Whitehall. The room is quite lofty, at 25 feet in height, and it is lit by two windows of almost the full height of the room, one of them a bay or oriel built when the room was altered in 1535; a row of smaller, high-set windows also light the room from above. The surviving roof and wooden ceiling also date from 1535, and demonstrate what is meant in the Works accounts by a 'fret' ceiling: a patterned system of ribs radiating from pendants, carved in relief and painted, and with heraldic badges in roundels set within the lozenge-shaped spaces between the ribs. The walls are hung with tapestries to a height of 14 feet, as they were in the sixteenth and seventeenth centuries. Otherwise the appearance of the room is rather plainer than it was before the Restoration: the decoration of the upper parts of the walls was removed in 1700.[38]

St James's

Parts of the Tudor St James's Palace also survive today. Its turreted gatehouse in brick is approached from modern Piccadilly down the road called, simply, St James's. The palace is still a royal residence and is not open to the public, but one may walk around the outside, observing the Catholic Chapel on Marlborough Road, built by Inigo Jones and which served Queen Henrietta Maria, who lived at the palace in the 1630s. The two-storey Tudor range on the opposite side of the road contains the former Guard Chamber or Great Chamber. One may also attend Sunday service in the surviving Tudor (Anglican) Chapel, with its elaborate ceiling, which lies next to the gatehouse within the remaining parts of the old palace complex.

St James's was never a large palace, although after the Whitehall fire of 1698 it became the principal London residence of the English monarchs, and was extended; Queen Victoria was living there at the time of her accession. It perhaps is better described, in its original form, as a large Tudor house. It was built by King Henry VIII between 1531 and 1541, on the site of the hospital of St James, which gave it its name.[39] It lay, and lies, not far from Whitehall, across St James's Park, which in Tudor times was enclosed, and contained deer and game. Its projected function may have been to serve as a court for the male heir to the throne, but it was only in the Stuart years that it came to fulfil this role. Prince Henry took up residence there in 1604, when he was a boy of ten. He died at the palace eight years later, and his elaborate processional state funeral began within its chambers. In the intervening years he kept up a culturally lively court which, it has been claimed, drew more attention than that of his father.[40] His brother Charles succeeded him as principal resident of the palace until he assumed the throne in 1625, following which the palace, with a specially built chapel and quarters for Catholic priests, was placed at the disposal of the queen. Marie de Medici, Henrietta Maria's mother, visited England in 1638, and stayed at the palace; a contemporary account of the visit is illustrated with some rather fanciful but generally informative engravings of the interior of the palace at that date (Plate 10).[41]

COMME MESSIEVRS DV CONSEIL PRIVE VIENNENT SALVER LA
REYNE DANS SA CHAMBRE

10 An engraving of the interior of St James's Palace at the time of the visit of the French Queen
Mother, Marie de Medici, in 1638.

Theatrical entertainments at the palace began, so far as surviving records indicate, in the Stuart years; they would always have been more intimate events than the festival plays at Whitehall, Greenwich, Richmond, and Hampton Court, since the largest chamber at St James's was the Chapel; there was no hall. The palace was planned as a series of courtyards, which have been referred to by different names over the course of the centuries. What is now Colour Court was, in Elizabethan times, simply called the outer court or the base court. Beyond it to the south-east lay a smaller courtyard around which the royal apartments were positioned. Elizabethan nomenclature usually designated it the inner court; today it is called Friary Court, but is no longer an enclosed courtyard, as the consequence of an extensive fire which destroyed the south-eastern part of the palace in 1809.

Two rooms appear to have been used for theatrical spaces at St James's, although as the chambers were differently used by their successive inhabitants their titles tended to change accordingly, and this can confuse.[42] Although plays were probably presented at the palace soon after Prince Henry took up residence there, the earliest specific references to them are from 1610 and 1612. The earliest mention of a precise location, from the Works accounts of 1615–16, is of 'the Councell Chamber',[43] and it appears that this room was consistently used until the 1630s. In 1633–34 a second room, 'the presence Chamber', was prepared for plays, and it continued to be used until records cease.[44] Both rooms, I believe, lay in the ranges which formed the inner court, and they were chosen because they were the largest spaces available. Both lay on the second storey adjoining the north-western corner of the inner court, at the head of the stairway which led up to the royal suite from the outer court. By the time it was used to accommodate theatrical performance, the Council Chamber seems no longer to have been used for the purpose suggested by its title: in 1610–11 it is referred to as 'the olde Counsell Chamber'.[45] When a reigning monarch had lived there, as did Queen Mary, and occasionally Queen Elizabeth, then the Privy Council would have met there, but a Prince of Wales did not have such administrative responsibilities. The room was contiguous to the royal suite, and survives in what today is called the Guard Room. Although somewhat altered, its present size of roughly twenty feet wide by forty feet long gives a fairly accurate idea of the space available for a theatrical adaptation. Although the Works accounts refer to the usual provision of 'degrees', or ranked wooden seating, and a 'halpace', or platform for the royal seat, the effect of the finished auditorium and stage can only have been far more intimate than a similar conversion within the Hall at Whitehall.

11 The Armoury Room, St James's Palace. Formerly the Tudor Guard Chamber, and, under Queen Henrietta Maria, the Presence Chamber.

The second room used for theatre at St James's was of a similar size. It too survives, probably less altered in interior dimensions than the former Council Chamber. What is today called the Armoury Room (Plate 11) measures just less than 20 feet wide and similarly less than 40 feet long. It is lit by two windows to the east, one of them a bay, and it has a Tudor fireplace. This room was the first chamber in the Tudor royal suite: the Guard or Great Chamber (despite its fairly modest dimensions). Beyond it lay the Presence Chamber (the Tapestry Room today), then the Privy Chamber, with the royal bedchamber beyond that, on the southern range, looking towards the park. The Tudor functions of the rooms changed, however, during the residence of Queen Henrietta Maria, when we learn that plays were presented in 'the presence Chamber'. First, in 1631–32, some kind of adaptation was made to the Council Chamber by dividing it with wooden partition walls and hence rendering it unsuitable for theatrical use.[46] Meanwhile, as a heraldic document reveals, by 1630 the former Great Chamber was 'now called the Presence',[47] the queen presumably having banished the guard to some other room below stairs to create rather more space for her own entourage. It was in that room that plays were presented, from 1633 onwards, under constraints of space similar to those in the Council Chamber.

Somerset or Denmark House

This was the second of the smaller royal houses close to Whitehall which were used by the extended families of James I and Charles I. The palace, which stood on the site of the Somerset House which now houses King's College and the Courtauld Institute, between the Strand and the river, had belonged to the Dukes of Somerset, but had become a royal possession after the arrest and execution of Edward Seymour in 1551.[48] It was given the name Denmark House possibly as early as 1603, when James granted it to his queen, Anne of Denmark, but the old name did not pass entirely out of use, and was increasingly revived after Anne's death in 1619; from now on I will use the older name for the sake of consistency, and will attempt to indicate where the name given the palace in contemporary references could be confusing. Both queens of the Stuart monarchs were enthusiastic patrons of drama, and both participated in royal masques as disguised and costumed dancers. Anne's court, like that of her son Henry, saw a certain amount of independent patronage of theatrical performance–probably rather more than has been recorded in contemporary accounts.

There is little precise information about the rooms within Somerset House. The palace had an impressive frontage on the Strand, from which a gateway admitted one to a large courtyard with ranges of buildings around it. In Elizabethan times it had a full suite of traditional chambers—'the w[th]drawing Chamber the prevy Chamber the pnts [presence] the greate chamber and Councell chamber'[49]—which were probably located on the second storey around this court; a contemporary account also speaks of 'the Queenes Chamber nexte the Streate'.[50] In the Jacobean period much of this block around the Strand court was rebuilt; the construction was not completed until 1613, and Queen Anne may not have taken up residence until around that year.[51] The house also had a hall, of quite large dimensions (60 feet by 31 feet),[52] which was certainly used to stage drama in the Caroline years, and may have been so used earlier.

The surviving accounts indicate that it was during Queen Henrietta Maria's residence at the house that it was most extensively used for theatrical events. One of the most elaborate occasions involved the building of an entire theatre within a courtyard—the so-called Paved Court theatre of 1632–33.[53] This was a wooden hall 76 feet long by 36 feet wide (and hence not a great deal larger than the Hall), with a scenic stage at one end. We do not hear of it again after the pastoral and masque that were presented there, and presumably it was taken down after they were over. It was therefore more an unusually elaborate temporary conversion than a permanent court theatre like the contemporary Cockpit.

In the following year, the Works accounts tell us that a pastoral play with a scenic stage and 'wth diuse motions' (that is, presumably, machinery to change the scenes) was presented in the Presence Chamber, while, in the Privy Chamber next door, seats were set up 'to behold the dancing'.[54] Neither room is likely to have been much larger than the similar chambers at St James's, and quite why such an elaborate show should have been mounted in such a small space is hard to understand. Miniaturisation, it appears, may have been one kind of court fashion accompanying the more usual royal taste for grand and expansive effects.

Windsor

Windsor Castle is among the most impressive of the royal properties to survive today. A castle has stood on the site since Norman times, built on a high point above the river Thames; from the level of the river or from aeroplanes approaching Heathrow it offers a striking view. The castle continued to be altered, but was definitively shaped by King Edward III in the fourteenth century.[55] The buildings at Windsor were, and are, arranged in two courtyards with a central keep, built on a mound, separating them, and together forming a figure-eight plan. The royal apartments were situated in the upper bailey, on the east. The

Hall built by Edward III lay on the northern side of the courtyard of the upper bailey, on an east–west line, with windows facing the court. It became known as St George's Hall, since it was used for the ceremonies of the Order of the Garter, and it is shown in an etching made in 1672 by Hollar, as an illustration to Elias Ashmole's book on the order (Plate 12). As may be seen, the Hall was a long rectangular space with a high wooden roof and a range of high windows and clerestories along its southern wall; nine bays are shown in Hollar's depiction. No record of its dimensions remains, but it evidently was as large as the Tudor halls at Richmond, Hampton Court, and Whitehall. It was subsequently altered, in 1678, then altered once again and enlarged to about twice its original size in the nineteenth century, as part of a thorough 'renovation' of the buildings which changed their character substantially. The Hall as designed by the architect Wyattville was heavily damaged by fire in 1992; in its recently restored form it has yet another appearance which differs from the medieval original.

The medieval royal apartments had distinct suites for the king and queen, each with its Great Chamber and a successive number of rooms. The King's Great Chamber, the basis of the Victorian Ball Room, was a long rectangular space roughly 75 feet long by 25 feet wide. The palace was extensively renovated for the queen's use in Elizabethan times. Like Hampton Court it was regarded as a suitably isolated retreat from infection in London, and was a staging point at the start and end of summer progresses: King James was presented with the third performance of Ben Jonson's entertainment, *The Gypsies Metamorphosed*, at the castle in September 1621, as he returned from travel in the Midlands. We have little clear information, however, about the Elizabethan chambers and how they were used. Court Christmas was held there only infrequently during the years surveyed in this book, and apparently not at all after the early 1580s (see appendix). The Revels Office attended to manage the dramatic entertainments; in 1582–83 a number of playing companies presented plays, and there was a mask. Quite where the revels took place is not clear. The Hall was the largest space, but there were certainly other chambers of considerable size which might have served as a temporary theatre. Yet despite its size, the palace seems not normally to have been used as a regular gathering place for court festivals, apart from those associated with the Order of the Garter.

Other Palaces

The buildings surveyed above were those most regularly and commonly used as places where the English monarchs and their families saw dramatic entertainment

The Prospect of the inside of
S. GEORGES HALL.

The Soveraign sitting at dinner   4. Knights sitting at dinner   5. Attendants.   6. Court Attends. that serve the Knights Table   7. Garter principall King of Armes   8. Officers at Armes
Per 7. Treasurer of the Houshold.   2. Controler of the Houshall.   9. Server.   10. Pensioners waiting the second course.   11. Cofferer.   12. Master of the Houshold   13. Yeomen of the Guard

12   Wenceslaus Hollar, etching of St George's Hall, Windsor, in the 1670s, as prepared for a feast of the Knights of the Garter.

between 1558 and 1642. Other places were occasionally used for royal shows, however, apart from the aristocratic houses and gardens, town gates, city streets and other places where kings and queens would have seen shows, pageants, and dramatised speeches while on progress or during processional state occasions. At least once, King Charles took a troupe of players on progress with him–they travelled with the royal party, and were provided with a tent for accommodation–so that he might commission entertainment for his hosts in the various places he visited.[56]

The records of the Office of the Works have scattered and infrequent references to preparatory work for plays at other royal properties, and they are probably not inclusive: more occasional entertainments are likely to have been presented at the smaller and more remote royal houses than the remaining records show. A mask was presented at Nonsuch, in Surrey, in 1559, for example, during the period when the house was not the property of the crown (1556–92);[57] the 'Stage' made in the Privy Chamber of Queen Henrietta Maria within the palace in 1631–32 is likely simply to have been a dais, without any theatrical significance.[58] Nonsuch, and the smaller house of Oatlands, to the south-east and the south-west of Hampton Court respectively, were frequently used by Queen Elizabeth during the summer and autumn, and also as retreats by the Stuarts. The only known theatrical entertainment at Oatlands was provided for Queen Elizabeth in the last summer of her life, when a visiting group of *commedia dell' arte* players presented a play to her in August 1602, an occasion about which little else is known.[59] Such places, built as hunting centres for King Henry VIII, were not on the grand scale of the larger royal buildings, and hence not planned for the display of a full court, but it seems quite likely that, especially in the Stuart years, they occasionally accommodated the more intimate and private kind of royal entertainment patronised at St James's and Somerset House.

Records for the preparation of chambers at other provincial palaces further from London also come from the Stuart years. James I acquired two houses north of London, at Newmarket in Cambridgeshire and Royston in Hertfordshire, as bases for hunting parties. Fairly unassuming buildings were enlarged, at Royston to include a great chamber, presence chamber, and so forth.[60] We know very little about the buildings, the size of the rooms, and their appointments, but it seems that neither house had great pretensions, even in a translated state. In 1616, however, students from Cambridge presented a play before the king in the Presence Chamber at Royston.[61] At Newmarket, at some time in 1631–32, a play was presented 'in the Queenes presence Chamber';[62] once again the scale of the space is likely to have been similar to that in St James's Palace rather than that of the larger court rooms elsewhere. The old palace at Woodstock in Oxfordshire–a medieval foundation enlarged and adapted by King Henry VII–also appears in the accounts of the Works as a place where theatrical space was prepared. In 1616–17 an entire temporary 'roome' was built there 'for a maske', and in August 1621 a quite elaborate theatre was built in the Hall for a play presented before the king by students from Oxford.[63] The palace was destroyed in the eighteenth century and not a great deal is known about the buildings, but the Hall there was built in the early thirteenth century, and its internal plan appears to have been rather different from the large Tudor halls; an observer in 1634 described it as a 'spacious church-like Hall, with two fayre iles, with six Pillars, white, and large, parting either ile'.[64] The Woodstock performance was a large-scale event, then; we know rather more about the provisions for the conversion than we do about many other occasions, and I will have more to say about it in subsequent chapters.

The rarity of records of preparations for plays or other theatrical occasions at houses other than the few commonly used and larger palaces is probably indicative: that is, it was unusual for royal patrons to see drama when visiting the smaller properties farther away from London. The records, as always, are unlikely to be giving us a complete and exhaustive record of such occasions. Plays may have been seen rather more frequently at Nonsuch or at Woodstock, as well as having been presented at other royal houses, like Oatlands, about which the Works accounts are silent.

3 Royal Theatres

O, for a Muse of fire, that would ascend
The brightest heaven of invention!
A kingdom for a stage, princes to act,
And monarchs to behold the swelling scene!

...

                       But pardon, gentles all,
The flat unraisèd spirits that hath dared
On this unworthy scaffold to bring forth
So great an object.
William Shakespeare, Prologue, *Henry V* (London, 1623)

Shakespeare's apology for the mismatch between the epic scope of the story of England's hero-king and the restricted resources of the Globe Theatre uses a word frequently employed in the Works accounts covering preparations for royal theatrical shows. Scaffolds held kings and courtiers as well as actors. *Henry V* was performed at Whitehall before the king and court in January 1605,[1] and we might ask whether the prologue was performed quite as it was printed in the Folio edition of the play. Dare an actor have suggested that the facilities provided by the munificence of the king were in any sense unworthy? Manners aside, however, the actors would have recognised many similarities among the spaces in which they performed at court, their own playhouses, and other playing places elsewhere. One type of London playhouse, from as early as 1576, was a converted medieval hall, with wooden seats and galleries framed inside the confines of stone walls and Gothic windows. The two distinct theatres at Blackfriars had this character, and the Paul's theatre, somewhere within the precincts of the medieval cathedral, is likely to have been similar.[2] Indoors or out, however, wooden structures supported stages and theatrical seating. The outdoor playhouses were built of heavy timber frames; seating facilities in provincial town halls and inn yards, in college halls at the universities, and in the halls and chambers of the county aristocracy and gentry would have been made in the same way as the carpenters of the Office of the Works built their scaffolds and degrees. Most court theatres were raised on wooden frameworks.

These royal structures can be understood as part of a long and widespread tradition of temporary wooden buildings for festivals. The word 'scaffold' was used for such places in Chaucer's day, and for his contemporaries it could mean both a place for performance and a stand from which an audience watched, just as it could 200 years later. The parish clerk Absolon, in *The Miller's Tale*, has played the part of King Herod on a scaffold, and the same word describes the dispersed playing stations on the surviving manuscript plan of the layout for the play *The Castle of Perseverance*, from the early fifteenth century. At the same time in York a Latinised version of the English word was being used to describe what are plainly stands for an audience.[3] Both actors and audience using such wooden structures in France can be seen in the famous manuscript painting by Jean Fouquet of a play on the martyrdom of a saint, from about 1460.[4] In the court of King Henry VII of England, some thirty years later, a version of these wooden frameworks and platforms was set up in the old palace of Westminster for the revels at Christmas, and the Office of the Works recorded expenditure '*super factura certorum spectaculorum sive theatorum vulgariter scaffalds infra magnam aulam Westmonasterii ut ludi sive la disguisyngs nocte Epiphaniae populo exhiberentur*' ('for making certain viewing stands or theatrical seats, in common language scaffolds, at the low end of the Great Hall at Westminster, to show the plays or disguisings to the people at Twelfth Night').[5]

Once the court was re-established after the Restoration, the habit of building temporary scaffold theatres died out, but the larger context which had contained the Elizabethan and early Stuart court theatres did not. That is to say that wooden platforms, steps, and viewing stands were still built for royal events, usually for great occasions such as coronations and banquets, although not exclusively so, and the technique of constructing them remained the same as it had been in the medieval period.

My survey of the palaces in the preceding chapter reveals that the size of temporary court theatres must have varied considerably from the very largest, set up within the great halls, to the smallest, in rooms of relatively modest size. Such variation would certainly have affected the size of the audience, and we might also think that it governed the kind of show presented: relatively small-scale, intimate plays might have been chosen for the smaller spaces, while plays such as

Henry V would have been presented where there was some space for their *brio* and dynamism. It is certainly true that the elaborate staging of the masques, with scenery, dancing, and large groups of musicians, could not be successfully realised in small rooms, although we might note that an entertainment with scenery and dancing was somehow put on in the relatively small rooms of the royal suite at Somerset House. Plays by the professional actors, however, do not seem to have been closely matched to the space in which they were performed. Plays of quite large scale, in terms of their length, the number of scenes with more than three or four actors on stage, and their stage effects–Shakespeare's *Richard III* and *Julius Caesar*, for example–were performed in the small chambers at St James's Palace.[6]

The amount of space available in a given chamber would also have affected the size of a stage. Stages are only infrequently mentioned in the Works accounts, and even more infrequently are dimensions given, so that we must infer that building them was a matter of course, and that their size was scaled to the total amount of space available. For professional actors, who were used to playing their pieces in varying venues when they toured provincial towns and cities, a stage platform of a few feet deeper or shallower would not have been of great consequence. There must, however, have been a required minimum of area to stage any play, and the King's Men could not have put on *Richard III* on a table-top. The smallest stage mentioned in surviving records was built in the Great Chamber at Richmond in 1588–89: it was 14 feet square, and actors from various troupes played on it. When compared with stages which preceded and followed it, this is an unusually small platform, and in unusual proportions. The stage at the playing place at the Red Lion in Stepney in 1567 was 30 feet deep by 40 feet wide, even larger than the best-known stage dimensions of the Shakespearean period, those of the Fortune playhouse of 1600, the measurements for which are usually understood to be 43 feet in width by $27\frac{1}{2}$ feet in depth.[7]

These measurements are typical of most stage spaces from the period that we can see in drawings or plans or of which we have verbal descriptions. Stages generally were wider than they were deep, even when, as at the Rose playhouse, the stage was not in the shape of a regular rectangle. Stages smaller than the extensive platforms of the Red Lion and the Fortune, however, must have been common enough. We do not know the exact size of the stages at the indoor playhouses at Blackfriars, Paul's, the Cockpit in Drury Lane, or Salisbury Court, but we do know that the theatres were all smaller halls, and thus that the proportions of the stage platforms in these places would have matched the reduced size of their auditoriums.

What is rather odd about the stage at Richmond, therefore, is that it was put up in one of the larger court rooms. The theatre made in the Hall at Woodstock in 1621, a very large chamber, was not provided with an extensive stage (24 feet wide by 16 feet deep), although even those modest dimensions provided a platform double the area of that at Richmond. Since the Elizabethan stage was provided for plays at Christmas before a large assembled court, the entire entry covering the preparation suggests that the Richmond Great Chamber must have been filled with people. The Works carpenters were paid for

> fframynge postes and Railes for plaies setting vp degrees in the greate Chamber Nayllinge one bracketts and boordes for the people to sitt one making new halpace there for the Quenes Ma^ts vse and a new stage of xiiij foote square for the plaiers to plaie on, and halpaces for the lordes and ladies to sitt on and iij other halepaces for the people to stand on, and after the plaies eanded for taking downe and removinge the prouisions.[8]

This assembly of scaffolds is likely to have had an impressive finished effect, filled with people and brightly lit by the candle brackets and the suspended chandeliers hung across the room by the Revels Office. But what kind of a theatre was it? It is unlikely, I think, that it looked like the transformed hall at Christ Church, Oxford, in 1605, or entirely like the arrangement made in the Hall at Whitehall for *Florimène* in 1635, which included a large stage with a proscenium and perspective scenery, a fashion of presentation only just beginning to influence English stage practice at that date. What the three theatres at Richmond, Oxford, and Whitehall had in common was the carpentered units on which they were raised, and before turning to the question of configuration–how the audience was arranged in relation to the stage, and quite how the stage and its surroundings may have looked to that audience–I would like to give a little more attention to these wooden frameworks. Though they may have been unworthy of the sustained admiration a good performance drew from its court audience, the success of such an occasion rested on their solidity.

The framing of a scaffold used to accommodate an audience would have varied with where it was built and with the weight it had to bear; evidently 'degrees' in a smaller chamber would have been made from lighter timber than that used for the main support posts of the largest of such structures in the halls. Scaffolds constructed outdoors–like many of the medieval theatrical structures, viewing stands for tournaments and processions, and the building scaffolding used by the Office of the Works–differed somewhat from indoor scaffolds. On unpaved ground a scaffold could be made secure by driving or planting the upright poles on which it was raised into the earth. A fairly light version of such a structure can be seen in the etching by Francis Barlow of horse races near Windsor Castle in 1684 (Plate 13). In the right middle ground Charles II, surrounded by his courtiers, stands on a roofed viewing platform with a waist-high guard rail; the façade of the structure has been decorated with arras hangings. The effect is not unlike the boxes or enclosed galleries that we can see in other plans and pictures, and it incidentally shows that audience accommodation, even for royal viewers, did not necessarily involve seating. Several Works accounts for theatrical preparations make a distinction between places where people could sit and other raised areas where they could stand, and we should take it that they mean exactly that. It was not only at the outdoor playhouses where part of the audience stood to watch a play, and those who stood were not invariably noisy vulgarians, as they are characterised by some contemporary playwrights and by the broad-brush descriptions of some modern popular accounts of the early stage.

If the construction of wooden scaffolds outdoors was a technique known and practised across Europe from the middle ages onwards, so was the adaptation of such structures for theatrical and other festival occasions indoors. The theory accompanying such practice begins to be recorded in books which celebrate the architectural taste of Italian Renaissance courts. The first and most famous of these is Sebastiano Serlio's *Archittetura* (1545), to which we must return, but the rather later compendium of techniques suitable for court theatres, Nicola Sabbatini's *Pratica di fabricar scene e machine ne' teatri* (1638), has more pertinent things to say about the kinds of structure which were most often used in the contemporary English courts. Sabbatini's diagram (Plate 14) shows a framework supporting 'degrees' or stepped seats. Since his commentary stresses the importance of avoiding damage to the walls or floor of the room in which the seating is built, the unit is meant to be independently stable, the triangle ABC representing a vertical frame connected to a series of similar frames by horizontal timbers at the apexes, and by the seating across the sloping front. It may be doubted whether such a simple model could be entirely relied on, especially for larger, heavier banks of seating. Though it is perfectly adequate as a rough plan it clearly presents considerable practical problems at the point C, for example, where the vertical supporting post is connected to two horizontal timbers running along the floor, and where the strength of the connection keeps the entire frame together.

This problem raises a further question about the Works scaffolds: were they built out of solid prefabricated units joined together on the site, or, in accordance with sixteenth- and seventeenth-century practice, were they framed before they

13 Francis Barlow, etching of King Charles II watching horse-racing near Windsor Castle in 1684 (detail). The viewing stand is simply built of wooden poles and planks, with woven cloth hung over the front. Members of the King's Guard stand on the steps.

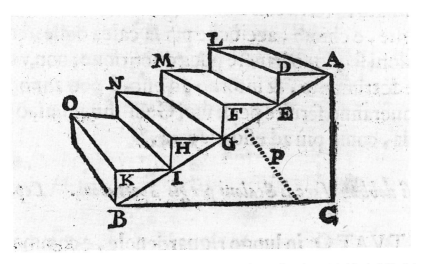

14   Woodcut illustrating the construction of a bank of theatrical seating, 1638. Nicola Sabbatini,
Pratica di fabricar scene e machine ne' teatri.

were erected? Such carpentry, used in the building of houses, barns, and outdoor
playhouses, employed tightly fitting joints to sustain the strength of the completed structure at points of stress. And if a custom-built prefabricated auditorium
was made for a given room, was it stored, once disassembled after the plays were
over, for subsequent events? An elaborate wooden stage and theatrical galleries
were kept from year to year for use at one Cambridge college hall, at least, during
our period.[9] One might be led to connect this practice with the rather puzzling
entry in the Works accounts for 1571–72, in which workmen at Whitehall were
paid for 'setting vp the frame in the halle for Playes maskes and Tragedies at
diuers tymes'.[10] If *the* frame was set up at various times then it undoubtedly was a
fairly elaborate demountable timber structure which would have been stored in a
special place when not in use. The term is not used again in subsequent years,
however, and it may be simply the accountant's way of saying that the usual
theatrical physical provisions ('the frame' was a completed temporary theatre)
were set up on a number of occasions. On the other hand, an entry in the
accounts for 1591–92 for the building of a 'greate removinge Scaffolde' at
Hampton Court certainly suggests that the timbers of some temporary structures
were kept together for re-assembly.[11] Since the bare term 'scaffold' covers a
variety of frameworks used for different purposes–including building, painting,
and plasterwork, the constant business of the Works operations–it is hard to tell if

the Hampton Court entry has any immediate theatrical significance, although the odds are that it does not, since both Christmas and Shrove in that year were celebrated at Whitehall. An entry for the following year at Whitehall is perhaps more suggestive: 'setting vp two removing Scaffolds and fitting sondrye peices that were warped with ioystinge and bordinge the saide scaffoldes sondrye time with ij° flowres one over another'.[12] I think that these structures are more likely to have been employed as work platforms for construction or restoration operations. Although raised boxes, which may well have been made with one floor over another, were certainly used at court assemblies, the continued rebuilding of the floors of these particular structures seems to indicate the heavy use and repeated movement of construction equipment. Thus a 'removing scaffold', like the modern mobile platforms used for working on high ceilings, for example, was distinct from those fixed into the ground or braced against a vertical surface in one position.

On balance, I consider that most of the evidence suggests that scaffolds used for court theatre were commonly built anew for each occasion, and that they were built in such a way that the lumber could have been re-used for other jobs when they were taken apart again. They were indeed made from pieces of wood designated by the names of their most common functions. An early Elizabethan Works account gives a summary of work completed during the preceding two short reigns of Edward VI and Mary I, and it includes an account of setting up seating in Westminster Hall for the state trial of the Duke of Somerset and others in 1551. On that occasion the scaffolds, which were probably large to match the size of the hall and the political significance of the event, were made of 'tymber, boordes Rafters quarters Ioystes Rayles & Yronworke'.[13] In this list 'tymber' probably refers to the longest pieces, which were probably not much trimmed and squared, used for the upright supports. A general account from the reign of King Henry VIII specifically lists 'Skaffolde Tymbre', as well as 'poles' and 'mastis of ffire'.[14] A list of supplies from the 1640s reveals that scaffold poles at that date were 22 feet in length.[15] Boards would have been required for the degrees themselves, to form bench seats and floors, as in Sabbatini's diagram; quarters were also a kind of board, generally of longer and thinner dimensions. Rafters and joists were squared pieces of timber used for building: made to span the width of a structure and to support considerable weight they were long and strong, and evidently were used as the horizontal members in a structure of the kind illustrated by Sabbatini.[16]

The most precise information we possess in the form of a written account about a specifically theatrical scaffold tells us about seating for Ben Jonson's

Masque of Augurs, performed in the newly completed Whitehall Banqueting House of Inigo Jones in 1622. The Works account tells us that there were eleven 'bays' of degrees, each bay 16 feet long, with eleven levels of seating divided into two sections, 'on both sides of the banquettinge house'. Since the Banqueting House is constructed in only seven bays, with 16 feet between the centres of the columns which define them, the description cannot mean what it might be taken to on first reading. Presumably the degrees, of eleven bays in total, were built around the perimeter of one part of the room, leaving space for a stage, dancing place, and music boxes at the other end, in a fashion similar to the *Florimène* plan. This confusion aside, the account gives detailed information about the job performed under the supervision of the master workman, which is worth quoting at length:

> Ralph Brice Carpenter for frameinge and setting vpp xj[en] baies of degrees on both sides of the banquettinge house every bay conteyninge xvj[en] foote longe, beinge twoe panes in every of them; the degrees belowe beinge seven rowes in heighte; and twoe boordes nayled upon every brackett the degrees in the midle gallery beinge fower rowes in heighthe and twoe boordes nailed vpon brackettes also with a rail belowe and another raile in the midle gallery being crosse latticed vnder the same; working frameinge & settinge vpp of vprighte postes wroughte with eighte cantes to beare the same woorke[17]

Several points of structural interest emerge from this entry. The 'Rayles' which are listed in the 1551 account quoted above are revealed here to have been used to separate distinct areas of seating. The rail at the foot of the entire structure prevented over-enthusiastic spectators from rushing towards either the performers or the king, and the upper rail, with the added barrier of latticing, prevented the easy migration of spectators in the upper, less desirable sections of seating into those nearer the performance, as happens in a modern theatre or concert-hall after the interval. The incidental indication is that seating in the court theatres was hierarchically arranged, as might be expected.

The supporting posts for *this* structure were not rough timber poles, as I suggested above, but specially cut vertical members 'wroughte with eighte cantes' (i.e., octagonal in section). One might suppose that degrees built in 16-foot sections within the Banqueting House were partly supported by the free-standing columns which are a feature of the room, but the provision of octagonal posts rather suggests that at least *some* of the bays may have been angled rather than having been arranged in a strictly rectilinear fashion following the walls of the room (as in the *Florimène* plan), and that the resulting auditorium may have approximated to a neoclassical curving form, like that followed at Oxford's Christ Church Theatre of 1605. What is more likely for a masque theatre is that only the seating at the end opposite the stage would have taken such a form, producing a plan like that of the Teatro Farnese at Parma (1618–20), with a long area of open floor surrounded by galleries on three sides.

The Christ Church plan and its annotations provide the most precise and reliable information we have about a temporary theatre in the years covered by this study. Although not strictly a court theatre, it was made for a visit by the king, and was planned and built by the staff of the Office of the Works. Its elaboration, evidently, is atypical of regular court practice, for either plays or masques. As John Orrell has pointed out, it is a consciously Serlian design – based, that is to say, on the model of a court theatre propounded by Sebastiano Serlio, with a curving, classically inspired auditorium in one high, rising rank, facing a stage with scenery designed in the conventions of linear perspective. Such a stage did not suit either performances by professional actors, whose performing spaces elsewhere did not employ perspective wing scenery, or the court performers of the masque, who required an extensive space in front of their spectacular scenes on which to dance. The 1605 experiment was something of a *cul-de-sac*, therefore, but its structural details are likely to be indicative of the practices of the Works in building temporary theatres and auditoriums elsewhere.

With immediate reference to the Banqueting House auditorium of 1622, the notes to the 1605 plans tell us that the first seven rows of degrees in the Oxford theatre took up 14 feet of linear depth and rose to 6 feet in height. Thereafter the seats rose by 8 inches per row, so that a spectator in the back row of a Banqueting House auditorium built on the same principles might have sat with his or her head 11 to 12 feet above floor level.

The Christ Church plan is also quite clear about the hierarchical ordering of the parts of the auditorium, which became less comfortable and roomy the further one was removed from the stage and from the king, whose position on the original plan was to be on a platform level with the stage at the very front of the auditorium, to give him the best view of the perspective effects. (Following some argument about this rather odd position, from the point of view of court protocol, the royal dais was moved further back.) The first seven rows of seating were 'for Ladys & the Kings servants';[18] the benches were 8 inches wide, with 16 inches of knee room in front, and 2 feet of height for the legs. Behind this section were thirteen further degrees of more cramped dimensions: seats 6 inches wide, with only 12 inches of knee room. At the rear, and partly supported by the hall screen over which they were raised, were two sloping floors for standing observers, which, it is noted, 'should have barrs to keepe them from overpressing one another'. Given the evident discomfort of some of the seating, which must have been more like the folding supports at some modern bus-stops than anything approaching a twentieth-century theatre seat, a crowded standing may not have been as inconvenient as it may at first sound.

Of even more interest, however, is that these dimensions are accompanied by an estimate of the seating capacity of the completed theatre, a calculation which the Office of the Works is likely to have made elsewhere, since the form and size of theatre conversions must have been partly dictated by the Lord Chamberlain's stipulations about the nature of the occasion, and of its guest list. Notations in one corner of the plan calculate that 'The first seven seats will conteyne 200 persons to sit at ease' and 'The seconde 13 seats, will conteyne 350.' The two areas for standing spectators at the rear are reckoned to be able to hold 130 each, for a total audience of 810 people 'without pressing'. With a little pressing, we infer, the theatre may have held 1,000.

At the very rear of the theatre (which we might note in passing was the 'low' end of the hall, a matter of location we must consider shortly), the highest section of the rising bank of the auditorium was built on the support of the hall screen, which sustained the weight of the sloping platform on which 130 people stood. Otherwise the temporary timberwork of the Works carpenters was raised from the floor, and it had to withstand the weight and movement of 680 people. If one guesses an average weight per person of 140 pounds, the dead weight of a seated audience would have approached 100,000 pounds; the movement of this weight as the audience assembled and dispersed would have put further stress on the stability of the structure. It seems that the changes to the king's seat probably involved some reduction in the size of this massive bank of seating, although these adaptations were made after the theatre had been completed according to plan.

I repeat that the Christ Church arrangement was an unusual one, and it was perhaps not repeated elsewhere because of the difficulties encountered in build-ing it. It safely fulfilled its purpose, however, and solutions were evidently found to its particularly challenging engineering. How was it constructed? The Christ Church theatre emulated a Serlian form, perhaps at the instigation of Inigo Jones, who had no formal connection with the Works at this date but who had been given charge of the stage scenery at Oxford. In Serlio's book his famous three scenes, for tragedies, comedies, and pastoral plays, are accompanied by a plan and a section of a converted theatre; Serlio's assumptions are that theatres are temporary conversions of court halls, and that the auditoriums in such places are to be built as nearly as possible to the Vitruvian model, that is as a copy of the semi-circular seating in a Roman theatre. The section of the rising auditorium (Plate 15) may give some hints of how the Works proceeded in the Oxford conversion.

Serlio's plan is schematic, and can hardly be relied upon as a guide to solid construction, but it does show one principle that Sabbattini's sketch does not: the diagonal brace, which supports a right-angled joint by a second connection between the two members, and by distributing the stress and load. Modern metal scaffolding, typically, is built in rectangular or square units with diagonal braces, which are placed both horizontally and vertically to help hold the assembled structure rigid. There is no specific mention of this technique in the Works records, but the drawing of the 1610 conversion of the Court of Requests (Plate 4), shows three kinds of diagonal bracing under the raised galleries at the end of the room.

Despite Sabbatini's concern not to damage the chamber in which temporary seating was set up, safety must have been the first concern of the Office of the Works. Wear and tear on the physical fabric of the palaces was entirely their

15   Illustration of wooden scaffolding supporting a large bank of theatrical seating. Woodcut from the first English translation of Serlio's *Architettura*, 1611.

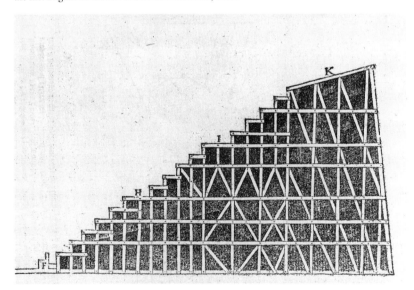

business to repair, whereas the politically symbolic embarrassment caused by the collapse of a royal structure would have been a strong inducement to make sure temporary stands and seats were thoroughly strong and stable, quite apart from the usual calculations of safe construction. As it was, royal woodwork occasionally gave way at sensitive moments. The famous Spanish ambassador Count Gondomar narrowly escaped serious injury when the planking of the wooden gallery which ran around the Paved Court at Whitehall broke under him in 1620.[19]

A narrative account in Latin of the 1605 theatre in Christ Church Hall suggests that it was partly supported by bracing against the stone walls of the building; it has been translated thus: 'From the floorboards of the hall right up to the lofty trusses of the roof, wedges (of degrees) were fixed [*affinguntur*] to the walls in a great arc.'[20] Such 'fixing' could have been done without structural work to the walls themselves. Whereas scaffolds for repairing or building masonry were frequently set into the wall, by removing bricks or stones and inserting supporting timbers for a work platform, a largely free-standing structure could have been propped or wedged against a wall with padded supports. If seating reached as high as the roof timbers, as is suggested in the rather rhapsodic description above, then part of the structure could be lashed or otherwise secured at that point. When the Whitehall Cockpit was converted into a permanent theatre, the seating at the upper levels was made secure in precisely this fashion. The Works accounts speak of 'framinge and setting vp the Degrees in the galleryes over the Cockpitt Cuttinge fyttinge and naylinge Brackettes vppon the same woorkinge and settinge of vpright postes to the Ceelinge for the better Strengtheninge therof'.[21]

On at least one occasion the wooden theatrical structures were also anchored into the floor. In January 1607 much of the paving of the Hall at Whitehall was 'taken vpp to place the degrees stages and devises' for Thomas Campion's masque at the marriage of Lord Hay.[22] It seems that the security of the scaffolds for seating would have been assured by every possible means–certainly by firm construction and by fixing them to any convenient permanent structure, and probably, on floors which could not be 'taken up', also by using sandbags and other ballast around the substructure, to prevent the weight and movement of the audience on the upper front surface from shifting the framework.

The arrangement of these seating units into a completed theatre, with a stage, a royal state, and at the performance of masques a dancing floor and boxes for musicians, could take various forms. The Stuart masques, grandiose performances which drew large audiences, quickly established a spatial model from which

87

little variation was made after the early seventeenth century; their Tudor ancestors, the masks and disguisings, were an entirely different matter, and could take a
variety of physical shapes. The staging of plays allowed more variety of theatrical
layout within the general defining conventions of space and theatrical facilities
that the players would have expected anywhere; we have already had the
opportunity to observe that large chambers could contain small stage platforms,
and that famous companies presented sweeping historical drama in intimate
palace chambers.

Even in the face of considerable counter-evidence, theatre historians used to
claim, up to a decade or so ago, that the staging of plays indoors, in court halls, in
aristocratic halls and chambers, in the halls of the inns of court and of Oxford and
Cambridge colleges, could be understood in terms of a simple, universal model:
the king or other important member of the audience sat at the 'high' end of the
room, on the dais, and faced the actors who performed at the 'low' end. In halls
this resulted in their playing in front of the screen, which, it was supposed, was
used for entries and exits, with the screens passage, or that part of the hall floor
that lay behind the screen, serving as a tiring house. The common two-entry
plan of many hall screens, like those at Hampton Court and the Middle Temple
in London, and the upright wooden wall with a gallery above, served as a model
for the actors, it was argued, when they came either to build themselves or to
have some say in the design of permanent playhouses. Indoor playing in halls led
to what we see in the Swan drawing, simply stated.[23]

The book which argued this position with the most strength and consistency,
Richard Southern's *The Staging of Plays before Shakespeare*, was published in 1973,
shortly before the validity of such a model began to be called into question, and
its authority to crumble. In fact, no simple, unitary model can easily be made to
fit the variety of late-medieval and Renaissance staging in England, whether at
the court or elsewhere. Certainly in the time since Southern's book appeared we
have come to realise or have been reminded that the staging of plays and
entertainments indoors was not necessarily connected with a hall screen. Southern was not incorrect: some plays certainly were presented at the screens end of a
hall, whether or not the screens entries were used theatrically. His account,
however, was incomplete: plays were presented in chambers without a screen,
and, as the Oxford plan demonstrates, the screen could be ignored as a theatrical
façade and used rather as an audience gallery. At Cambridge college theatres set
up in halls, this indeed seems to have been the rule rather than the exception, and
even more radically, in comparison to professional practice in the London
playhouses, an important section of the audience sat at the high end of the hall,

with the stage between them and the rest of the audience[24] The actors' 'houses', consequently, were at the sides of the stage, and hence the patterns of actors' movements must have been considerably different from what we imagine to have been the traffic of the stage at the Globe, for example.

Academics, perhaps, have other ways of doing things. The Cambridge model, if there was such a thing, will not do for all cases either. Theatre historians have been fond of evolutionary explanations, whereby practices at a certain date lead on to other, more developed practices at a later date. While there might be a bedrock of common sense underlying such an approach, it can also be misleading and reductive. Southern's thesis is one such example; another we should be suspicious about is Sir Edmund Chambers's, expounded in his chapter on 'Staging at Court' in volume II of *The Elizabethan Stage*, first published in 1923. Chambers's claim, simply put, is that the staging of plays at court changed radically with the collapse of the Revels Office as an arm of production, and that by the end of the 1580s the kind of physical space used for the presentation of plays before the queen had become a great deal simpler. I will be examining the truth of this assertion as I proceed, but it can immediately be appreciated that it is difficult to distinguish between changes dictated by the court itself and those arising from practice in the acting profession. It was during the 1580s that the larger acting companies emerged and concurrently that the dramaturgical and literary character of dramatic texts took on new complexity and richness. Plays, and hence performances, were characteristically quite different by 1590 from what they had been, as far as we can now judge, in 1580.

Turning back to theatres, if we begin with one indisputable diagram of a stage at court, that for *Florimène* in the Hall at Whitehall in 1635 (Plate 3), we might note, first, that the audience did indeed sit facing the low end of the hall, but that the screen was entirely hidden from view behind a proscenium and perspective scenery: the screen served no theatrical function beyond that of helping support the backstage construction. The form of the stage which the court audience watched on this occasion was, like the Cambridge academic stages, foreign to the contemporary practice of the professional theatre. As in the theatres for masques, an area for dancing was placed between the stage and the royal seat. Dancing took place in the *intermèdes* between the acts of the play, and probably in the antimasques which concluded it; the scene design includes steps down from the stage level to the floor below.[25] The auditorium, however, set out in the rather more than half of the hall floor area remaining, might well be taken to be representative of such structures elsewhere and at other times: that in the Great Chamber at Richmond at Christmas 1588, for example, with degrees 'for the people to sit one', a platform for the queen's seat, and other raised platforms both for the nobility to sit and also for people to stand. It is likely that these raised wooden platforms followed Sabbatini's model, and were set back against the walls of the room for support, thus forming the rectilinear plan we see at Whitehall in 1635.

Protocol demanded that the monarch be in a central position, a rival with the entertainers as focus for the gaze of the assembly. As it was at Oxford in 1605 or Whitehall in 1635 the monarch's 'halpace', or platform of state, would have been placed at Richmond on the centre line of the room, directly facing the stage, and surrounded by the seats of leading members of the court and visiting dignitaries.[26] No seats intervened directly between the monarch and the stage. In the masques the performers habitually made use of the direct and uninterrupted confrontation with the king for address and invocation, both solemn and comic, and plays also could be adapted for court performance to acknowledge that most important member of the audience who was first in the actors' eyes as they looked directly outwards from the stage platform.

In short, if we make the adjustment to the *Florimène* plan of a rather simpler and smaller stage platform we have a plausible model of a court theatre set up for plays. To take an example roughly contemporary with the theatrically unrepresentative *Florimène*, in 1631–32 Hampton Court Hall, of very similar dimensions to the Hall at Whitehall, was prepared by the Works through 'setting vp Degrees and Rayles and fitting and p^rparing of the greate Hall for Playes to be Acted there'.[27] If the same configuration was followed with a rather smaller stage then a correspondingly larger auditorium might be built, by moving the royal state closer to the stage and enlarging the depth and height of the degrees behind it, possibly with 'Rayles' for standing observers at the very back, as at Oxford. Such a theatre would follow, on a larger scale, the general layout of the indoor theatres of London at that date: the Blackfriars, the Phoenix or Cockpit in Drury Lane, and the Salisbury Court. The stages in these theatres lay across one short end of a rectangular hall, with most of the audience facing it from seats at the floor level, and from galleries which were built against the other three walls.[28]

We know, however, that not all court theatre conversions followed this plan. The 1630 adaptation of the Cockpit was constrained by the particular shape of the building; Jones's solution to the question of hierarchy was to set the royal seat in the central wedge of space under the galleries, directly facing the stage (Plate 7). The remaining six sections of seating on the ground floor lay, rather unconventionally, in front of the monarch, but he did not exactly have to look at the backs of his subjects' heads. Two sections of seating faced the monarch at right angles, in a traditional fashion (compare the *Florimène* plan), while the others are inclined towards the royal seat at a 45° angle. What is more unconventional is that most of the audience in the galleries would have been unable to see the king, or he them. One might regard this as an awkward accident compelled by an idiosyncratic Tudor structure, as a sign of the declining hieratic importance of the royal presence, or as indicative of the cultivation of relatively private, intimate space in the Caroline court. In 1605 a great deal of fuss had been made about the inability of the Oxford audience to see the king in the odd position in which he had been placed to enjoy the visual pleasures of single-point perspective scenery. Two kinds of seeing came into conflict: the audience had come to see the king as much as the play, and he had to be on show. On this occasion political considerations overrode aesthetics. By 1630, perhaps, despite the absolutism of Charles's style of government, both king and subjects felt differently about such ceremonial display.[29] The Cockpit, of course, can never have been intended for occasions of great state significance, elegant though its appointments may have been: its scale is calculated for private and select amusement.

The arrangement within the Cockpit is not entirely unrelated to the *Florimène* plan; once again the stage forms one limit of the entire space, and in the remaining area seats are set in rows defined by the interior walls, to face the actors. A more radical departure from the contemporary or modern theoretical models we might think of in considering stage and audience space–the Rose or the Globe playhouses, Southern's account of performance before hall screens, or the *Florimène* plan itself–is presented by an entry from the Works accounts for construction at Whitehall in 1601–2. I quote the most surprising information in its context.

> makeinge ready the haule with degrees the boordes vpon them footpace vnder the state framing and setting vp a broade stage in the midle of the haule makeinge a standing for the Lorde Chamberlaine makeing and setting vp viij pticons in the haule and entries and setting vp a flower in it the ground (*round*) windowe in the haulle for musitions[30]

If these preparations were made for plays–and the Works and Chamber accounts for this court season are at odds about when the Hall and the Great Chamber respectively were used–then actors in 1601 must have found it a very strange arrangement. By that date even the rawest actors, like Bottom, Quince, and company in *A Midsummer Night's Dream*, were accustomed to thinking of performance as taking place on a flat area of stage space (or 'This green plot') adjoining a place of concealment, used for entries and exits: the tiring house (or 'this hawthorn brake'). The tiring house abutted the stage on one side, so that the observing audience could watch the action from the other angles around the stage area, depending on quite how the stage might be placed within a yard, chamber, or other surroundings. A 'broade stage in the midle of the haule', if indeed it was 'in the round' and entirely ringed by spectators, would have put professional actors at a considerable disadvantage, used as they were to timing entries, listening for cues, and making quick costume changes to re-enter as a doubled character from an immediately adjacent tiring house. Moreover, if a tiring house were provided in its traditional position it would have blocked the view of the stage from one side, and wasted space.

We might doubt, however, that this account entry, although it is placed in the context of dramatic records in the Malone Society collection of extracts from the Works documents, is connected with theatrical activity; the Chamber accounts tell a rather different story.[31] Together, the two sets of records suggest that the Hall and the Great Chamber were both prepared for revels, at Christmas and again at Shrove. The Chamber records specifically say that the Hall was prepared for Twelfth Night, when the Works accountant says that the Great Chamber was prepared for that day ('againe', rather bafflingly), for both plays and dancing. I think that the two rooms must have been used throughout Christmas, one for plays and one for dancing, although not necessarily consistently with the same kind of entertainment in the same chamber. A broad stage in the middle of the hall, in conjunction with a special box for musicians, is far more likely to have been built for an exhibition of dancing than for plays. A stage, like a scaffold, might have served a variety of purposes.

Two years later, however, a very similar entry appears. Shrove 1604 was part of the first English court season of the new king, James I, and at Whitehall the Works were employed 'making readie the hall with degrees and footepaces vnder the state with a Stage in the middle and making of soundrie pticons with bourdes in the entries and passages for plaies'.[32] This is both similar in its phrasing to the earlier entry and quite clear that these particular preparations were for plays. A little later in the same passage there is a second reference to making a box for the musicians in the bay window; if it is connected with the occasion of the plays, it should give us further pause in interpretation.

If both these early seventeenth-century records describe similar struc- tures–large playing platforms placed in the geometrical centre of the hall with seats around them on four sides–they form a unique category in the various forms of court theatre. Such an arrangement was not habitual practice, and, to repeat, actors would have found it extremely difficult to use, precisely because it was unlike the playing spaces they employed elsewhere. If these were not theatres in the round, however, what were they? I think that the 1601 stage is more likely to have been a dance floor, and in either case there is some latitude surrounding what the phrase 'in the middle' might mean. The monarch's state was also invariably in the middle of any temporary theatre, if one means by that that it was placed on the centre line of the room with the rest of the seats grouped around it; it directly faced the stage or performance area, which was also centrally aligned. While the 1604 description may be taken to refer to an arena stage, therefore, the theatre may quite possibly have been set up in a manner generally similar to the *Florimène* theatre.

The early Jacobean Works accounts are unusually informative about stages, that part of the temporary theatre which is of most interest to modern enquiry, but some of the information is rather odd. Generally it might be said that the Works entries tend to be most detailed about unusual or particular jobs, while regular tasks repeated from year to year, like putting up degrees to watch plays or stages on which to perform them, are either recorded formulaically or not recorded at all. Stages and tiring houses must have been made when chambers were prepared with seats for plays, but the accounts rarely say so.

The new court of King James was evidently establishing its character partly through lavish spectacle, one manifestation of which was the production of the court masques, which often included special stage effects. The simplest of these–stage shutters which opened to reveal another painted view, for example–did not require much in the way of carpentry, but the first collaboration between Ben Jonson and Inigo Jones, *The Masque of Blackness*, presented in January 1605, featured a large moving platform, described in the Works records as 'a great stage in the bankettinge house xl^ty foote square and iiij^or in heighte wth wheles to go on'.[33] This evidently created the effect at the start of the entertainment when a landscape painted on a curtain fell away, and, in Ben Jonson's words, '*an artificial sea was seen to shoot forth, as if it flowed to the land, raised with waves which seemed to move, and in some places the billow to break*'.[34] While the account provides some useful dimensions, particularly as regards its height, this stage can hardly be regarded as typical of what might have been set up for visiting players. Similarly something quite unusual–it is difficult to tell exactly what–was built in the Hall at Whitehall at some time in the seasons of 1607–8 and 1608–9. The Works recorded expenditure for 'making a stage three foote highe from the ground vpon the Trestles all the lenght and breadth of the hall, making a haullpace railed aboute vnder the kinges state being all made ready for plaies in the hall'.[35] In attempting to interpret this structure we are once again at the mercy of phraseology which may be approximate, and is certainly not telling us everything. Were no degrees, for example, built for an audience on this occasion? If the entry literally means what it says, the entire area of the Hall was raised three feet on a wooden floor, but what purpose could that have served, why would the term 'stage' be used for such a structure, and why would mere 'trestles' have been trusted to support the considerable weight of an assembled audience on top of it? A stage raised on trestles sounds far more like a theatrical platform for the actors, but such a thing would certainly not have been as wide and long as the Hall itself.

This entry is an isolated piece from a lost jigsaw: it seems impossible to give a plausible account of the theatre built on this occasion from such an odd single detail. It does tell us, however, that a stage was raised on trestles, the angular supports which are still used to make light tables, or to serve as sawhorses. The same account corroborates this information in describing the stage made for *The Masque of Beauty*, presented in the newly built Banqueting House in January 1608; it was 'a great Stage fower foote highe from the grounde vpon Trestles'.[36]

We might then take it that stages were frequently constructed in this way. Trestles were part of the common furniture of the court; since the larger chambers contained very little in the way of permanent fittings, tables in particular were made to be easily movable, with a top supported on folding trestle legs. Modern caterers rely on similar furniture for receptions and parties in spaces not regularly used for eating and drinking. The height of a useful table, of course, is a good deal less than four feet, and we should not too readily suppose that stages were assembled like a rather larger table; trestles in a variety of strengths and heights must have been kept in store for many purposes. Stages too probably varied in height to suit the size of the room. A masque in the Banqueting House was a large-scale event in every way, and the prominence and visibility of the stage from some distance would have been an important consideration. So it might be asked whether in the very smallest chambers, like those at St James's Palace, a stage was required at all, and whether actors simply performed on an area of the floor of the room. The general silence of the accounts in the matter of stages leaves us free to imagine this, and undoubtedly actors on tour must on occasion have played simply on bare floors, or even the bare ground outdoors. It seems to me that at court, however, the formal division of space would have been marked in some way, even if the actors' stages were on some occasions fairly low platforms–what in the Works accounts are generally called, in a variety of spellings, halpaces (that is half-paces, or a low step in height).

Even the areas for dancing in masque theatres could be low stages. Of more practical interest to the dancers than the pictorial stages which dominate our impressions of the masque today, the dancing floor, we might expect, could simply have been a vacant area of the chamber floor. A stone or a tiled surface, however, would have been hard on the feet. At Somerset House in 1620 the Works prepared 'a false floore of tymber and boordes for the Prynce and Noblemen to daunce vppon';[37] such platforms are likely to have been built elsewhere in masque theatres. Certainly all masquing floors were covered with cloth, perhaps to muffle the sound of the steps somewhat, and to give the dancers' feet a softer and less slippery surface. Traditionally the cloth was green–Busino saw the coloured floor appear as the audience for *Pleasure Reconciled to Virtue* settled down after the king's entrance. The preparations for a masque at Somerset House in 1626 involved one Ralph Grinder in supplying materials and labour in laying the floor: 'one hundred fower-score and three yards of greene Cotton to Couer a floore at Denmarke house where the said Masque was performed and for threed and Workmanship in fitting and laying the same, and two thousand black tacks imployed therein'.[38]

To sum up, then, the crucial spatial principle of court theatres from the largest to the smallest was that the royal seat should directly face the stage, and hence both state and stage were aligned on the central axis of the chamber. The truly important matter about the stage's being 'in the middle of the hall' was that it should be in the centre of the sovereign's view. He or she should also be able to hear well. If King James's seat at Oxford was moved back so that more of the audience could see him, in 1603–4 the Works were busy 'altering of a Stage in the hall to bring it nearer the king'.[39] The audience was then grouped around these two central elements of stage and state. Court theatres generally were not made to give the best possible view of the stage to the greatest number of people; the 1605 Oxford theatre was regarded with suspicion because it did precisely that. Audiences at court came to see the entertainments, naturally, but they also came to watch the monarch watch, and to register their own presence at such an occasion. Lesser members of the court watched the greater, and so on. The seating, turned towards the royal seat as much as to the stage, reflected a double spectatorial function, though in effect display and observation at court assemblies must have been complex and many-layered.

What the monarch watched changed somewhat between 1558 and 1642, reflecting changing styles in entertainments and the ways in which they were mounted, but considerable variety in royal shows might be noted at any given period. There was also some continuity. Late in the years of his London court

King Charles watched plays from early in Shakespeare's career, mounted by the same company which had first presented them, and whose professional forebears could have acted them before Queen Elizabeth. Actors in the 1630s undoubtedly performed and staged these plays in a fashion rather different from the styles and practices of the 1590s, and changing theatrical style would have been reflected at court. Professional theatre practice, however, was only one influence on the changing taste apparent in the wide variety of royal entertainments presented over the eighty-four years of this study. In considering such change there are certain clear markers: the sudden reduction in the budget of the Revels Office, for example, or the sudden fashion for the elaborately staged masques of the Jacobean court. In the chronological surveys which follow I will attempt to distinguish changes and continuities in the English court theatre which seem to be of particular significance.

The early Elizabethan period, 1558–1583

One constant throughout our entire period was constituted by the early Tudor palace chambers adapted for use as theatres for over a hundred years. Whether it held a Jacobean masque or a Tudor interlude the Hall at Hampton Court would have imposed a certain character on the occasion. The qualities of Elizabethan taste in particular in visual and architectural matters might be more accurately gauged from the descriptions of the successive banqueting houses erected at Whitehall, and referred to in chapter 1. These were largely light-hearted festival buildings, put up to honour successive embassies from France on the difficult business of negotiating marriage with the English queen, and the Revels Office was responsible for decorating the first two of them. These buildings are of interest because there is a good deal of overlap between their decorations and the kind of preparations which were made in court rooms and halls for the presentation of revels, and I will return to them in chapter 4.

From an early date it seems that one of the effects desired at court gatherings on festive occasions, precisely when plays were most often presented, in the Elizabethan years, was strong illumination. It is hard to create what one might call a blaze of light with candle flames, but as far as chandeliers, wall sconces, and reflectors could produce intense dispersed illumination, every effort was made to do so. The intention was not to illuminate a stage–the practice of the modern theatre–or rather not to illuminate a stage alone, but to create an inspiriting atmosphere throughout the hall or chamber. At the fifty-first parallel of the northern hemisphere, Christmas and Shrove both occur at dark times of the year, and the festive effect of as bright a light as massed candles might produce would have been both gay and impressive: a flood of light no doubt also signified the power and magnificence of the monarch. The responsibility of the Revels Office for maintaining and hanging the fittings which produced this blaze was not in the first place specifically theatrical; the Office was set up to manage royal festivities of various kinds, and the Christmas and Shrove feasts were primarily holiday gatherings of the court. When, at the end of Shakespeare's tragedy, Romeo opens the tomb and sees the wife he supposes to be dead he imagines that her appearance creates radiance in the gloom: 'her beauty makes / This vault a feasting presence full of light'.[40] The word 'presence' here would have particularly reminded Elizabethan listeners of the great court festivals, splendidly illuminated.

Plays, then—even solemn ones like *Romeo and Juliet*—were presented in a glow of candlelight which surrounded actors and audience alike. Chambers 'made ready' for plays had their regular means of illumination supplemented many times over through the rigging of lines across the room, from which decorated chandeliers, each bearing multiple lights, were hung on wires and cords, with pulleys to lower them in order to trim and replace the candles. The management of this overhead network of open flames, dripping a certain amount of hot wax and occasionally setting light to stray pieces of decorative trim, must have been rather a tense affair,[41] but the effect of the bright overhead glow must have been magical, transforming the character of the chamber entirely, and constituting one of the chief atmospheric effects of the occasion of a play at court. As we have seen, the Revels jealously guarded the prerogative of producing this delight, and the soft yellow shimmer of many candles lighting the faces of the actors and the audience remained a mark of the court theatre until its disappearance in the 1640s.

Although the largest spaces—the great halls of Whitehall, Greenwich, Richmond, and Hampton Court, and the Whitehall banqueting houses—gave the fullest opportunities for the spectacular effect of massed lighting, they also presented the greatest challenge: light could easily be diffused in the vast spaces of their high wooden roofs. Lighting fixtures were therefore placed, whenever they could be, against vertical surfaces, including those surrounding the performance area, and also on stands placed on the floor. In 1605 the Banqueting House at Whitehall was lit by sixteen hanging candelabra, eight of which were large and held 'fiftin great Lightes Apece',[42] and by eighteen standing candlesticks. The last act of *Othello*, which was performed there by the King's Men on this occasion, would have been brightly and evenly illuminated; Othello's candle would have shone out in a darkness that would only have been imagined. When the smaller Cockpit theatre was set up in 1630 it was illuminated by at least fifteen chandeliers, some of which were placed 'round about and before the Stage'.[43] Such attention to lighting the stage was not new, as we might expect; I shall return to this issue below.

At the beginning of the reign of Queen Elizabeth, the Revels Office continued to provide the kinds of entertainment which it had in the preceding two short reigns of Queen Mary and King Edward VI. The surviving account lists and inventories of the Revels for the thirty years between the mid 1540s and the mid 1570s are the most informative material we now have about English royal entertainment in the middle of the sixteenth century. They have a great deal to say about the manufacture of costumes, properties, and scenery, and they generally give the impression of a lively and imaginative theatrical culture. We can have only a hazy conception of the context of theatrical shows at this date, however, because we have very little in the way of extant dramatic texts through which we might understand the production activities of the Revels Office. In later years, precisely when we would like to know quite how *Measure for Measure* and *The Tempest* were mounted for the Jacobean court, the ratio is reversed: many interesting surviving texts, both of plays and masques, but far fewer details of court production than we could wish for, even in the case of masques, for which a rich if rather patchy archive survives in the drawings and sketches of their chief designer, Inigo Jones.

Dramatic entertainment at the early Elizabethan court was of two kinds: plays and masks. Although the distinction is not a clearcut or watertight one, I use the English spelling of this word–more usual in the Elizabethan period–as a convenience to distinguish the form from the considerably more elaborate Stuart masques, which we tend to treat today as *texts*, to be read, written by Jonson, Campion, Davenant, and other authors. In fact the opening sentence of this paragraph raises the theoretical question of quite what might be meant by 'dramatic' entertainment, or indeed by 'theatrical' entertainment. We know what a play is, and if asked to give a rough definition we might say that it is a fictional narrative in which the characters speak and move, performed in our presence by people who assume their roles. A play text is a written record of those words and movements. A Stuart masque might fit within this definition with qualifications to the effect that some characters do not speak, but move, especially in dance, to music, to which other characters sing. A sixteenth-century mask, however, would not fit the definition at all.[44] As far as we know, on many occasions there was very little speech, if any, involved in the show, and little narrative or individual personation. A group of characters dressed in matching unusual, exotic, or grotesque costumes entered the chamber with their accompanying torchbearers, and danced, both together in rehearsed choreographic numbers, and then with members of the audience. In such an entertainment the maskers were usually men, and hence they habitually danced with women from among the spectators. These elements—disguised dancers entering with torchbearers and performing two sorts of dance—remain in the more sophisticated Stuart masques, so that the two forms are certainly connected, but the production demands of *most* Elizabethan versions were considerably less elaborate. Plans for masks at a proposed meeting between Queen Elizabeth and Mary Queen of Scots in 1562 demonstrate an allegorical programme as well as some considerable scenic elaboration, while the surviving text of a mask played at court in 1595 by the legal fraternity of Gray's Inn – *Proteus and the Adamantine Rock* – demonstrates a mixture of dramatic dialogue and song not far removed from the Jacobean model.[45] By contrast, masks of 'ladies', presented on at least two distinct occasions for Queen Elizabeth, were not performed by women, as at the Stuart courts, but by boy actors in costume.[46]

The Tudor mask, then, like the Stuart masque which followed it, was in itself a Protean form. The occasion of the entry of the maskers offered the opportunity for various kinds of spectacle beyond the fancy dress of the dancers. Floats and waggons with surprising or amusing special effects could appear, and be pushed across the dancing area: the entry was a kind of parade, and like a parade all kinds of promiscuous details could be added to it—its main purpose was to be novel and striking. The Elizabethan mask might include scenic elements, then, but they were very differently conceived from the unified pictorial settings of Inigo Jones and his imitators.

The mask could be and sometimes was described by the rather more inclusive English term, the 'disguising'. I raised the question of what we might mean by dramatic or theatrical entertainment because disguising—putting on a special costume, and sometimes giving a prepared speech as the character in costume—was widespread in other kinds of court activities that we would not readily be inclined to call theatrical. We might say, however, that a certain theatrical attitude governed formal occasions at court and elsewhere; adopting self-consciously fictional poses was regarded as elegant and stylish. So the kind of cultural activity which manifests itself in the mask might also be observed in tournaments or barriers – the martial exercises of the male court aristocracy[47] – at formal welcomes when the queen moved from one palace to another, or at special entertainments put on at times other than the two regular winter feasts: to honour important foreign guests, for example. The Revels Office was responsible for providing material for many of these events.[48]

To be more precise, then, there were two court feasts at which revels in the shape of plays and masks might be presented. As with the Stuart masques, masks were produced principally within the court; the costumes and any properties and scenic devices were prepared by the Revels Office, and the maskers were members of the court community. King Henry VIII and his principal courtiers had put on masking costumes and danced; his second daughter enjoyed dancing, but did not, as far as we know, disguise herself as a masker, as did Queen Anne after her.

Plays, as in later periods, were largely the product of outside groups, both professional and amateur, both adult and child actors, although some of the children's groups, particularly, were connected with the court–the choristers from the Chapel Royal (at Greenwich) and also from Windsor Chapel, for example. It was not only the professional troupes of the principal nobles who entertained the queen. Talented schoolmasters might occasionally show off their pupils' skills in drama, and the best-known play of this early period which received a performance at court, *Gorboduc* (1562), was acted by amateurs, the gentlemen students of the law at the Inner Temple. Costumes, properties, and scenic effects for these visiting shows, even those presented by the professional troupes, were provided by the Office of the Revels. Scenery in particular was occasionally elaborate, and the productions which included it must have looked very different from the version of the Elizabethan stage conjured up by modern notions of its bareness and non-representational character. Rocks, clouds, trees, towers, and other large items, built of painted timber, wire, and canvas, were constructed by the craftsmen of the Revels Office, and appeared on the court stages.

There is no reason to think that the general physical provisions for adapting court rooms to theatrical spaces which have been described above were any different at the beginning of the Elizabethan period. Scaffolds and degrees had been set up for audiences for many years before the new queen came to the throne, and chambers continued to be prepared in the same way into the 1640s. At Greenwich at Shrovetide 1573, for example, the Works noted the 'making of a halpace for hir ma^tie in the great chambre and settinge vp the great Scaffolde and Railles'.[49] Most usually there was not, as we have seen, any sharp distinction between seats for audiences at plays and those at any other large gathering, so that while we might not want to call a chamber in which the court assembled to watch the maskers dance a theatre, exactly, the layout of the seating for such an occasion was probably in a similar configuration to that for the presentation of plays. At Christmas the hall might be prepared for audiences who watched a series of different entertainments on successive nights. The degrees remain securely fixed in the same position, although the stage, I have suggested above, may have been moved to and from 'the midle of the haule'.

The distinguishing physical feature of a dramatic performance, then, was its stage. Generally the actors required a stage, or a reserved playing area on the floor, which, lacking other evidence, we should take to have been placed regularly at one end of a rectangular room, as in the *Florimène* arrangement, with the state facing the stage, and degrees grouped behind and on either side of the royal seat.

The appearance of the stage—what the assembled court audience looked at under the shimmering candles—is of considerable interest in this period. Anyone who has made even cursory enquiries into what stages at the time of Shakespeare looked like is bound to have encountered a reproduction of the famous drawing of the Swan theatre in 1596, made by a Dutch visitor to London and copied by his friend: the copy survives.[50] The effect of the stage in that drawing is of Spartan plainness, apart, perhaps, from the classical pillars which hold up the stage roof. What looks like a very large stage terminates at a blank wall, labelled '*mimorum aedes*' (the actors' house, or tiring house). There is a partitioned gallery with figures sitting in it over this wall, and there are two symmetrically positioned doors piercing the wall at the back of the stage. They are round-headed, double-leaved wooden doors, and they look heavy, rather like church doors. One would not describe what one sees in this picture as elegant or well proportioned: the stage and its surroundings look dull, plain, and rustic.

If we assume that something like the physical provisions at the Swan were set up in court theatres before 1583—that is, a fairly large projecting platform stage with a tiring house at the rear—it seems altogether unlikely that they were left as plain and bare as we see them in the drawing. Before the Revels Office lost its budget for production, visual splendour was one of its central principles. Stages were hung with curtains and painted cloth, some of which was clearly scenery, in that it represented places to which the action of the play referred. Painters were consistently employed by the Office, and we might imagine that the stage which faced the queen in court chambers was richly coloured, both with painted wood and cloth hangings, and with reflective gold and silver fringes catching the light. Costumes too were probably more gorgeous than modern naturalistic decorum would find appropriate, but we should remember that the play, whatever its subject, was part of a festival occasion, and a reflection of the splendour of royal style. Elizabethan visual taste was rarely restrained.

In the first two decades of the reign, at least, the Revels Office was primarily responsible for the decoration of the stage, but also partly for its construction. Perhaps the Works provided the playing platform, as they did in 1588, but the accounts from this period, as frequently is the case, are silent about stages as such. The Revels, however, built structures which are referred to not as tiring houses but as players' houses, or simply as houses, and usually in the plural, even when the preparation was for one play. Theatre historians have made various guesses about what these may have been, what they looked like, and how the actors used them in putting on their plays, but, without either plans or drawings of these structures, guesses are as far as one can go. It is possible that they were dispersed along the upstage edge of the platform rather like the system of 'mansions' in medieval French staging, so that as characters in a play conventionally moved from place to place they would station themselves in front of different schematic frameworks.[51] My own guess about the early Elizabethan 'houses' is that collectively they probably were not much different from what is later called the tiring house: that is, that they were a series of curtained or painted points of entry to the stage, with space at the rear which constituted the Elizabethan 'wings' and dressing room in one. I shall try to substantiate this guess in more detail below, by examining a surviving text of a play performed at court which makes reference in its stage directions to houses, the stage term used by the Revels Office.

Not all plays presented at court in this period, however, were mounted within the conventions of a raised wooden platform stage with upstage entries from 'houses'. At least one play, put on by the professional troupe of the Earl of Warwick's Men in 1579, called on scenic effects so elaborate that it seems to me unlikely that they would have been confined to a stage platform. Within a court hall, the entire surface of the floor which was not taken up by seating could be used by entertainers. Dancers in Tudor masks and Stuart masques made use of it, as did fencers and acrobats. The play which survives only as a title, *The Knight of the Burning Rock*, was evidently some kind of romance story, but with spectacular stage effects. The rock was a physical location, and it was built by the Revels Office staff. Not simply a painted cut-out, it was three-dimensional, and large. A wooden frame was covered with canvas, and inside it there was machinery and room for stage hands to work: an elevating chair could rise through a trap in the rock, while flames and smoke produced with burning spirits could be made to appear from other crevices.[52] The story of the play evidently had something to do with enchantment, and the rock was a kind of hell. The forces in control of it were symbolically defeated by the powers of good, who employed siege ladders to attack it. This sweeping action would have called for as many actors as could be drafted, and such dramatic turmoil is most unlikely to have taken place on a platform 14 feet square; or indeed on any platform, since the evident place to plant what was clearly a very large, solid, and heavy scenic unit would have been on the chamber floor.

One kind of early Elizabethan court staging, then, employed dispersed settings, with actors moving across the wider arena of the open floor of the room. The fragmentary information about *The Knight of the Burning Rock* which one may piece together from the Revels accounts does not make clear whether there were other scenic units in the play: evidently the actors must have had some point of entrance and exit. If I am right about the stage arrangements for this play then perhaps 'players' houses' could on some occasions have taken the form of a number of isolated structures dispersed around the extent of the playing area. Such staging is reminiscent of the grand scope of *The Castle of Perseverance*, from 150 years earlier, the action of which also features an elaborate siege to an emblematic stronghold. Scenes of battle, perhaps more like military tattoo than a developed drama, were also presented in court chambers during the middle ages, and perhaps *The Knight of the Burning Rock* had some connections with such a tradition.[53] Certainly there was an overlap between entertainments of this kind, produced by actors, and the shows and parades which frequently accompanied tournaments and indoor combat such as barriers and sword fighting.

The rock made for this show is only one of a series of elaborate scenic units made by the workmen of the Revels Office, and although *The Knight*, for example, was staged by a professional troupe, who at the date of the production may have been performing at the playhouse at Newington Butts, south of London Bridge, it seems unlikely that such lavish effects formed part of the regular presentation of plays at public performances.[54] Productions at any date from this period until the Civil War had to be adaptable to playing in a variety of conditions as the actors toured, and the economics of mobile troupes of players did not allow for a large volume of material to be taken on the road; the costumes required to mount three or four plays would have presented enough of a challenge to carry from place to place. The habit of touring may have been one factor which governed the plainness and simplicity of the stage we see in the Swan drawing.

I think it would be wrong, however, to suggest too extreme a distinction between production at court and contemporary production in playhouses and other playing venues of the 1560s and 1570s–between elaborate and showy conditions on the one hand, with richly decorated stages and stage appointments, and bare, stripped facilities on the other. There are likely to have been degrees of variation in both court and public productions; certainly the actors would have attempted to copy impressive spectacle and decoration, as far as they could afford it, in their own theatres. One might ask what the skilled property-makers, painters, and costumiers hired by the Revels Office did for the rest of the working year, and whether they did not have some connection with the growing theatrical business of London. I will turn to this question in more detail in the next chapter.

The later Elizabethan period, 1583–1603

By any measure, the last twenty years of Queen Elizabeth's reign saw a remarkable and unprecedented surge in the quality and quantity of dramatic activity in London. One can be rather misled by a modern interest in the remarkable texts produced by this activity in gauging the difference of the later years from the 1560s and 1570s. As has been pointed out several times in recent scholarship, the breadth and variety of dramatic activity in England as a whole was actually reduced during Elizabeth's reign: the provinces suffered in favour of the growing metropolis, and many small groups of players succumbed to fewer, larger, tightly organised groups under the patronage–and control–of leading members of the court.[55]

The breakthrough in dramatic writing represented by the plays of Marlowe, Lyly, Kyd, Greene, Peele, and the young Shakespeare is, in the end, difficult to account for. There was certainly a market for new plays to tempt jobbing writers, but this market had existed in the 1570s.[56] The generally more expansive form of the drama from the later eighties onwards (as in *The Spanish Tragedy*, for example) was related in part to theatrical conditions. A longer play, rather than a 1,000-line interlude, for example, was designed for a whole afternoon in the theatre–Shakespeare's 'two hours traffic of our stage', or somewhat longer. The numerous characters in many plays were calculated for playing by a troupe of ten to twelve actors (such as the members of the Chamberlain's Men), with apprentices and hired men, and with considerable doubling of roles. The late-Elizabethan repertory called for a sustained and vigorous rhythm of playing, embodied in the conventions of a platform stage with entries from the tiring house at its rear. Once again we can be misled by the paucity of plays surviving from the earlier decades, but it is probably largely true to say that theatrical practice became more confident, vigorous, and uniform as the century drew to its close, and hence that the usual habits of the players in mounting their plays in theatres and provincial playing spaces are likely to have governed the arrangement of stages at court.

Simultaneously the production activities of the Revels Office largely came to an end; as they did so the burden of creating elaborate shows such as *The Knight of the Burning Rock* devolved on to the players. Although spectacular effects were undoubtedly popular in the playhouses also, they were realised there in the relatively simple conventions of platform staging, which the actors would have followed in performing their plays elsewhere. Consequently, there was perhaps less variety in the physical presentation of plays at court in the later Elizabethan period.

However true that may be, in the late 1580s there are still signs of differing forms of staging at court. The playing platform 14 feet square, for example, in the Great Chamber at Richmond at Christmas, 1588, served a number of playing companies. Four years after the Richmond performance one of them was to begin using the newly built Rose playhouse, where the stage was neither square nor rectangular, but trapezoidal, about 16 feet in depth—quite comparable to the court platform—but with a maximum width of more than twice the depth. Such a ratio of width to depth seems to have been the norm in the play-houses, and if the actors' practices were increasingly reflected in court staging, then the proportions of the Richmond stage would not have been frequently repeated.

In the Works account for 1586–87 I think we have an incidental indication of the position of a court stage, a detail which we do not know in the case of the Richmond platform. In that year the wiredrawer Edmund Burchall, who appears on the payroll of both the Works and the Revels over the course of a number of years, was paid for his work at Greenwich Palace 'for sondrie sortes of wierworke by him done aboute the skrene at shrouetide'.[57] A wiredrawer, as this entry suggests, did not make wire so much as work with it, rigging it for support or suspension, and forming it into metal objects. Burchall's speciality was lighting: he set up taut wire cables for hanging lights, and he made candle-holders and hanging chandeliers. He first appears on the Revels payroll in 1578, and in the year following the Works payment he was back at Greenwich working for the Revels, and providing 'wierworke & branchis [chandeliers] in the hall at Grenewch, at Twelftid and Shrovetid'.[58]

At Shrovetide in 1587 he was also providing lighting for plays: Paul's Boys played on Shrove Sunday, and the Queen's Men on Shrove Tuesday.[59] The Works entry shows, first, the overlapping and grey areas of responsibility be-tween Works and Revels as the latter was beginning to scale down its production activities; in the event, the Revels retained its responsibilities for lighting. Second, and more importantly, it shows where the stage was placed on this occasion. Wirework 'about' the screen probably means that candle sconces were set up on its vertical surface, and therefore that the screen was not obscured by a bank of seating, as at Oxford in 1605. Richard Southern's model of staging at court is correct in this instance, it seems. The screen wall may have been used as a stage façade, but it was certainly used to mount lights, probably with reflectors placed behind them to throw the light outwards into the chamber, and onto the stage below.

In late February of the following year, 1588, the amateur actors of Gray's Inn presented a play called *The Misfortunes of Arthur* before the queen in the Hall at Greenwich. For this occasion the Works made 'a greate Scaffolde with degrees and pticons'.[60] Possibly the stage was placed before the screen, as in the previous year, but the published text of the play makes clear that the performance featured stage houses: even if the screens end was the place of the stage the screen doors were not used as stage entries. The Office of the Revels certainly was still building houses in this season. The carpenter John Mildney was paid 'for timber bordes and workemanshipp in mending & setting vp of the houses', payment was made to 'Russell & dyvers other paynters for there worke & collours for paynting of houses', and the Office bought 'Canvis for the houses'.[61]

The Misfortunes of Arthur is a singularly turgid and unreadable play to modern tastes; no record survives of what the queen may have thought of it on the occasion of its first performance. Since it is unique in including references to court production methods in its stage directions, however, it is of considerable importance to theatre history. Although the printed text of the play does not correspond absolutely with what was performed, it gives us a fair indication of what the actors would have required from the Revels or Works carpenters who prepared the stage for their show. An analysis both of the stage directions and of indications of stage movement and business within the dialogue reveals that the stage required a trap, for an initial apparition of '*three furies*', and that it had at least three points of entry: three vaguely nominated 'places' from which characters enter are named in the fourth of the dumb shows which precede the acts. As far as 'houses' are concerned, two are named, the first for Mordred and the second as 'the house appointed for *Arthur*'; these two characters are the chief antagonists of the play, and we might guess that the houses were symmetrically arranged at opposite sides of the stage. In the first act a '*Cloister*' is nominated as a point of exit, but it is not called a 'house', and is not used or referred to after the third scene. The fourth dumb show also suggests that a fourth part of the stage was localised, when in a piece of emblematic barbarism a babe in arms is snatched from its mother by soldiers and flung 'against the walles'. (Since the violence is the major theatrical point here the detail of physically realised 'walls' would seem to have been by no means necessary.)

In putting this information together, we might assume that 'houses'—at least in the case of this play—were largely points of entry, perhaps constructed as projecting booths. The three places nominated in the first act—Mordred's house, Arthur's house, and the cloister—are not referred to subsequently by those names in stage directions, and they may be identical with the three distinct but unlocalised 'places' of entry required later in the play. In other words a tiring house at the upstage edge of the playing platform was provided with three entries, two of which could serve as 'houses'—distinct locations connected with a character—when required. The decoration of the tiring-house façade perhaps reflected such a division into distinct places, although the design of both houses in this play—both the castles of military leaders—is likely to have been some form of painted stonework, hence providing 'walls' for the show of infanticide.[62] In short, 'houses' need not have been a great deal more complex than a decorated tiring-house wall. If they were independent structures distinct from the kind of neutral, flexible stage-entry which the doors of the tiring houses at the playhouses provided they are likely, once again, to have been inconvenient to the actors. An isolated 'house' would leave an actor marooned; having made an exit he would have to wait there for his re-entry. The complex stage traffic of plays written from the late 1580s onwards assumes the fluidity of movement possible with stage entries communicating with a common backstage space: the tiring house.

Although the 'houses' disappear from the Revels records, therefore, we need not think of a radical change in the visual style of the stage at court. The houses, one might say, became subsumed under the singular house, the tiring house used by the actors elsewhere; if so, we are observing a difference in terminology rather than a considerable difference in the use of the stage between the earlier Elizabethan period and the later. Not every tiring house looked like that at the Swan; players on the road would have expected to set up a tiring house for their performances, but the only constant was its function. Tiring houses would have varied in size and appearance to suit the spaces in which they were set, and the audiences they faced. If cloth hangings could have been carried with the costumes from town to town and attached to locally borrowed scaffold poles, performances at aristocratic houses were probably more lavishly furnished with the household's own material—and so at court. Stages there did not suddenly lapse into a Swan-like plainness with the scaling down of the Revels operations, we may take it. One or more of the other royal Offices—the Works and the

Wardrobe, principally–would have been charged with ensuring that what the queen and court looked at was fittingly decorated, and matched the splendour of the rest of the theatre, and of the audience.

The simplest tiring house would have been built as the other parts of the theatre were, from a wooden skeleton, with those parts of the entire theatre which were not hidden by gorgeously clothed human bodies–as were the stage and the seats–concealed by richly decorated hanging cloth. Tapestry and arras, subtly coloured and decorated with figures and scenes, was probably also used in the playhouses when the troupe or management could afford it. The cheap alternative, canvas painted to imitate the effect of woven tapestry, may also have been used at court, but the real thing was readily available. The Wardrobe kept an extensive stock of woven cloth and curtains in various sizes, and could quickly have created a lavish vertical wall of drapery, suitably hung in sections to provide entries, on a framework erected by the Works, and to serve as a tiring-house façade. It also seems unlikely, however, that the tradition of painted stage decoration died out entirely between the ending of the elaborate Revels preparations and the beginning of the period when scene-painters' skills, applied in a rather different manner, were in demand for the mounting of the court masques. Among the many necessary tasks which are simply passed over in silence in the accounts it seems likely to me that the Sergeant Painter and his staff, under the direction of the Works, continued to create painted decoration on court stages, including the decoration of scenery when it was called for. I will explore this issue at more length in chapter 4.

During the last twenty years of Elizabeth's reign, court theatres continued to be large structures, built within the halls and great chambers of the major palaces, where the Christmas and Shrove festivals were habitually held. Whatever the queen's own taste for dramatic entertainment, her court patronised the players on only two occasions in the year; however much the quality of London playing might have improved over the course of the reign, the traditional frequency and function of plays at the court remained the same. The large spaces within the halls on such occasions, with the correspondingly large audiences they might contain, must have resulted in performances with the scale and register of those in the larger outdoor playhouses. As I observe above, it would have been challenging to act in the cavernous space of Hampton Court Hall, with its daunting emptiness high overhead. Theatres in the smaller areas of the great chambers, with generally lower ceilings, would have corresponded more in scale and acoustics with the indoor playhouses, and they were probably far better suited to the less powerful voices of the troupes of boy players, for example. This consideration evidently did not carry much weight, since boy companies were required to perform in the Hall at Whitehall, and in other large areas. Whether they could have been heard in the upper reaches of the seating furthest from the stage is open to question. The Elizabethan court, however, did not watch and listen to plays in spaces smaller than the great chambers, as the Stuarts later did, and the queen appears not to have seen plays in her own residences in conditions more intimate than those of the festival seasons.

If Elizabethan court patronage of the drama can look rather conservative and ungenerous when compared with the Stuart years, the court did respond in some ways to the changing conditions in the theatrical world outside. The foundation of the Queen's Men in 1583, for which the leading adult professionals of the day were drafted from their respective companies and brought together into one troupe, appears to have been an attempt to advertise royal status through association with a genuinely popular entertainment, and to follow the lead of principal nobles, chiefly the Earl of Leicester, who had used playing troupes in a similar manner in the preceding decade.

Although their status as royal servants was largely nominal—apart from receiving a livery of scarlet cloth they were expected to pursue their own living as a professional troupe playing to the public—the Queen's Men became favoured as a visiting troupe at court for the decade following their foundation, and if the combined skill of this group of actors set new standards in performance it is perhaps significant that in the second decade, from 1593 to 1603, the companies appearing at court were predominantly those of the leading adult professional troupes, especially the two increasingly dominant companies, the Admiral's Men and the Chamberlain's Men. The company to which Shakespeare belonged first appeared at court in the Christmas season of 1594-95, and thereafter was to play before the queen in each remaining year of her reign. Court entertainment was increasingly made up of the plays from the adult professional theatre: the schoolboy and legal amateurs patronised in the earlier part of the reign no longer appeared at court, and even the trained boy players, partly as an accident of the career of such troupes, dropped entirely out of view at court throughout the 1590s. The result was that the court was seeing the best—presumably—of the dynamic professional theatre of London, as if, in the 1970s, the Royal Shakespeare and the National companies were to have played several of their best productions of the year for a few nights of command performances at Buckingham Palace. In addition, there was a direct communication between the stages of the Theatre, the Curtain, the Rose, and the Globe, among other playhouses, and the stages at court. However different court stages may have been from those in the playhouses before the 1590s, by 1600 the arrangement and layout of stages and tiring houses at court would have been made to suit prevailing professional practice. Court stages for plays had become spaces entirely for professional players, and predominantly for adult players. To repeat, I do not think that this would have meant that they became plain and ascetic: the signs are rather that the actors emulated court style in their public playing places. The Puritan complaints about the gorgeousness of playhouses, beginning in the late 1570s, suggest that the players attempted to decorate their stages and tiring houses with something of the *élan* of royal magnificence.[63]

With the termination of the detailed Revels accounts we hear a good deal less about masks, but it would be wrong to assume that these entertainments disappeared entirely. It may be significant, however, that the most remarkable mask we know from the later Elizabethan period was presented by a group from outside the court: the young law students of Gray's Inn, who put on *Proteus and the Adamantine Rock* in the Hall at Whitehall at Shrovetide 1595. On this occasion degrees were built on both sides of the Hall, and there was a 'standeinge' for the Lord Chamberlain near to the stairs leading to the Great Chamber.[64] This arrangement rather suggests that the performance area was at the other end of the Hall; the Great Chamber lay to the south-west of the Hall, and was accessible via a doorway in the western wall, which may be seen in the *Florimène* plan, at the top left, directly above the platform for the royal seat (Plate 3). So the layout in 1595 was probably very similar to that for the play forty years later: the maskers are likely to have performed their show in the space towards the screens end. Apart from the literary interest of the surviving text of this mask, which is probably a good deal more complex than most Elizabethan entertainments to which the title 'mask' was applied, the production also used scenery, though of a traditional kind. The rock of the title—so similar to that of the play performed in 1579—concealed the eight maskers, and it was made to open to release them after the dialogue which precedes the dancing. The magic rock, as we have observed, had been a motif in court productions for many years.

The Jacobean period, 1603–1625

The 1595 mask may be regarded as prophetic of developments in the Jacobean court, which saw the transformation of the old disguised entry and dance with new literary, musical, and scenic elaboration. Even *Proteus*, unusually textually elaborate though it is, used a completely traditional scenic emblem, presumably traditionally built from a wooden frame covered in canvas, which had been employed in plays, processions, and parades since the middle ages, and which might variously represent, for example, Mount Sinai, Mount Olympus, Fortitude, and so on. That is, it was a three-dimensional built piece, placed on the floor of a hall, on a stage, in the street, or even on a wagon. Its meaning was plain from wherever one might see it. The Jacobean masque, under the guidance of Inigo Jones, soon adopted the principles of a unified visual scheme, to be seen from one principal direction, and of visual surprise, entrancing the observers with some remarkable theatrical transformation. Although surprises and theatrical tricks were also a traditional part of court festivity–the account of the wedding pageants to celebrate the marriage of Prince Arthur and Catherine of Aragon in 1501 describes a number of them–in the context of the first principle, of a single visual focus, the theatrical result at the Jacobean court was a stage which could be framed and masked, with wing, cellar, and fly space, and a front curtain to conceal the scenery set on the stage. The early seventeenth century saw the arrival of the proscenium stage in England. The scenic representations on such a stage were conceived in a painterly, two-dimensional fashion, so that while the stage space became more complex the carpentry of scenery became a good deal simpler. The machinery of Jones's stages, which produced revolves and flying effects, and which we might be led to think of as innovative, was in itself traditional: it used principles and technology well-known to stage machinists in the middle ages, which had been employed on occasion for spectacle in Elizabethan court shows, like *The Knight of the Burning Rock*. Its application by Jones, to produce effects within a focussed stage picture, was what was truly new.

The masques of the new court were considerably more elaborate than their Elizabethan predecessors, however, and, after some experimentation with spatial layout in the early Jacobean years, a tradition of staging was established which called for a particular form of theatre. Theatres for the masques were large, being built either in the halls, or the successive Whitehall banqueting houses. They drew large, crowded audiences, to accommodate which large banks of degrees were built, and they required two performance spaces. The first was a pictorial stage of the kind described above, which was the focus of the preliminary dramatic action, and from which the masquers eventually appeared, frequently prefaced by some special spectacular effect. The masquers' dance followed, for which steps were required from the stage down to the open floor in front of it; this area was flanked by the boxes for the musicians who played for the songs and dances. The form of the complete theatre therefore required that there be no seating for some distance directly in front of the stage, since the ballet which was a major part of the entire entertainment (and of which masque *texts* give us very little conception) was performed there. When we look at the Jones sketches for masque scenery we must remember that the stage picture was viewed at some distance even by its ideal observer, the king, who sat at the centre of the theatre, at the point of view from which linear perspective scenery is composed. Other viewers nearer the stage would have seen it from the sides, from seats in either rank of degrees against the side walls; thus the pictorial conventions of the new scenic stage, in conflict with an auditorium built to watch a ballet performed in an arena, could not always have shown themselves to great advantage, even without taking into account the considerable challenge of lighting an enclosed scene with sufficient brilliance, using only candles and oil lamps.

The curious mixture of theatrical styles and conventions in such a masque theatre was not solely English, however, and need not be regarded as a failure to apply the principles of Italian scenery with proper thoroughness. No visual representation of the entire effect of an English court hall set up as a masque theatre survives, but there is an interesting etching by the famous illustrator, Jacques Callot, of an entertainment at the Uffizi Theatre in Florence in 1617 (Plate 16), which gives some impression of the combination of a proscenium picture at one end of the theatre and of a ballet performed across a large arena in front, surrounded on three sides by audience. The Jacobean masque theatres must have been very similar to what we see in this picture.

The assembly of large numbers of people for the culturally ambitious productions of the masques, advertising splendour and sophistication, was evidently an important project of the Jacobean court; whether or not James himself was enthusiastic about the project he certainly acquiesced in it, and continued to play his roles as paternal observer–benefactor, and as the usually patient recipient of rhetorical and musical praise for several hours each Christmas season. Another sign of its importance is the priority given to the Banqueting House at Whitehall, the site of many masque performances up to the mid 1630s, and its fitting architectural dignity in which the king *does* seem to have taken some personal interest. A new wooden building, to replace 'the old rotten, sleight builded banquetting house'[65] erected in 1581, was begun in 1606 and finished the following year. As I have described it in my survey of the Whitehall buildings above, its style was in some respects probably not unlike the stone building which replaced it after it burnt down early in 1619. Quite full records concerning its decoration and appointments are given in the Works accounts, but these have not been as widely cited in histories of the theatre as have the similar Cockpit records, for all the significance of the Banqueting House in Jacobean court

16 Jacques Callot, etching of a court ballet in the Uffizi Theatre, Florence, 1617. The first
intermezzo of the entertainment *The Liberation of Tirreno*.

theatrical culture and as the first structure at Whitehall to announce a clear stylistic break with the Tudor past.

The interior was a large open hall with two orders of columns supporting a gallery around three sides. It was famously observed in January 1618 by Orazio Busino, a member of the Venetian ambassadorial staff, who attended the perform-ance there of Jonson's masque *Pleasure Reconciled to Virtue*, twelve months before the building disappeared forever, and whose description is among the most informative documents we now possess about court performance. At the ceiling level, Busino noted, there were 'festoons and angels in relief with two rows of lights'. This may sound rather awkwardly antiquated and Gothic, but we should consider that, if the classical character created by the columns was carried through, they are more likely to have been conventional swags and *putti*. The Works accounts reveal a great deal of very detailed decorative work on the building. Doric and Ionic columns were painted, marbled, and gilded, the roof had carved pendants in 'Antique woorke' (Busino's 'festoons'?), and the 'angels' are called 'boyes of Elme Tymber to hange over the roofe'. Other carved 'boys' also formed part of the decoration, and presumably were indeed *putti*.[66] Though the general theme of the building was classical, then, it must have exhibited considerable exuberance and festivity of a distinctly theatrical flavour, suitable to its purpose.

Busino's description of the disposition of the hall in 1618 is as follows: 'A large hall is fitted up like a theatre, with well secured boxes all round. The stage is at one end and his Majesty's chair in front under an ample canopy. Near him are stools for the foreign ambassadors.'[67] By 'boxes' he is perhaps describing the effect of sections of degrees around the walls divided by the columns, although we should also remember that the Works accounts frequently mention 'parti-tions' in conjunction with 'degrees', indicating that the entire rank of seating was divided into sections which could be reserved for particular groups. Busino's own account tells how his party were led to their places by the Master of Ceremonies. Though he had some reservations about the standards of the music, and about the early-morning rowdiness of the audience after the show, Busino was favourably impressed by the effect of James's building and by the theatrical occasion at which the heir to the throne, the seventeen-year-old Prince Charles, danced. The masque and its physical setting were designed to work together in creating an effect of royal splendour and generosity.

We can still admire the splendour of the building which was immediately planned to replace it, following the accidental fire. Jones's stone Banqueting House was not structurally complete until three years later, when Jonson's *Masque of Augurs* was presented there in January 1622, masques in the intervening period having been mounted in the Hall and other spaces. It was used as a theatre as its predecessor had been, by building temporary stages and seating within its walls in the general shape described by Busino. Its function as a masque theatre was ended only by a further glorification of King James. Once the painted ceiling panels commissioned from Rubens and depicting the apotheosis of the late king were placed in position, ten years after his death (they are still to be seen on the ceiling of the Banqueting House), King Charles decided that the room must no longer be used for theatrical performances because the expensive paintings were not to be 'hurt with Lights'.[68] This concern gives us an incidental indication of one aftermath of court theatrical events: blackened and scorched ceilings, which required washing or repainting.

Masques largely remained part of the Christmas feast at court, although a number of them celebrated particular events, notably noble and royal weddings. As part of the festival season they were prepared for partly by the usual court Offices, although a good deal of the work on costumes and scenery was financed through other budgets. Most of the masques shown at court were produced there, and featured chief court figures as performers in the dancing. The series of 'queen's masques', beginning with the first Jacobean Christmas in 1603–4 and lasting until 1611, featured Queen Anne herself as the principal masquer, with leading court ladies as her companions. They were not exactly 'amateur' productions, however. Not only was the scenery for the masques designed in a fashionable international style and executed with great elaboration and skill, but the music for the songs and dances was provided by the very best players and composers in London, professional musicians permanently or temporarily in royal employ. Dancing masters trained the royal and aristocratic masquers in their steps, and professional actors from the leading companies took speaking parts in the prominent dramatic episodes that Ben Jonson and other writers composed to frame the choreographic part of the entertainment. Numerous artists hired to mount the annual court masques were involved in the world of the professional theatre, as actors, musicians, and costumiers, so that the influence that lavish court entertainment had on the professional theatre in the middle of the sixteenth century could be regarded as continuing in some degree during the first three decades of the seventeenth.

The patronage of drama increased at the Jacobean court. The renaming of all the chief acting troupes of London at the start of the reign, giving them all patrons in the royal family, was not necessarily connected with a direct interest in the welfare of the professional players, but its symbolism can only have been advantageous to the actors.[69] Like the Elizabethan Queen's Men before them,

Shakespeare's troupe after 1603 bore the title of the reigning monarch, and could wear royal livery. Shakespeare himself, like his fellows, had the status of a groom of the chamber (a fairly lowly post, were it not a largely nominal title). As knighthoods lend modern actors a certain senior status and authority, however, so the royal title must have eased many negotiations in the company's professional life. As far as direct monetary patronage was concerned, James was no more generous than Elizabeth: the King's Men were expected to function as royal servants when they were called to court, but in practical terms they made their living as they always had, by playing to a paying public in playhouses and other performance spaces.

Their living *was* helped by the consistency and frequency with which they were called to court to perform, receiving for each performance a reward of ten pounds, a considerable sum in comparison to what might be expected from the daily take at the playhouse. Between December 1603 and February 1604, for example, the King's Men performed nine plays at court.[70] Typically, the Jacobean season for plays began somewhat earlier than in the days of Queen Elizabeth, in late October and early November, also continuing after Christmas, blurring the boundary between Christmas and Shrovetide. Lent was usually observed as a fast, without the frivolities of revels, but thereafter plays could be called for at court until well into the spring. The traditional Elizabethan focus on the twelve days of Christmas and the two or three days preceding Ash Wednesday for revels became extended, and a longer, continuous winter season was established, during which actors might expect to be summoned to perform at court at any time.

One reason for the expansion in the number and extent of entertainments was the considerable increase in the size of the court, which in effect became a series of connected courts, inhabiting a number of the palaces simultaneously. That of the king was based principally at Whitehall, the queen's courts were at Somerset House and Greenwich, and the courts of the Prince of Wales (Prince Henry was invested in 1610, and Prince Charles, following the death of his brother, in 1616) at St James's and Richmond. Plays were no longer necessarily seen by the entire assembled court with the reigning monarch present; the royal children were entertained by players independently and in more intimate circumstances than those of the large assemblies in palace halls. Thus a greater variety of chambers was called on for theatrical conversions, and hence Jacobean court theatres came in a greater variety of size and configuration than did those of the Elizabethan years. Not only were players performing more frequently at court, but they were playing in differing physical conditions.

While the large court chambers continued to be used for large assemblies to see plays, the desire to enjoy entertainment in the company of more intimate, 'private' audiences, formed from the immediate members and guests of a particular court group, led to the conversion of court rooms which had never been used as theatrical spaces before. As far as we can tell, the Cockpit at Whitehall was first used as a theatre in this period, possibly as early as March 1604, but certainly by December 1607. Why such an unconventional building, as compared to the habitually rectangular chambers used for court playing spaces, was chosen for conversion to a temporary theatre is a question to which only speculative answers can be offered. Perhaps its location, far from the busiest parts of Whitehall Palace around the Hall and the royal suite, was an advantage. The disruption caused by the assembly and dismantling of the heavy wooden scaffolding for theatrical seating would not have been as great an inconvenience in a building which was relatively isolated, on the edge of St James's Park, and which perhaps was not otherwise in very frequent use for its nominal purpose, cockfighting. This answer assumes, however, that physical preparations for plays in the Cockpit were similar to those made in halls and great chambers. In fact, the Works accounts make no mention of making stands or degrees in the building before the major conversion began in 1629. The Cockpit from the beginning had been furnished with permanent seating, since its function was to serve as an arena, and the seats were repaired and refurbished periodically over the years. Permanent seating for an audience might be regarded as another advantage the Cockpit had over other spaces; it could be prepared for plays relatively quickly and inexpensively, perhaps, except that the seating was arranged in a continuous ring around the central area, a very inconvenient layout by the standards of the usual hierarchy of seating in court theatres. The ring of seats in the Cockpit surrounded a raised circular table on which the cocks were set to fight, and which we know to have been 12 feet in diameter. In itself this can hardly have served for a stage, though it seems likely that it may have supported a larger platform laid on top of it.

If so, the stage would have sat more or less in the centre of the building. As I have argued above, the players when they came to court would have required facilities matching those in their habitual playing places, and specifically a tiring-house space at the rear of the stage, which so placed in relation to a central stage in the Cockpit, would have rendered a whole segment of the circle of seating unusable for an audience. In any case the important patron of the occasion of a play–and we know that Prince Henry, for example, watched plays at the Cockpit in the early Jacobean period–would have sat directly opposite the stage, and the assembled audience accompanying him are likely to have been grouped around the royal seat to the rear and the sides, the habitual configuration of seating at plays and masques. The result in a circular arena would have been something like a half-circle, or a grouping following five sides of the octagon of the interior walls. In short, the eventual conversion of the building into a theatre by Inigo Jones perhaps preserves in its plan something of the layout followed in the temporary use of the Cockpit for royal plays (see Plate 7). Rather more than half of the original full ring of seating, at ground level and in the second-storey gallery, was used in the permanent theatre, as it would have been in the temporary arrangement I describe above.

However close the match may have been between the plan of the 1630 theatre and those of temporary theatres set up before that date, the building must have proved itself, visually and acoustically, to be well suited to dramatic performance in order for the conversion to have been undertaken. The Cockpit in fact had a longer career as an occasional, converted theatre than as a permanent theatre building, even counting the few years that the refurbished theatre served the court of Charles II after 1660.

The courts of the two successive princes of Wales, Henry and Charles, constituted an important nucleus of patronage of dramatic activity. Both princes were regular participants in the masques, both patronised playing companies, and both paid from their own household accounts for visiting players, independently of the larger court festivals. Henry's residence at St James's Palace appears to have seen the beginning of the staging of plays there, in the relatively small spaces I have described above. These chambers – fairly narrow, low-ceilinged Tudor rooms – cannot have held a large audience, but the plays presented within them were drawn from the regular playhouse repertory and performed by the full company on facilities which, while they were no doubt scaled down to suit the chamber, cannot have been miniaturised. In a room barely 20 feet wide the players would have preferred their playing area to have stretched from wall to wall. A tiring house cannot have been so modest in depth as to be impractical, and the same would have been true for the stage space. The performance facilities as a whole, then, may have claimed about half the floor area in a small chamber such as those at St James's. The remaining 400 square feet or so cannot have accommodated many people, even if some of them stood against the walls, but all of them would have been in very close contact with the performers. Theatre at St James's was an intimate experience, in which the actors could be observed and heard with a detail possible only in small studio theatres in the modern period. We are left to imagine how actors fresh from playing at the outdoor playhouses to audiences numbering in the thousands might adjust the nuances of their acting to conditions of such intimacy, an intimacy charged with the consciousness of the rank and status of those listening to them. As Jacobean court theatres varied in configuration and size, so may the Jacobean acting seen and heard in them have displayed a range of style and subtlety.

The Caroline period, 1625–1642

The seventeen years defined in the heading above take as their ending the year in which King Charles retreated from London in the face of opposition to his rule and, rather later, the theatres were closed by the well-known parliamentary decree, but the active years of court culture had ended somewhat before that. King Charles was absent from London for much of 1639, engaged with the rebellion in Scotland, and for the following two years of his residence in London was preoccupied with constantly increasing political difficulty. The last of the Stuart masques extolling wise and beneficent rule, Davenant's *Salmacida Spolia*, was presented in January 1640, its naive idealism appearing in retrospect grimly ironic in the face of Charles's mishandling of his disaffected people. Regular visits by the players to court seem to have ended at about the same time, although the courts of the queen and the royal children continued to see plays occasionally until the serious crisis of 1642. The accounts of the royal Offices tail off and disappear around 1640, as the normal rhythms and functions of court life were increasingly interrupted and suspended. Some of those who worked for the crown went unpaid, and parliament later had to settle their appeal for back pay. If the actors also did not receive their fees, they may have become increasingly reluctant to give up a day's playing to entertain at court.

The reign began, however, with considerable optimism and energy. Charles had grown up in surroundings of some sophistication, and he had more personal taste for the arts, as a connoisseur and collector, than the two monarchs who preceded him on the English throne. Immediately upon his accession he married a French princess, the sister of Louis XIII, who also had a lively interest in theatre, music, and literature, and whose own experiments in production and performance contributed considerably to the theatrical culture of the Stuart court.[71] Her first undertaking, a performance in French of the play *Artenice*, at Somerset House in February 1626, initiated the use of perspective scenery, set on a proscenium stage and designed by Inigo Jones, for drama, as distinct from masque. Such experimentation influenced the professional stage very little before the Civil War, but plays with 'scenes' were increasingly regarded as possessing a certain chic and elegance.

Having seen from his boyhood the leading London actors playing both the latest plays and the famous older repertory from the Elizabethan years, Charles was an enthusiastic patron of plays and theatrical culture, continuing, but expanding still further through the year, the court season observed by his father, during which players might be called to court. The fifteen years between Charles's accession and the end of the 1630s is the most consistently lively period of theatrical activity at court in the entire 'long Elizabethan' period. (The adjective 'Elizabethan' is sometimes loosely applied, especially in the context of drama, to the entire period from 1588 to 1642.) The King's Men continued to be a favoured group in terms of the frequency of their playing at court, and although they had no closer ties as royal servants than those James had instituted in 1603 they were, for example, taken on more or less as 'players in residence' at the Christmas court held at Hampton Court in 1636–37, when London was in the grip of severe plague and the playhouses were closed.[72]

The court theatres of King Charles's reign continued to be built in the traditional locations. The Banqueting House designed by Inigo Jones was still a relatively new addition to the Whitehall landscape at the start of the reign, and it was favoured for the continuing seasonal production of masques until the installation of the Rubens ceiling. Soon thereafter the king commissioned a Masquing House, a long rectangular hall built of timber, to be put up in the space adjoining the elegant new stone building to the east. Also designed by Jones, and erected quickly in 1637, the Masquing House served to accommodate the masque at the next Christmas season: *Britannia Triumphans*.[73] It was as large as the Banqueting House itself, and was set up as a theatre in a similar fashion. While it would seem appropriate for a wooden theatre designed to stage masques to have permanent ranks of seating, and even a permanent proscenium stage, this does not appear to have been the case. Its continuing function, when it was first erected, does not seem to have been assured, and, in the years that followed, the Works were involved in the usual preparations for each masque as it was presented. As events dictated, *Salmacida Spolia* was the last masque staged there, but the building was adapted in the following April to accommodate a visiting Spanish embassy, and 'diuided into two roomes' in a fashion which suggests that no large ranks of theatrical seating occupied the interior.[74] The Masquing House, despite its title, was simply another large court chamber which might serve a variety of functions. We know of no further use of this large wooden building until five years later it was pulled down by parliamentary order and the timber sold off to pay some of the wages owed to royal servants.[75]

A free-standing temporary wooden theatre built from the ground up was not entirely a new kind of structure, and one might regard it as either within the tradition of the earlier Elizabethan banqueting houses or an elaboration of the substantial timber theatres framed within existing stone walls. Some years earlier an entire theatre had been raised for one or two performances of Walter Montagu's pastoral play *The Shepherd's Paradise*, a second production mounted by the queen and featuring her as performer. The building, erected in 1632, enclosed a courtyard at Somerset House; it was made to abut existing exterior walls, so that in effect the courtyard was roofed over, and its area formed the floor of the theatre.[76] The theatre therefore can be regarded as midway between the temporary wooden theatres enclosed in an existing building and those, like the Masquing House, built entire, with walls and roof.

A surviving plan of the theatre was identified by John Orrell in 1977 (Plate 17), and it shows seating arranged in a familiar layout, with a large bank of degrees rising behind a central royal seat which faces a stage with wing scenery; degrees are also placed along the side walls to either side of the state. The entire theatre was 75 feet long, and the auditorium 34 feet wide. The stage, which was built in a wider end of the courtyard, was about 50 feet wide and half that dimension in depth–a very large platform–although the plan shows that the downstage area defined by the wings used only about half the full depth of the stage, and about 30 feet of width at the proscenium opening. Montagu's play, like *Florimène* which followed it in 1635, was produced with Italianate perspective scenery designed by Inigo Jones, of the kind usually seen only on the masque stages.

The plans of this Paved Court theatre of 1632–33 and of the conversion of the Hall for *Florimène* in 1635 together give us a clear idea of how audiences were accommodated at a court play, but the stages in neither plan correspond with what would have been set up by the Office of the Works for the King's Men to play *Othello* in Hampton Court Hall, for example, as they did in December 1636.[77] The theatre that King Charles created for the players at Whitehall, also designed by Inigo Jones, had quite a different stage from those at the queen's theatres. This was the one at the converted Cockpit, opened in 1630, and I wish here simply to add some comments on the stage itself to my earlier discussion of that building. The surviving drawings of this theatre are particularly significant in that they are unique in showing us a stage at court on which the actors performed the plays they brought from the London playhouses.

Jones, I have suggested, may have followed in his plans for the permanent conversion the arrangements made in temporary translations of the Cockpit into a theatre before 1629. He had to accommodate the theatre to an idiosyncratic building, and he had to consult the requirements of the players, but he also had

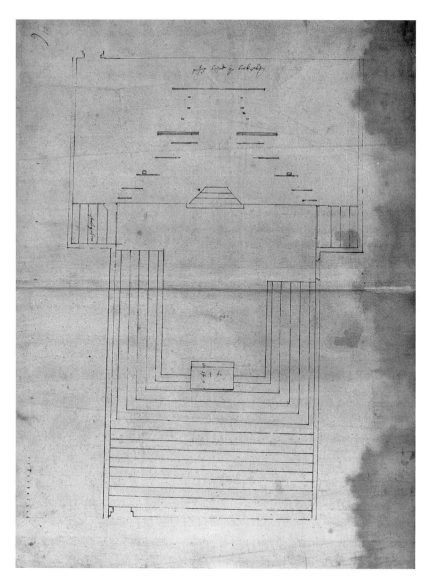

17   John Webb, plan of the theatre made by Inigo Jones in the Paved Court, Somerset House, for the staging of *The Shepherd's Paradise*, in 1632–33.

his own architectural scheme in mind, based on his study of Palladio and Vitruvius. When we look at the plan and elevation of the theatre (Plate 7), we see a five-entry *frons scenae* which stands behind the open stage, with its larger central *porta regia*, columns, busts, statues, and an inscription, all characteristics of the Roman stage generally, but which are more specifically alluding to the neoclassical Teatro Olimpico, Palladio's elegant creation at Vicenza in 1583, which Jones had visited and drawn. The scene wall curves, to follow the octagonal plan of the pillars supporting the Tudor gallery and lantern roof, producing an effect never seen in a Roman theatre, nor ever seen, we used to think, in a tiring house at a playhouse. The scene wall in the drawing of the Swan is flat, running parallel with the stage front. The discovery of the foundations of the Rose playhouse in 1989, however, demonstrated that the tiring house there may well have had a concave shape, following the line of galleries behind the stage, and its entries may have been set at angles to the centre, exactly as in the Cockpit plan. The players may not have needed five entry doors–the number is significant for the learned observer of theatrical architecture only–but any combination of symmetrically opposite entries and a central door communicating with a common backstage space would have suited them quite well. It is unlikely that the Cockpit stage and tiring house are modelled on those at any of the London playhouses, but their essential theatrical features are shared with what the players knew elsewhere.

In front of the scene wall is a simple open platform, which in the first half of the seventeenth century was the main physical medium professional players relied on. The area of the stage at the Cockpit also seems a perfectly suitable one for players whose stages at the indoor playhouses were not particularly large. The platform is 34 feet in width across the downstage edge, and roughly half that in depth at the centre of the stage.[78] In general the theatre would have been similar in size and character to the indoor playhouses of the 1620s and 1630s: the Blackfriars, the Cockpit in Drury Lane, and the Salisbury Court theatre.

In addition to her participation in occasional plays as well as masques, the queen patronised players in her own household, which inhabited the two royal properties of Somerset House and St James's. In the latter place she continued the fashion for intimate entertainment which had begun while Prince Henry was resident there. Both palaces were provided with facilities for Catholic worship, and accommodated Henrietta Maria's French ladies-in-waiting and a varying number of priests. Because of these special circumstances, Richmond served as the chief palace assigned to the royal children. The royal couple had a young family at the outbreak of the war; their eldest son was born only in 1630, and the future King Charles II was not formally created Prince of Wales before 1642.

Notwithstanding, he saw plays on his own account at Richmond between 1639 and 1641, which were paid for from his own household funds.[79] These were staged, according to the Works records, 'in the Guardchamber',[80] that is the Great Chamber, where Queen Elizabeth had watched plays surrounded by her court. King Charles II, whom we think of first in relation to the new drama of the Restoration, to the radically different playhouse of the later seventeenth century, and especially in his personal relations with the new professional actresses of that period, was in fact the last monarch to have watched plays staged at court as they had been in Shakespeare's time.

4 Artists and Artisans

Then did I flourish, then my spacious rooms
Were hung with Arras, nay with Persian looms.
Then did my walls drest in rich colours vie
With Roman Pallaces for Imag'ry:
Mosaick paintings (though I'm now folorne)
Did then my costly gilded roofs adorne.
Statues of Parian Marble such as might
The amorous *Pigmalion* invite
To laugh at his dull workmanship, did grace
My walks and gardens.
Henry Glapthorne, 'White-Hall' (London, 1643)

While court stages and tiring houses for players had in their essentials to match theatrical facilities elsewhere, structures built and decorated by artists employed by the crown resembled other royal physical appointments. As a kind of interior decoration, court stages reflected prevailing styles in the treatment of rooms and furnishings. Certain styles remained constant across our entire period–most early sixteenth-century rooms remained virtually untouched, and the covering of large areas of interior wall with tapestry hangings continued–while others did not. The unchanging intention to create impressive and magnificent effects through architecture and interior finish, to awe the observer with richness and grandeur, continued to inform the principles of royal building, but an increasing appreciation and application of neoclassical style altered the forms in which it was expressed.

Given the weight of the surviving evidence we tend to think of the court theatres of the Stuart period as having achieved the highest point of visual splendour. The designs for masques and a few scenic plays made by Inigo Jones dominate our impressions. These were made for a form of theatre which was new in being specifically pictorial: it aimed to create a visual impression through painted perspective scenery. By contrast, stages of theatres at the Rose, the Globe, the Blackfriars, and the 1630 Whitehall Cockpit presented a visually neutral space within which the dramatic fiction was enabled to shift quite radically in imagined location, while the semiotic stress lay on actors' costumes, movements, and groupings, and on any particular properties or scenic pieces brought on to the stage–King Richard the Second's looking-glass, or the witches' cauldron in *Macbeth*, for example.

The theatres Jones built for his new scenery were made expressly to present a picture, viewed through a frame or a pierced façade: the proscenium arch. Court theatres for professional plays presented the façade itself, one might say, in front of which the playing platform extended and the actors performed. The painters who worked for Jones in preparing the elaborate scenery of the masques, however, were those regularly employed by the Office of the Works, under the general supervision of the Sergeant Painter, and their work on scenery cannot be regarded as entirely distinct from their other decorative tasks elsewhere, including any on the theatres made for the players. In his survey of the painting of interiors in England, Edward Croft-Murray points out 'how closely allied are the two arts of scenography and decorative painting. After all, the same artifices were used in both: ingenious foreshortening, play of perspective, and painting of false architecture and sculpture–in fact all the tricks of *trompe l'oeil*.'[1] More recently, in his study of Jones's designs, John Peacock repeats this point quite specifically. Speaking of the mixture of Italian and French influences Jones wrought into his own particular manner in the 1630s, he writes:

This 'royal' style came to be used not only in the court theatre but for schemes of interior decoration in the King's and Queen's residences. The association is a logical one, given the idea of seeing the stage 'pictures' and their 'frames' as large decorative projects . . . Clearly [Jones] regarded his ornamental style as a versatile medium adaptable to either architecture or theatre, just as he regarded his theatre projects as an integral part of his work overall.

Other artists also saw the Jonesian style as versatile, and adaptable from stage design to interior decoration. The figure of Truth on the Tragic Scene proscenium, for example, reappears in different contexts. She is on the ceiling of the Single Cube Room at Wilton, decorated by Jones's assistant Matthew Gooderick. And in slightly altered pose she figures in the frieze ornaments designed by Edward Pearce, another Jones assistant, published in 1640. Pearce here also uses motifs from Jones's decoration of Henrietta Maria's palace at Oatlands, which he seems to regard no differently from the scenic ornament.[2]

Both Gooderick and Pearce were on the staff of the Office of the Works before the Civil War; the former worked on the decoration of the Whitehall Cockpit in 1629–30.

What can be demonstrated to be true at court in the 1630s, because the evidence survives, is likely to be true of earlier periods. Court painters, many of whom were portrait and subject painters, were regularly employed by the Works and other royal Offices in decorative tasks, and in the mid sixteenth century they were demonstrably working for the Revels Office. The distinction between 'high', or so-called fine, art and what we now call decorative or applied art was not as extreme or as widely recognised in the Renaissance. Even so famous and rich a painter as Rubens, an outstanding contributor to the fine art of the seventeenth century whose painting we now look at in galleries throughout the world, did not regard it as beneath him to provide designs for engraved title-pages for the Plantin press in Antwerp. Although most Sergeant Painters at court since the time of Henry VIII had painted portraits, principally of the monarch and royal family, and other figurative paintings (with varying degrees of success, it must be added), when Robert Streeter was appointed to the post after the Restoration his patent stated that he was to be responsible for 'all our works as well belonging to our royal palaces and houses as to our Great Wardrobe as also within our Office of Revels as also for our stables, ships and vessels, barges, close barges, coaches, chariots, caroches, litters, waggons and close cars, tents and pavilions, Heralds' Coats, trumpets, banners and for funerals to be solemnized'.[3] An impressive ambit indeed, and one which still recognised a tie between the Sergeant Painter and the Revels Office. Streeter, who painted the surviving ceiling of the Sheldonian Theatre in Oxford with celestial figurative designs (1668–69), was no mere jobbing decorator, and evidently much of the Sergeant Painter's job was supervisory, directing the teams of workmen who carried out his schemes of design.[4]

To understand what painters may have done for the Revels or the Works in the long period when we have no explicit record of their work on court theatres, we will need to look at the wide sphere of responsibilities described above; descriptions of other tasks and some surviving examples of court painting will give us a clearer sense of how royal theatres are likely to have been decorated. The example of Jones's reliance on other artists and designers, so thoroughly demonstrated by John Peacock, may serve as a more general model. Jones's scenes and figures are composed from details taken from Italian and French printed pictures especially, with both theatrical and non-theatrical subjects. In doing this he was perhaps showing some of the tentativeness of the draughtsman who was largely, for all we know, self-taught. The modern view of copying the work of others was not shared in the sixteenth and seventeenth centuries, however, when visual models and types were widely employed, even by the most accomplished artists, and alluded to a tradition of representation. Jones's sources, as demonstrated by Peacock, are consciously on display, proclaiming the connection between his own art and that of the masters whose style he is following. As literary cognoscenti might admire Jonson's adaptation of Horace's manner in English verse, so the knowing viewer would recognise certain continental European treatments of landscape or of perspective in Jones's visual schemes.

To compose his scene and costume sketches Jones was using published prints: of Callot, Tempesta, Sadeler, De Gheyn, Parigi, and many other artists. In doing so, however, he was simply following a standard practice of artists and designers which began soon after woodcut and metal prints began to be made, in the last quarter of the fifteenth century. Designs and pictures in loose prints as well as within books became part of a graphic artist's vocabulary, and pictorial styles could migrate internationally with considerable speed. Jones's own interests were in Palladian architecture and Italian perspective staging, but English artists had used foreign prints long before him. Lacking a strong native graphic style, English artists and decorators drew constantly on printed pictures and designs from continental Europe.[5] The Revels Office in 1553 paid ten shillings 'to an Italian for dyuers printed patterns',[6] for example. The 'patterns' were probably used as designs for mask costumes, possibly for the 'Greek warriors' of that year, but they were imported prints, and it seems likely that other mask costumes from this period for which we have verbal descriptions–the 'Lanceknightes' (= *landsknechts*, German soldiers) of Christmas 1573–74, for example–were also composed with reference to prints. Single-sheet and collected group prints of the *landsknecht* figure, extravagantly dressed and armed, were produced by many artists in the sixteenth century.[7]

Although English portraiture of the second half of the sixteenth century, particularly, has been characterised as antiquated in style and closed to the vibrancy of continental techniques in painting,[8] one can make too much of England's isolation and benightedness in the fine arts. Not only did the circulation of imported prints make continental style easily available for copying, but many artists working both at the court and in London were 'strangers', foreign visitors or immigrants whose training and technique were more advanced and sophisticated than those of native artists, but who would have passed on their skills to others in their workshops. Henry VIII had patronised many foreign artists and craftsmen in the decoration of his buildings; the most famous among the many foreign painters at his court was undoubtedly Hans Holbein, who worked in England over the course of almost twenty years. Renowned for his portraits, Holbein also worked occasionally on decorative painting, notably for the banqueting and disguising houses at Greenwich in 1527, and on designs for metalware and jewellery. Holbein never became Sergeant Painter, however; in the early sixteenth century the post was the preserve of the native English painters of the Painter-Stainers guild.[9]

This English monopoly was broken in 1544 by the appointment of Anthony Toto, as the Anglicised version of his name was usually written; his full name was Antonio di Nunziato d'Antonio, a Florentine who had worked with Ghirlandaio and Torrigiano, and who had come to England at some time after 1519, probably to work for Cardinal Wolsey.[10] Between 1548 and 1553, among his other responsibilities, he served the Revels Office in 'drawyng patrons' (patterns, or designs), 'drawinge & devisinge for painters and others', 'settinge oute woorkes to the painters and makinge patrons for them', and drafting 'certen patrons by him drawen after the Masters device for maskes & other percelles of the premisses in paper for syte & shewe of the forme in colours before the woorkmanshipp began'.[11] Toto, trained in early sixteenth-century Florentine style, was directing the painted design of scenery and making costume designs for tailors well before Inigo Jones engaged in similar work. No identifiable work by his hand survives, although it has been claimed that painted panels at Losely Park, Surrey, are by him. These are fragments of grotesque decoration and heraldic motifs, painted on canvas, with some figurative painting.[12] They may have been part of some royal decorative scheme in the later 1540s; that this was connected with the Revels is indicated by their being at Losely, the house of Sir Thomas Cawarden, the contemporary Master. If they are indicative of Revels painting, whether for a banqueting house or a theatrical occasion, they demonstrate considerable detail, skill, and liveliness, being elegantly executed in a fashionable mannerist style. The style continued into the Jacobean period: the surviving panels on the organ at Hatfield House, painted in 1611, after a model in a German pattern-book, by Rowland Buckett, master of the later court painter Edward Pearce, are in a very similar manner.[13]

Other foreign artists working for the Revels in the mid sixteenth century included Nicholas Bellin of Modena, a designer and sculptor, who had previously served at the court of Francis I of France at Fontainebleau (as had Sebastiano

Serlio), and the property-maker Robert Trunkwell.[14] The tradition continued in the early Elizabethan court. The accomplished portraitist Hans Eworth contributed designs to the Revels in the early 1570s.[15] The successor to Toto as Sergeant Painter was Nicholas Lizard (or Lysory), who was French, and held the post from 1554 to 1571. His sons were prominent in the Revels and the Works as painters and property-makers: William, John, Nicholas junior, and Lewis Lizard all were employed by the Revels and other Offices at one time or another until the mid 1580s.[16] During the same years the names of other painters recorded in the payment lists of the Revels indicate that many were foreign-born and -trained; in the 1572–73 season, for example, 'Pangrace Inglishe', 'Andro Depree', 'Haunce Kisbye', and a man identified simply as 'Balthazer' received wages along with the Lizard brothers.

Family groups of graphic artists seem to have been quite common, as sons, and occasionally daughters, followed fathers in the same trade, and hence received a training, in the case of children of foreign-born workmen, which maintained techniques and practices of the native paternal tradition. Painters were not alone in such familial avocation, but their interconnections are perhaps more noticeable than those of other trades and crafts; they suggest that matters of style, technique, and finish would have been shared, and passed on to English apprentices, for better or worse. In terms of purely professional contact Robert Peake, portrait-painter to Prince Henry and one of two Sergeant Painters to the crown from 1607, was working as a Revels painter in 1576–77 in the company of the Lizard family. Thus a man who had perhaps trained in decorating the Revels 'houses' lived to see the very different painted stages of Inigo Jones, whether or not he had any share in decorating them. In the Jacobean period, Peake also ran a business as a publisher and printseller, with a shop in Holborn; he produced the first English translation of Serlio's books of architecture (1611), and he must have been thoroughly familiar with the contemporary art of continental Europe in the form of engravings and etchings.[17]

His colleague as Sergeant Painter, John de Critz, who served for the entire Stuart period until the wars, was also of foreign origin, as his name suggests. He was allied by the marriage of his sister to Marcus Gheeraerts, the portraitist, son of a Flemish artist living in London, and part of a community of Flemish and Dutch artists permanently or intermittently resident in England: the famous De Passe family of engravers were among its most distinguished members.[18] Gheeraerts was also the brother-in-law, through the marriage of his own sister, of Isaac Oliver, the French-born pupil of Nicholas Hilliard, whom Oliver followed as a miniaturist and portrait-painter; Oliver was also patronised by Prince Henry.

The English art world of the mid sixteenth to the mid seventeenth centuries was therefore characterised by a good deal of interconnection, but it was far from being ingrown and cut off from artistic ideas from outside the country. Whether or not they chose to put them into practice, graphic artists in London between 1550 and 1640 must have been well informed about developments in composition and technique in painting and drawing in Italy, Germany, France, and the Low Countries, although the increase in the collecting of continental paintings and sculpture under the Stuart kings must have vastly facilitated the study and absorption of new techniques.[19] Inigo Jones's *application* of what he saw and read was unique, but this knowledge in itself was not, we may say.

To return to the rather more mundane day-to-day work of the successive Sergeant Painters, it is clear that whoever held the office had to be experienced in painting on cloth, which was used in a wide variety of decorative applications, from clothing (the heralds' armorial tabards, brightly coloured in red, blue, and gold) to large surfaces serving as curtaining, or as walls and ceilings. For the Wardrobe in the 1560s Nicholas Lizard painted and gilded designs on taffeta, velvet, damask, satin, silk, and canvas, while John de Critz painted 'funeral stuff' for the burial of Queen Anne in 1619, which included hatchments and banners carried in the procession, but also the carved effigy of the queen which lay on top of the hearse.[20] One royal Office initially connected with the Revels was that of the Tents (see chapter 1), which as its name suggests looked after the manufacture and storage of tents for the monarch's use in war and peace: in war for the battlefield, or for treaties and ambassadorial meetings, and in peace particularly for the travelling court on royal progresses. (Tents for entertainers on such journeys were also provided from time to time.) The glorious days of the Office were those of the chivalric wars of Henry VIII; after the 1520s its importance subsided, but it was never dissolved, and continued to supply elaborate tents for the progresses of Queen Henrietta Maria in the 1630s, for example. Royal tents of the sixteenth and seventeenth centuries were not simply the rather drab canvas colours of the days before nylon–nor are the bright blues and reds of modern camping tents particularly similar in effect to a Tudor royal encampment.

Tudor tents *were*, however, brightly coloured and painted–by the Sergeant Painter and his staff–in a variety of finishes. Early sixteenth-century painted designs (what the Revels Office designated 'patterns') survive for elaborate tents, probably for Henry VIII's meeting with Francis I of France at the Field of the Cloth of Gold in June 1520. They show whole ranges and suites of connected tents in rectangular and circular shapes, a palace under canvas, in a number of colours, and covered with filigree designs in gold, badges and mottoes, the ridge poles decorated with gilded fretwork, and with heraldic beasts bearing arms crowning the upright poles.[21] That such extravagant design continued is apparent from the later accounts of the Office of the Tents. In 1627–28 tents for the queen had gold *fleurs de lys* painted on blue calico, and poles and ridgetrees decorated with gilded pyramids and star patterns.[22] At some time in the next two years the Tents created a mock castle in cloth for the queen, with 'ffower Turrets', 'lardge square houses painted like Stoneworke', and 'A lardge ffower square wall of Canvas embattayled and painted like a Stonewall with battlements and peeces of Orden^aunce.' Painters further embellished the tents with 'hatchments, valence, lily pots [sculpted finials in *fleur de lys* shape], vanes' and 'pyramids'.[23] This playful conceit was nothing more than a large piece of theatrical scenery set *en plein air*, a mocking invasion of the English landscape by a French conqueror. (It was erected at Wellingborough, Holdenby, Tunbridge Wells, and Oatlands.) The widespread dislike of Charles's queen seems particularly sour in the face of such testimony to her sense of humour.

The overlap between structural and decorative work is particularly apparent in the case of Tudor banqueting houses, which were generally lightly built festival buildings put up for occasional use, and extravagantly decorated in a rather hectic style. One must distinguish such structures from the dignified stone palace hall created by Inigo Jones in the 1620s, the chaste elegance of which is very different from its rather gaudy ancestors. In fact, large tents of the type discussed above could have served very well as banqueting houses in the earlier style, since they were thought of as temporary structures set up in gardens and parks for amusement in the warmer months of the year. Following the Field of the Cloth of Gold in 1520, a large circular tent, 120 feet in diameter, was erected in Calais to serve as a banqueting house; unfortunately it proved not to be equal to a gale-force wind, which destroyed it before it could be used.[24]

More fortunate structures were put up jointly by the Works and the Revels in the Elizabethan years. Two distinct banqueting houses were erected at Whitehall for the embassies of the Duc de Montmorency in 1559 and 1572. The Revels accounts for preparing the second of these are full and detailed: the Office made a kind of indoor garden-house for the June occasion, with birch branches, ivy, pinks, privet flowers, honeysuckle, and roses apparently woven into wicker frameworks that covered the walls; the floor was strewn with rose leaves and scented with rose-water. Amidst such natural artifice, other decoration may have seemed redundant, but painted and gilded pendants as well as heraldic roses and *fleurs de lys* formed part of the décor.[25]

This festive building, with a light wooden frame with canvas on the exterior, was taken down after it was used, exactly as a tent would have been; its floral charms were calculated to last for hours rather than years. Even so it was used not only for a banquet but also as a theatre space to present a mask and a tourney, if accounts can be believed. The next banqueting house at Whitehall, built in 1581–82, immediately for the reception of the Duc d'Alençon, was more ambitious, and lasted until King James ordered its demolition in 1606. Like other festival buildings it was a canvas-covered wooden framework, except that the timbers were more substantial, including framed and glazed windows, and the decoration of both exterior and interior was more elaborate than the floral dressing of the 1572 structure. It was described in Holinshed's *Chronicles* as a building:

> made in maner and forme of a long square, three hundred thirtie and two foot in measure about; thirtie principales made of great masts, being fortie foot in length a peece, standing upright; between everie one of these masts ten foot asunder and more. The walles of this house were closed with canvas, and painted all the outsides of the same most artificiallie with a worke called rustike, much like to stone. This house had two hundred ninetie and two lights of glasse. The sides within the same house was made with ten heights of degrees for people to stand upon: and in the top of this house was wrought most cunninglie upon canvas, works of ivie and hollie, with pendents made of wicker rods, and garnished with baie, rue, and all maner of strange flowers garnished with spangles of gold, as also beautified with hanging toseans made of hollie and ivie, with all maner of strange fruits, as pomegranats, orenges, pompions, cucumbers, grapes, carrets, with such other like, spangled with gold, and most richlie hanged. Betwixte these works of baies and ivie, were great spaces of canvas, which was most cunninglie painted, the clouds with starres, the sunne and sunne beames, with diverse other cotes of sundrie sorts belonging to the queenes maiestie, most richlie garnished with gold.[26]

Holinshed's description of exterior rustication (*trompe l'oeil* painting to simulate stone blocks and mortared joints) and of the various kinds of painted effects on the canvas ceiling are in accord with decorative techniques practised over the course of a considerable period by royal painters, and which might be turned to theatrical applications as much as to the decoration of buildings.

The building continued to be embellished with decorative painting. The Sergeant Painter, George Gower, in 1583–84 added 'ij° Personadges done about the Arches & Pillers'[27] – an intriguing detail in the light of Jones's later designs for proscenium arches, frequently supported by painted figures. In the following year the elaborate ceiling was redone entirely. On strained cloth, Lewis Lizard and a team of painters laid on 'sondrie kindes of colo^rs with Diamondes furtage [fruitage: garlands] and other kinde of woorke' in water colour. Armorial devices were painted on 'a greate border' at either end of the hall, and Edmund Burchall hung wire pendants with gilded metal flowers which presumably supported the lights.[28] A few years later, in 1588–89, George Gower 'mended' the ceiling and other parts of the painted decoration, and added an entirely new motif: 'vpon the walle one the westeside an order with prospective in sondrie Oyle Coullers'.[29] While certainly neoclassical in general theme, the design may have been either a colonnade in painted relief ('prospective' in the sense of shadowing and fore-shortening) or an archway framing a view ('prospective' in the sense of receding landscape); both are of interest in a theatrical connection. The building was painted for the last time early in the new reign, before James decided he needed something better. The Sergeant Painter by this date was Leonard Fryer, who painted an entirely newly sewn and strained canvas ceiling, 532 square yards of it, with 'worke called the Cloudes in distemper', and at the ends the new royal arms and 'Piloste^rs', perhaps extending Gower's decoration.[30] By the following year, when *The Masque of Blackness* was performed there, 'other devices' as well as the clouds had been added to the ceiling painting.[31]

Painted skies, sometimes with stars, the sun and the moon, the planets, and zodiacal signs or figures were a common decoration for ceilings, and it is frequently assumed that the 'heavens' or stage ceilings in the contemporary playhouses were so decorated, although no conclusive proof of this can be offered. In its role as a theatre, the Banqueting House was embellished with a cloudy heavens between 1603 and 1606. A blue calico ceiling with golden stars was also a feature of the Whitehall Cockpit theatre of 1630, although it must be said that painted skies were not confined to theatrical decoration.[32]

The Jacobean Banqueting House completed in 1607 was more substantial than its predecessors, although most of its interior was built of wood and relied on faux finishes in paint to give the impression of more massive and costly materials. As the columns on the stage of the Swan Theatre – the visiting De Witt had noticed – were cunningly painted to resemble marble, so in the new White-hall building the Sergeant Painter, John de Critz, was in charge of 'pryminge stopping and casting into marble & other stone Coloures' the two orders of columns, as well as the balusters and rails of the gallery. Gilding and 'rich Bisse' (a blue or green pigment) decorated the frieze. The thirty putti in relief which hung in the ceiling were also gilded.

False finishes, so important to scenic painting, were evidently common. The stonework painted on the wae walls of the Banqueting House in 1582 or on the tents for the queen in the late 1620s was an ancient motif, and painters had been producing it for royal shows and celebrations since at least 1501, when a pageant to welcome Catherine of Aragon was 'empeynted like frestone and whight lyme, so that the semys of the stone were perceyved like as mortur or sement had been between'.[33] The technique was also used indoors, to disguise temporary wooden platforms as more substantial and imposing stone steps. At the end of Queen Elizabeth's reign, Leonard Fryer was paid for 'pryminge stopping and woorking of vj foote paces [platforms] stonne woorke like vnto the pavements'.[34] Although much of the regular maintenance and touching up the Sergeant Painter was called on to supervise, at least, must have been repetitive and unimaginative work, he also acted as conservator and restorer of the royal art collection, refreshing and revarnishing old pictures, repairing and gilding frames, and so on. The tasks each master workman performed through the financial year are frequently listed holus-bolus in the annual account, so that the payments to De Critz for his decorative work on the Cockpit in 1631–32 are mixed in with his repairs to royal paintings, by Palma and Titian, among others. Many historians of the stage, misled by the casual listing of the Works accountant, have assumed these paintings were hung in the theatre, which is altogether unlikely.[35]

We have seen that George Gower, about twenty of whose panel paintings survive,[36] included figurative work in at least one of his decorative projects. Other royal painters, notably Holbein and Eworth on surviving evidence, might have produced decorative work which included figures with complexity and sophistication. We have little that survives from the hand of De Critz to be able to judge how accomplished a draughtsman and colourist he may have been, but the fuller Stuart Works accounts show that not all the labour he undertook was conventional or routine:[37] he was also responsible for original design, in the Jonesian sense, although like Jones he may have used pictorial models to help him compose. Early in King Charles's reign, for example, the accounts record this elaborate decoration at Hampton Court:

> John De Creits Sergeante paynter for paynting, and guilding with gold the chimney peece in the kinges p'sence in the middle of the peece a Circle Diciphered with a border of Stone, and vulcan forging, paynted in proper Collours within the same Circle the rest of the peece donne with anticke woorke in gold the ground the bases, and Capitalls guilded, and shadowed the Cornishe guilded with Egges anckors and leaves shadowed, the mantletree paynted and guilded as the rest [38]

At exactly the same time as he was working on the Cockpit Theatre, interpreting Jones's designs in paint and plaster, he decorated another 'chimney piece' at

Whitehall, 'payntinge vppon the fronte there the storye of Æneas Carryinge Anchises out of Troye wth the Scroules on each side of the fronte paynted to expresse them as they were carved'[39]–that is in *grisaille*, shades of grey painted on the flat to give the impression of stone relief. De Critz would have had as little trouble realising the scenic designs of Jones as he had with the architectural concept of the Cockpit.

To sum up, painters employed at court were expected to be able to work on both detailed and large-scale decorative projects in a variety of media, to be capable of executing designs and figurative representations, to create *trompe l'oeil* effects, to have knowledge of classical and mannerist styles of ornament, to have some skill in 'prospective', and to be able to work successfully on a variety of surfaces, including wood, stone, metal, plaster, and cloth. Any decorative work they undertook on the court theatres would not have presented them with difficulty. In the case of the masques we have Jones's drawings to give us some sense of what was produced in the theatres by the painters, although we should remember that in any period there is a difference between the effect of a conceptual sketch and that of the full-size, three-dimensional, completed setting.

The detailed Elizabethan Revels accounts run until 1589, and reveal that up to that date the Office employed the painters who regularly served in other departments of the court, chiefly under the leadership of William Lizard. That the Restoration painter Robert Streeter still had formal responsibilities to the Revels Office underlines the general question we should keep in mind: whether the simpler, more general accounts of the Revels from the late 1580s onwards really indicate that theatrical preparations became less elaborate, specifically with regard to the decoration of the stage and its surroundings. For the thirty years of the detailed Elizabethan accounts, painters worked for the Revels in three main areas: the decoration of properties and lighting fixtures, the painting of large scenic pieces or free-standing cars and floats used in masks and entries, and the painting of canvas and other cloth placed on the stage, as part of the 'houses'. An example of the second category may be found in 1572, when a mask was presented in June before the queen and the visiting Duc de Montmorency. Designed by Eworth, it featured two mobile floats, one a castle for Lady Peace and the second a 'Charriott', 14 feet long by 8 wide, on which scenic representations of Parnassus and Helicon accommodated Apollo and the Muses, who were probably the maskers. William Lizard decorated the castle, which was considerably more than canvas stonework. It contained a 'Rock & church'–an emblem of religious settlement, we may take it, which also included the effect of a 'lighte' shining from it. The castle was resplendent with gilding and classical ornament: 'The pillers

Arcatrye [architrave] frize cornish & the Roofe gilt w*ith* golde and ffine silver . . . the Armes of England and ffraunce vpon it'.[40] There was also 'A prison for
discord', perhaps beneath the castle, in the traditional location of hellish vaults.

In considering the provisions for the players, we once more encounter the
problem of interpreting verbal descriptions in the absence of plans or diagrams.
What is certain is that painters decorated the 'houses', built of canvas over a
wooden framework. I list a number of characteristic entries from the Revels
records below.

> [Following a list of seven play titles] . . . to ye whiche belonged diu*ers*
> howses, for the settinge forthe of the same as Stratoes howse, Gob-
> byns howse, Orestioes howse Rome, the Pallace of prosperitie
> Scotland and a gret Castell one thothere side (1567–68)

> . . . sundry Tragedies Playes, Maskes and sportes with theier apte howses
> of paynted Canvas & properties incident suche as mighte most lyvely
> expresse the effect of the histories ^plaied (1571)

> [Following a list of six play titles] Having also apt howses: made of
> canvasse, fframed, ffashioned & paynted accordingly (1571–72)

> Io^hn Rosse for poles and shyvers [pulleys and sheaves] for draft of the
> Curtins before the Senat howse (1573–74)

> Iohn Drawater for Cariage of fframes & painted Clothes for the players
> howses to hampton Co*or*te (1573–74)

> ffor Cariadge by water of a paynted cloth and two frames for the Earle
> of Leicesters to the Court (1576–77)

> [A list of plays and their theatrical requirements: extracts]
> A history of the Duke of Millayn and the Marques of Mantua . . . a
> Contrie howse a Cytte
> A history of Alucius . . . A Cittie a Battlement
> A history of the foure sonnes of ffabyous . . . A Cytie a Mounte
> The history of Cipio Africanus . . . A Citie a Battlem*ent*
> The history of [blank] . . . A Citie a Countrye house
> The history of Portio and demorantes . . . A cytie a towne
> The history of the Soldan and the Duke of [blank] . . . A Citie
> The history of Serpedon . . . a greate Citie a wood, A wood A Castell
> (1579–80)[41]

Collectively these entries suggest, first, that the houses were prepared by the painters ahead of time, in the work rooms at St John's. Further, although they were meant to 'lyvely expresse' the sense of their related plays, they sound distinctly formulaic–cities, battlements, woods, palaces, and castles–and some of them must have been re-used from year to year, like the generic wing flats of the proscenium stage. What 'Gobbyns howse' may have looked like is hard to say, but in the context of the other entries Gobbyn lived in either the city or the country. Given his name the latter seems likely, though hardly in a 'country house' in the social sense of that term. (The question of the relationship between scene and dramatic genre, I will return to shortly.) A third point is that only one play in the above list uses more than two locations. *Serpedon*, I think, had three, the repetition of 'a wood' being a simple scribal slip. Many plays have two visually defined locations, and in one case we are told that they lay on opposite sides of the stage. The 'frames' from which the houses were made also came in pairs, one entry reveals, but in that case with only one 'paynted cloth'. This can hardly mean one continuous piece, since then there would have been no points of entry for the actors. Perhaps even when a play required only one location, like *The History of the Soldan*, the stage background was still built as two three-dimensional projections, which is what I take the 'frames' to have produced.

The frames themselves evidently varied in substantiality and in the ways in which they were built. In 1572–73 it took two men, of unspecified trades, to put them together.[42] If they were set up on a platform built by the Works they would have required fixing in position, which is perhaps what the carpenter Rowland Robinson did with 'iij Elme boordes & vij Ledges for the ffames for the players & . . . Nayles &c'.[43] On occasion, however, the frames were also joined together with metal devices, perhaps clamps, tightened with a screw, which could simply have been released to take them down again. This I take to be the technique alluded to in the payment of 1584–85 for 'mending of the vices for the frames'.[44] 'Vice' is another rather variable term in sixteenth-century usage, but the range of tools it refers to were all used for pulling or tightening; there is also an account item from ten years earlier for 'Yron woorke for ffames' which includes the provision of 100 'vyces', 'keyes for vices', and the 'mending of vices and nvttes'.[45] The last item in particular may suggest that 'vices' were in fact threaded bolts, while 'keyes' were spanners or wrenches, so that the wooden sides of the frames were bolted together through pre-drilled holes. Frames which could be joined and taken apart in this fashion could have been easily and compactly stored from season to season, further suggesting that, although the size of stage platforms may have varied, the dimensions of the houses perhaps did not.

Cities and battlements predominate in the list of locations quoted above. Battlements we are in a good position to understand, as far as painted canvas is concerned, although if they were used as 'walls' in the manner of the later English chronicle plays the scenic house would have to have been built more substantially than a mere skeleton of poles. But how might a 'city' have appeared? Was it painted as a view of buildings, like Serlio's streets, or was it formally represented as a city gate, perhaps with a title scroll above it bearing the legend 'Rome', for example? Sir Philip Sidney, who is more likely to have seen plays at court than in the playhouses, speaks in *The Defence of Poesie* of '*Thebes* written in great letters upon an old doore' as a theatrical convention unlikely to mislead anyone.[46] The question of the city also raises the matter of the three Vitruvian scenes; as they were propounded by Serlio in *L'Architettura* they are firmly allied with genre, as in his Roman source: noble buildings for tragedies, middle-class townscapes for comedies, and rural scenery for satyr plays and pastorals. It seems unlikely to me that the Elizabethan stage at this date was using background painting in such a way, and demonstrably the display of more than one location simultaneously, which is what the houses allowed, contravenes Serlio's understanding of a single environment for the action. I have argued above (chapter 3) that the houses were principally points of entry, and if an actor had to enter through a painted view–to step through the backdrop, as it were–the effect may well have been ludicrous. Cities, however they were treated, came in a variety of sizes: the 'greate Citie' used in *Serpedon* was distinct from the 'small cities'–six of them–the painting of which William Lizard supervised in 1580–81.[47]

Although the two houses representing distinct locations may have been a common arrangement for plays at court until the later 1580s, it was far from being a universal model. When the Queen's Men acted at court at Christmas and Shrovetide in 1584–85, the stage provisions varied considerably to suit the plays. On 26 December they played a 'pastorall of phillyda & Choryn', which was staged with 'one great curteyne', 'one mountayne and one great cloth of canvas'.[48] Such scenery sounds a good deal more like that employed for the Jacobean masques, and makes no mention of houses or frames. For a pastoral the canvas was perhaps painted in the 'wood' style used for *Serpedon*. 'An invention called ffive plays in one', played on Twelfth Night, was provided with 'a greate cloth and a battlement of canvas and canvas for a well and a mounte'.[49] Once again, nothing in this list is called a house. The great cloth sounds like a hanging, while the well and the mount were perhaps built pieces set on the stage: two-dimensional and three-dimensional scenic elements in combination. When the Queen's Men entertained the queen on the following Shrove Tuesday at Somerset House with 'An Antick playe & a comodye' only 'one howse'–of unspecified character–was used.

Houses, then, were not always used on Elizabethan court stages, and when used they were not always of the same character. If the norm was a painted canvas-covered frame suggesting a location, the senate house for *Quintus Fabius*, played by the Children of the Chapel at Whitehall on Twelfth Night 1574, was more elaborate. It was built of deal boards and adorned with 'knobbs'. The curtain cord John Rose devised for it (see above) drew curtains with fringes for some discovery scene. Evidently without pretensions to historical verisimilitude suiting the classical theme of the play, it was a practical piece of scenery built to manage an effect called for by the action. If it was to reveal the senate in session it was probably quite large, and it was decorated with theatrical panache rather than classical decorum. A similar structure was used for 'A storie of Pompey' in 1581, 'ymploied newe' rather than having been drawn from a scenery store.[50]

The masonry and stone of walls, rocks, and mounts were executed with techniques the painters knew well. If cities and woods were indeed landscapes it is harder to judge their effects from the perfunctory verbal descriptions of the Revels accounts. It is clear, however, that the painters worked in a full range of colours, judging from the list of pigments bought each year. The painting was to 'expresse' the play, and it did so with colourful stage decoration, matching that of the rooms in which the stages were set.

The painting and gilding of the chandeliers for the Revels' lighting was also the responsibility of the painters; they were also frequently decorated with tassels and fringes of 'Assedew' or arsedine, a gold-coloured metal foil which would shimmer and catch the light. In the seventeenth century it was 'cutt small', probably to serve as spangles stuck to a painted surface, and to create a similar effect.[51] The painting of properties was an *ad hoc* responsibility, depending on the particular demands of an entertainment. William Lizard himself evidently had a range of skills: he is listed in the accounts both as painter and property-maker, and he also produced designs for costumes. The title 'property-maker' was fairly elastic, covering both our own understanding of the term–the manufacturer of small objects and special items of costume, like jewels or armour–and something more like a supervisor of special effects, or stage machinist, who worked on spectacular or amusing stage tricks. John Rose, who rigged the senate-house curtains, was such a craftsman, as was John Carowe, who had worked for the Revels since the 1540s. Both men had skills as joiners and carvers, as well as an understanding of stage engineering. Rose made the chariot for the Muses in

1572, while Carowe made a variety of properties for the same show. Carowe died in 1574, and his wife and executors were paid what was owing him for:

> propertyes vid*elicet* Monsters, Mou*n*taynes, fforest*es*, Beast*es*, Serpent*es*, Weapons for warr as gvnnes, dagg*es* [pistols], bowes, Arowes, Bills, holberd*es* borespeares, faw-chions [swords], daggers, Targett*es*, pollaxes, clubbes headd*es* & headpeeces Armor cou*n*terfet Mosse holly, Ivye, Bayes, flowers quarters, glew, past. pap*er.* and suche lyke with Nayles hoopes horstailes dishes for devells eyes heaven, hell & the devell & all the devell I should saie but not all.[52]

This promiscuous list, the freewheeling rhythm of which leads the accountant into a brief moment of bureaucratic light-heartedness, is certainly indicative of the great range of theatrical effects the Elizabethan Revels Office produced for plays and masks. The presence of 'fforest*es*' makes clear that not all sylvan effects were painted on the flat–this item must have been some kind of built tree, or a number of such trees.

John Rose also produced mechanical special effects in plays. He managed the rising trap which was built within the scenic rock for *The Knight in the Burning Rock* at Whitehall in 1579, and he probably also supervised the pyrotechnic effects which accompanied it. In the production of *The History of Loyalty and Beauty* in the same season a 'wagon' was used, and it was probably for the same show that Rose built a mechanical cloud which was drawn 'vpp and downe', perhaps for a celestial apparition, as in Shakespeare's *Cymbeline*.[53] Some years earlier, for the plays at Hampton Court at Christmas 1574–75, there is evidence of quite elaborate mechanical effects, although they are hard to connect with a specific play. Rose was paid for 'Long boordes for the Stere of a clowde', 'Pulleyes for the Clowd*es* and curteynes', 'Dubble gyrt*es* to hange the Soon in the Clowde', for sewing the fringed curtains and for wire to hang them, as well as for 'vyces for the pulleyes'. Concurrently, Rowland Robinson the carpenter was paid for boards, rafters, and quarters, in elm, oak, and beech, some of which were clearly brought to court for the Revels – one, 'A peece of Elme boorde for the clowde', quite specifically connected with Rose's project.[54] Taken together, these entries indicate a quite elaborate stage structure entirely unlike the lightly built houses. The effect may not have been a proscenium scene, exactly, but I think that a wooden framework, possibly with a sturdy stage grid to support actors and technicians, was built over the area where the spectacular show of the clouds and the sun was displayed–presumably the clouds parted to reveal the sun hung behind them. The scene was concealed by curtains which were opened from backstage by pulleys and 'vyces'–capstans or windlasses hidden from the view of the audience. Similar machines made the scenic sky move about, from side to side rather than up and down, although perhaps both. Boards for the 'Stere' of a cloud meant, I think, a wooden trackway to steer it, or direct its movement as the pullies worked their magic.

The reference to 'Dubble gyrt*es*', or fastenings, indicates that the sun was securely fixed, perhaps to stop it swinging ludicrously if nudged by the cloud machinery, or perhaps because it was heavy. Did the parting clouds reveal an illuminated sun, blazing with theatrical glory? The effect of stage lights in a pictorial scene is discussed by Serlio in a section of his treatise which relies less on Vitruvian theory than on the novelties of the court entertainments in Italy and France on which he had worked: 'When you need a specially strong light you put a torch behind a glass and behind the torch a barber's basin well burnished. This will reflect a splendor like the rays of the sun.'[55] Similar lighting effects had been used in some medieval religious shows,[56] and the techniques involved were probably international currency by the 1570s. The presence of 'A greate Lanthorne' among the list of metalware bought by the Revels for the wiredrawers is certainly suggestive.[57] For all Shakespeare's mockery of theatrical moonshine in *A Midsummer Night's Dream*, spectacular stage effects were certainly undertaken with what seem today to be inadequate physical means.

Hampton Court Hall, the theatre for the first Jacobean masque in 1604, had seen a spectacular show of some theatrical complexity thirty years earlier, and Inigo Jones's work may be regarded as a development of a certain kind of staging begun in the Elizabethan period rather than as a completely novel break with the past. The stage moon in the 1611 masque of *Oberon*, for example, is unlikely to have been unprecedented on court stages. The elaboration of the Revels stages in the first thirty years of Queen Elizabeth's reign raises a number of questions. Did it continue, although the records become silent? If not, what kinds of stage decoration were seen at court thereafter? And what was the relationship between the richly furnished stages at court and the physical presentation of plays in the contemporary London playhouses?

To repeat a point made above, our general sense today of staging in the early playhouses is of scenic simplicity against which rich and expensive costumes were set, which would have provided the chief visual interest on a stage like that at the Swan. By 1598, however, the Rose, at least, had a collection of large and small properties stored somewhere in the building which outdoes even John Carowe's in eclecticism. It too included 'the devell & all', in the shape of a hell-mouth, that standard *locus* of medieval religious plays. Among the miscellany recorded in a written list, many items are identified by the play in which they were used—for instance, 'Tamberlyne brydell', which must have been the reins and harness used for the striking entry of Tamburlaine's chariot, pulled by the captive kings. There are also items we cannot now connect to particular productions, however, among them 'the sittie of Rome' and 'the clothe of the Sone & Mone'.[58] If the city of Rome was also painted on cloth, then the professional theatre at the end of the century retained some of the style of staging at court in the earlier Elizabethan period. The actors may indeed have bought or been given some of the material used at court; players had rented or bought costumes from the Revels in the 1560s and 1570s, and in the 1630s court theatrical costumes appeared on the stage of the Blackfriars playhouse. But if 'Rome' was similar to the cities great and small painted by William Lizard, it was used, like the properties, for some specific play, and marked by being a special effect distinct from the regular techniques of staging.

If some kind of painted scene persisted on the playhouse stages until the end of the century, did the earlier Revels practices continue at court under different auspices? If so, there is no sign in the accounts that the Works, for example, picked up the responsibility for houses and painted hangings. The Revels continued to supply stage provisions for the actors in some degree, however. The first Jacobean account still includes payments to painters; painted cloth continues to be mentioned for a number of years thereafter. The look of the stages themselves, however, had changed, or was changing. In 1604–5, when the King's Men presented numerous plays at court, the account lists 'xij Eles [45 feet] of Canvas for the Offic of the Revelles for the Tiering house'.[59] The material is traditional, but the nomenclature is new: one tiring house, not multiple houses. Court stages by this date reflected the common practice of the players. The phrasing of the entry suggests either that this particular tiring house was used for the rehearsals at St John's (but duplicated the facilities at court) or that one tiring house, demountable and mobile, as the old frames had been, could now serve all plays—and therefore it would not have been decorated with motifs specific to one play only.

Painted cloth is not in fact mentioned in direct connection with a tiring house, although the 1604–5 structure must have been decorated in some fashion. Painted cloths were used to decorate the stage, rather generally, at court in 1610–11, and also on another structure, first mentioned in 1604–5: the music house. Music houses, however they were used, became a particular responsibility of the Revels; they continue to be mentioned in accounts up to the 1630s, appearing there far more frequently than tiring houses. Like other Revels structures they were wooden frames covered with cloth, but were provided with a door and a lock, so probably were quite solidly built. The front was open, but could be covered with light curtains, so that musicians might play while concealed from view. The most likely call on music houses would have been for the masques, although music had always been played at many royal ceremonies and entertainments, probably including plays. A clear connection between music and drama is signalled by a structure made by the Works in 1618–19, and called 'a musicke and attyring house for plaies'.[60] This phrasing indicates the construction: as musicians in the playhouses were accommodated on a second storey of the tiring house, so at court. The Revels 'music houses' are hence probably to be understood as two-storey tiring houses, with a gallery which might be used by the players as well as the musicians.

If painters continued to do some work for the Revels Office, property-makers disappear entirely from the account lists. There is only one hint that stage properties continued to be made for plays with particular demands. In the accounts for 1614–15 we find payment for 'Canvas for the Boothes and other neccies for a play called Bartholomewe ffaire'.[61] Jonson's famous play was acted before the king at Whitehall on 1 November 1614, and it was evidently given some special attention to create the atmosphere of the fair booths, so important to the action after the opening scene. What the other necessaries may have been we are left to imagine: a practical set of stocks, large enough to hold three people, is required in the play, for example, as well as the odd chair. While the general account of the change in Revels production given by most modern stage historians is that after the late 1580s the actors brought with them to court all the costumes and properties they needed, for some plays this would have involved a good deal of expense and trouble in what the Revels habitually called 'carriage'. By the 1630s some financial notice was taken of the difficulties of transporting playing gear to the more remote palaces; payments to companies playing at Hampton Court and Richmond were doubled, from the customary ú10 to ú20, in consideration of a lost afternoon of profit in the playhouse and for 'trauell & remoue of goodes'.[62] Although they were used to touring, I think it unlikely that players carried large items with them on the road, and rather borrowed locally or improvised simpler expedients to stage certain scenes. So the Revels Office probably maintained a stock of the bulky properties commonly used in plays – a bed is the principal example – and carried them to court as they were required. The accounts for 1629–30, for instance, include an item 'for diuerse Propertyes vsed about the Playes', for a charge of five shillings.[63] Such a sum would not go very far in making anything, but might well cover transport costs.

We might imagine that after 1603 the visual splendour of court plays was neglected at the expense of the masques, which absorbed a good deal of artistic energy in planning and production. I think that such reasoning would be incorrect; the mounting of plays must have continued to receive the attention appropriate to royal entertainments. It would be true to say, rather, that many of the older functions of the Revels in painting and building scenery and in creating costumes were revived in a new context, although now not supervised by the Revels Office. Court painters and carpenters worked on the new style of stage setting in the busy weeks before the production, and although they were asked to create scenes arranged in a new way, supervised by a designer with a unified effect in mind, there were probably some continuities between the older painted stages and the new ones. Particularly in Jones's earlier designs, for *Oberon* in 1611 (Plate 18), or for *Love Freed from Ignorance and Folly* in the same year, we see rocks and castles which the older painters on the court staff would have recognised as the motifs of masks and plays from the Elizabethan years. If we wish to understand how the burning rock or the Palace of Prosperity might have appeared, it is not too misleading to take Jones's drawings as one point of reference.

Court painters in 1570 were as sophisticated as those working in 1611, and the 'darke Rocke' for the opening of *Oberon*, although it was painted on a flat shutter rather than a shaped canvas, would not have been regarded as a radical challenge by Elizabethan craftsmen. The castle which appeared when the rock parted, for which two other sketches survive apart from that illustrated, is treated in rusticated stonework, an old theme of the painters. The classical detailing it displays was known to Eworth and William Lizard, while the fantastic finials and scrollwork are the kind of mannerist fancy which might have appeared on buildings fifty years earlier. Its character and its painted finishes could well have been produced by the Elizabethan Revels workmen, and we caricature the distinction between the earlier and the later styles in scenic painting if we think of the Elizabethan Revels houses as necessarily crude and rough, approximating to Snout's loam, rough cast, and stone in *A Midsummer Night's Dream*.

Painting a large, unified pictorial scheme—scene painting, as it was practised from the Jacobean years until the early twentieth century—was evidently something new, even though the covering of large areas of cloth with motifs and designs was not. Similarly, the decorated proscenium frame which masked the wing and fly spaces of the pictorial theatres was in one sense new, but in terms of schematic design was simply a large version of a border, similar to conventional engraved and woodcut designs on the title-pages of books, with supporting

18   Inigo Jones, scene design for the masque *Oberon*, 1611.

figures, inscriptions, and animal, floral, geometric, and other well-worn ornamental motifs. As George Gower had painted 'personages' in the old Banqueting
House, John de Critz turned himself to the decorated borders of proscenium
stages. The Works accounts record his 'payntinge of a great arche wth two
spandrelles, two figures and two pillasters on eyther syde' for a masque in
December 1613.[64] De Critz's general ease with the classical style is attested to not
only by the subjects and style of his decorative painting, described above, but also
by his role in the transformation of the Cockpit, in which he, rather than Jones
himself, acted as supervisor on the site, 'directing the Carvers and Carpenters to
followe the Designes and Draughtes given by the Surveyor'.[65]

The rather younger painters, Matthew Gooderick and Edward Pearce, belonged to a generation without deep roots in Elizabethan style; Pearce's published designs of 1640 demonstrate a confidence and fluency with Italian motifs

which he must have learnt chiefly from Jones, and from Jones's own sources. Pearce appears to have been in sole charge of painting the scenery for a masque at Richmond in September 1636.[66] There were four conventional settings of a landscape, a military camp, a triumphal arch, and a temple. The designer, perhaps Jones, is not specified; possibly such an entertainment, outside the Christmas season, was entrusted to Pearce himself.

From the beginning, the Stuart masques created scenic *coups de théâtre*–amazing or amusing transformations, appearances, disappearances, and other special effects to make the audience gasp. Such gimmickry was hardly in the tradition of ascetic Palladianism, but it might be said to be in one kind of classical tradition, and even Vitruvius speaks of revolving machinery.[67] Splendid and surprising effects, however, had a long tradition in court entertainments, and Jones seems to have been willing to meet the demand within the conventions of the new stage, where theatrical aces could easily be kept up one's sleeve. The vacuity of *mere* spectacle was famously mocked by Ben Jonson.

> and I have met with those
> That do cry up the machine, and the shows,
> The majesty of Juno in the clouds,
> And peering-forth of Iris in the shrouds!
> The ascent of Lady Fame, which none could spy,
> Not they that sided her, Dame Poetry,
> Dame History, Dame Architecture, too,
> And Goody Sculpture, brought with much ado
> To hold her up. O shows! Shows! Mighty shows!
> The eloquence of masques! What need of prose,
> Or verse, or sense, to express immortal you?[68]

All the effects Jonson refers to, and a good number more, were staged in *Chloridia* (February 1631), the last Whitehall masque on which Jonson worked, and in which he clearly felt his own (rather few) words had been swamped by Jones's celestial spectacular, as they probably were.

Ascents and descents, we have had occasion to notice, were not exactly new. Jones's carefully composed pictures gave them a new kind of focus, enhanced – in theory – by special lighting effects, while the scenic stage allowed the machinery to be more easily concealed. The same enclosure presented a practical challenge to lighting, however, and it was not overcome for two centuries. Cut off from the general radiance of the auditorium in an enclosed box, the painted pictures risked virtual invisibility at much distance from the stage: the farther upstage scenery or performers were placed the more obscure they would have become. Changes in the levels of luminosity were nothing comparable to the effects obtainable in the modern theatre, and light which could be neither concentrated nor projected, save with the means of reflectors, would have produced a glow rather than, as Jonson enthusiastically describes an effect in *The Masque of Blackness*, 'a glorious beam'. Nonetheless, relative changes in light levels would have been registered by those watching, and, however diffuse the light may have been, Jones certainly grouped oil lamps and candles on and around scenic pieces to create concentrated radiance, sometimes to reflect back on the masquers and sometimes in full view, as part of the decoration of the scene. The moment of the revelation of the masquers was when such effects were particularly used, retaining the old connection between masked entries and light.[69] Peter Thornton speaks of the mobile quality of candlelight, which flickers and pulses as the flames burn. He continues: 'When the level of lighting in a room is low, moreover, reflecting surfaces seem relatively bright. Gilding, particularly, stands out in the surrounding half-light.'[70] Hence, reflective fabric and gilded detailing were used frequently in masque costumes.

We know very little about the workmen who managed the lighting of the scenic stages, although it was the Revels Office in particular which had had long experience in lighting court dramatic festivals, and especially the wiredrawers who fashioned and hung the instruments which held the candles. The Revels records include general entries concerning lighting the halls used for masques, with few hints about what their responsibilities may have been on the stages. 'Armes of double plate to hold great wax lightes on the Postes in the Maske'[71] may have been used backstage, but on the whole sound more likely to have been employed in the auditorium, where the 'posts' supported part of the wooden seating. 'Plate' candlesticks were sconces with reflectors; double plates could be made to shine in two directions, for general illumination.[72]

We can speak a little more confidently about the management of Jones's mechanical effects. They were worked with the kind of machinery John Rose had used in court shows in the Elizabethan years, which consisted of hemp ropes running through pulleys to a hoisting mechanism, a windlass or a capstan, pulled by hefty stage-hands. Heavy items might be more easily lifted or lowered with the help of balanced counterweights, as they were in contemporary cranes and wells. Counterweights in theatrical machinery give the delightful effect of smooth, regular motion, entrancing perhaps because it is so unusual and inorganic: the operator simply releases a brake and one weight, out of sight, pulls the other–the god, cloud, or hellish blasphemer–upwards or downwards at a steady, even speed. The device could also be used, and still is used, to hoist or lower curtains. Proscenium stages had a good deal more space to conceal the ropes and pulleys needed for such equipment than did the professional playhouses before 1642, where hoisting machinery was probably fairly simple.

The Office of the Works had ample and long experience with hoisting and winding machinery, as applied to the business of building in both stone and wood, where cranes, lifts, winches, and devices to pull heavy loads laterally were constantly employed, powered by ropes, pulleys, blocks, and both man- and horse-power. Treadmills were also frequently used for heavy lifting, but these were too large and bulky for the theatre. Jones's theatre machinery was largely ready to hand, in the Works storehouses in Scotland Yard. There are fairly steady records of the provision of equipment by the Works; in the Caroline years the carpenter John Davenport seems to have been in charge of putting the machinery together. What are frequently called 'engines' or 'devices' were supplied with pulleys and rope, and soap to lubricate wooden moving parts and to prevent them from squeaking; 'two peeces of leather for Engins' were provided for *Salmacida Spolia* in 1640, perhaps to serve as strap brakes on windlasses.[73] Some machinery was custom-made: 'diverse wheeles and Devices' turned the 'greate throne of Cantes' in *The Masque of Beauty* (1608), while for *Luminalia* in 1638 John Hooker was paid for turning on a lathe 'a great spindle of elme for an Engin'.[74]

Our sense of how effects were worked from behind the scenes is helped by a surviving section plan of the scenery for the final masque, *Salmacida Spolia* (Plate 19).[75] The drawing shows five sets of wings or shutters, decreasing in height from downstage to upstage, and with matching border pieces hanging from the ceiling above them. At the rear of the stage is a moving chair, or tiered bench, shown in two positions. It was hoisted by ropes running over pulleys and down the supporting posts into a machine room below the stage cellar. Between the second and third wings is a similar hoisting device; in this case the windlass which powered it is drawn in position below the stage. While the diagram is informative, however, it is schematic in nature, and does not show either the full stage structure or the mechanical provisions for some of the effects. The windlass in the plan powered a flying chariot containing two performers which 'came breaking out of the heavens'. There must, then, have been a fly gallery and access ladders to reach it, which do not appear on the plan. The culminating revelations of the masque were of the king and queen. The king and the male masquers were revealed by opening shutters, sitting upstage in the Throne of Honour. They moved downstage as a cloud descended from above, containing the queen and

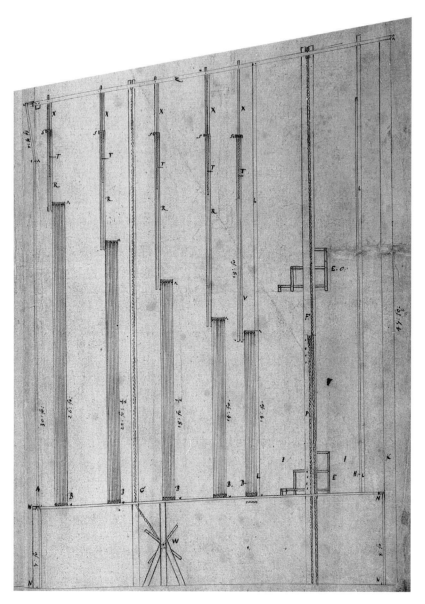

19　John Webb, section drawing of the stage and scenery made for the masque *Salmacida Spolia*, performed in the Masquing House, Whitehall, January 1640.

the female masquers, sitting on the chair device we see in the plan. As they did so, the Throne of Honour sank below the stage into the cellar: it lay directly below the cloud machine and moved in the same supporting grooves, but on a distinct hoisting system.

Evidently the plan misses out a good deal of the practical detail required for such an effect to work satisfactorily. Both suspended seats had to bear the weight of eleven people–people of very great consequence even if not of large physical proportions–and the hoisting machines to work them would have to have been extremely sturdy and powerful. A note on the plan tells us that 'The Capstalls for these Engynes were placed in the vault vnder the floore of the roome', incidentally giving us some information about the structure of the 1637 Masquing House, and indicating that the machinery was the same as that visible on the drawing: windlasses with bars pulled by hand. If we doubt that such devices could smoothly control a load of 1,500 pounds or more we should consider that extremely heavy loads were moved by ganging windlasses together in series, one pulling on or taking the strain of the winding shaft of its neighbour.[76]

When the Elizabethan Revels budget was cut back, I have suggested, the responsibility for the decoration of royal stages may have passed to the Works. Paintwork, however, whether for stages or any other royal property, was consistently expensive: the annual bill of the Sergeant Painter for the tasks he undertook for the Works was always high.[77] An alternative approach to the decoration of the tiring house and the front of the stage platform would have been to treat them like other vertical surfaces indoors, and to hang them with arras or woven cloth. The royal department of the Wardrobe looked after the preparation of rooms in this fashion, and their responsibilities could easily have been extended to the stage facilities. The chamber was 'made ready' with hangings covering the walls, and following a particular event the yeomen and grooms busied themselves 'takeing downe stuffe & laying it vp'–returning the valuable fabrics to the rooms or cupboards where they were stored.[78] The effect of a court chamber prepared with temporary seating and decorated with woven hangings may be observed in Abraham Bosse's etching of a ceremony at the French court at Fontainebleau in May 1633 (Plate 20). The room in this case, La Salle de la Belle Cheminée, the largest hall within the palace, was set up as a temporary chapel, provided with wooden galleries and boxes, covered with tapestries, to watch an investiture of an order of knights. Like English theatrical occasions, it has a raised canopied platform for the monarch, with the observing audience flanking the side walls. There is also a raised gallery with musicians playing, visible above the altar. The walls are also hung with large

20 Abraham Bosse, etching of the investiture of the Knights of the Holy Spirit at the French court, Fontainebleau, May 1633.

tapestries, tacked back to give access to a doorway behind them (in the left background).

Decorated cloth of various kinds conceals the carpentry of the framework of the galleries and of the royal state. Fringed cloth is hung over the gallery rails, and decorates the front of the platforms on which the knights and churchmen are seated. Tapestry forms the front façade of the ladies' box, which a contemporary account calls 'vn grand echaffaut', or great scaffold:[79] we see three distinct pieces with landscape designs, apparently 9 to 10 feet high by about 12 feet long, and the edge of a fourth. The very much larger pieces on the walls also have landscape designs.

The English court could easily have matched this kind of display. Henry VIII assembled a large collection of tapestries, some of them of a remarkably sophisticated design, in that they reflected Italian decorative motifs rather than Flemish figurative themes. James and Charles after him encouraged native tapestry weaving through their support for the Mortlake factory, which produced designs of a painterly style, most famously in a series depicting the Acts of the Apostles, based on drawings by Raphael.[80] That woven cloth was used to decorate royal auditoriums as well as stages is confirmed by Sir John Finet, who writes of 'carpets hung before and about' seats in the theatre made in the Hall at Whitehall in April 1640.[81] We know a good deal about the tapestries in the royal Wardrobe by 1642, because they were subsequently inventoried by the parliamentary assessors charged with selling off the assets of the crown after Charles's execution in 1649. Tapestries to hang in chambers came in matching sets, to form a sequence around the walls of a room, with mythical and biblical themes ('Six peices of *Vulcan and Venus*', 'Five peices of hangings of *King David*', etc.), but also in landscape designs, like those at Fontainebleau, and with other non-figurative motifs ('*Flower potts and pillars*'; '*flower Deluces*'; '*Beastes* bearing the *Arms of England*'; '*Pillars and Gallerys*'; '*Bloomes and such like*').[82]

Hangings came in many sizes and qualities, and although very valuable pieces would not have been used to decorate a stage there was a good deal of choice to be had in the Wardrobe's stores. For the important opening of the new Banqueting House with *The Masque of Augurs* in 1622, special hangings were brought from storage at the Tower.[83] They were no doubt hung around the walls, behind the galleries of seating. One contemporary representation of a playhouse façade shows what are either woven hangings or painted cloth at the rear of the stage, with figurative designs, certainly a very common motif.[84] If tapestry formed the tiring-house wall on a court stage, the actors might have appeared in front of other figures, represented in two dimensions in coloured weaving. Such a picture, naturally, would have remained unchanged as the various pictorial compositions of the action formed and transformed in front of it; it also might or might not have had some relevance to the theme of the play. *Hamlet* acted in front of 'One piece of *Hercules*',[85] for example, could have given the references to the mythical hero within the play a special kind of prominence, as well as adding further irony to the moment at which hangings are used as a practical location for the action, and Polonius is stabbed with Hamlet's sword.

The background behind the actors may equally have been a coloured landscape represented on the flat plane, and thus not unlike painted scenery in its effect, or a non-referential design may have been chosen by the Wardrobe, which had no 'story' to clash with the action of the play, nor the generic suggestions which woodland views or townscapes might create.

At the beginning and the end of the period covered in this book the theatrical craft most prominently patronised by the court was that of the costumier. The first twenty to thirty Elizabethan years of the operations of the Revels Office saw the continuation of their responsibilities for making and storing costumes, while for almost forty years of the seventeenth century the preparations for the Stuart masques involved a great deal of work by tailors and costume dressers in building the elaborate and fantastic clothes worn by the participants. The purpose of masque costumes, as of those of their Tudor predecessors, was to make a striking effect, but in two distinct ways, corresponding to the distinction between the masque and the antimasque. The disguised gentle, noble, or royal dancers wore impressive clothing which reflected their status: *en travesti* they were gods, nymphs, and heroes, in classical or medieval style. Masque costumes were also designed to be grotesque, bizarre, amusing, and outrageous–visual jokes and clowning were as much part of the entertainment as was refined fantasy. In England the performers in these roles were not courtiers, but rather professional dancers and actors. In the case of the Stuart masques we have many costume sketches by Inigo Jones, a few of which show the colours of the clothes, and which bring to life the verbal descriptions of the payments to mercers, tailors, and others involved in making them. They are generally more informative about the masquers' costumes, richly decorated and expensive, than those for the antimasquers. No pictures survive from the early Elizabethan period, which we must regret; they certainly once existed, as we have remarked. If the costumes were as lavish and expensive as their Stuart successors, it is not difficult to understand why a Lord

Treasurer in search of economy would have wielded the axe on the Revels wardrobe.

Extravagant costuming for court entertainments was an international European fashion, and novelties in disguising tended to travel from court to court, or to resurface after not having been seen for some years (the ape costume, for example, which appeared in shows at court in 1552–53, 1613, and 1632). Published books or prints about entertainments allowed styles and motifs to be copied. The famous Medici entertainments in Florence in 1589, designed by Bernardo Buontalenti, were given wide currency by the prints of Agostino Caracci, and Inigo Jones was copying them by 1611.[86] The taste for antique or outlandish designs in costume made prints or books of Roman or foreign dress particularly useful to court artists and craftsmen: one of Jones's repeated sources was the anthology of costumes of the world by Cesare Vecellio, first published in 1598. In the 1630s Jones appears to have drawn on the ballet designs of his French contemporary Daniel Rabel, who produced many extravagant and amusing sketches for entertainments at the court of Louis XIII.[87] Rabel's figures give more sense of the comic and grotesque side of entertainment costumes than do Jones's, and throw occasional light on motifs used concurrently in the English masques. The performance of *Pleasure Reconciled to Virtue* in 1618, for example, included a comic antimasque dance described by Busino as 'twelve extravagant masquers, one with a barrel round his middle, the others in great wicker flasks very well made; and they danced for a while to the sound of cornets and trumpets with various and most extravagant movements'.[88] A second observer spoke of 'the antimasque beinge of little boyes dressed like bottels and a man in a tonne'.[89] Very little in the way of designs for this masque survives, but a drawing for the *Ballet du Sérieux et du Grotesque*, performed at the French court in 1627, gives us some idea of the English antimasque of nine years earlier (Plate 21).

The chief item of expenditure at any period was on material rather than workmanship. Wages were relatively cheap, whereas the rich cloth favoured for costumes was very expensive. The Revels Office acquired materials from the Wardrobe, but also bought them directly from suppliers. In the earliest Elizabethan account the money spent on supplies of cloth is five times that of the tailors' wages, and in 1571–72 more than £1,000 was spent on cloth and haberdashery, much of it fine and rich fabrics: cloth of gold, satin, silk, velvet, and lawn.[90] Most of these were made up into costumes for six masks within that court season, the themes of which we do not know, apart from such hints as can be picked up from the accounts.

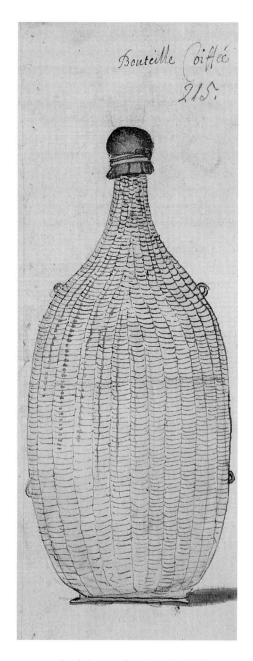

21   Daniel Rabel, design for a '*Bouteille Coiffée*', *Ballet du Sérieux et du Grotesque*, Paris, 1627.

Cloth of Golde .ij. of which one ^{maske} was yolow, garded with black velvett garnished with sylver Lace & fringe viz vj. long gownes having vj hattes of Black velvett edged with golde lace & for theier Torchebearers .vj. long Gownes of Changeable Taffata red & yolow garnished with ye lyke lace & frenge *with* hattes^{·vj·} answerable & vizardes, skarfes, ffawchions, buskins, wrestbandes & suche like necessaries incident. The tother ^{maske} was of Crymsen purple & greene cloth of golde. viz. viij Long Gownes garnished with silver frenge & lace & buttons. whose torchebearers had viij Long Gownes of Redd Damask likewise garnished & all furnished with straunge heades. ^{·xvj·} vyzardes skarfes fawchins Buskins garters & wrestbands according[91]

Once made, most costumes went into the Revels store after use, whence they were likely to be brought out and reworked in subsequent seasons, a practice which never seems to have been followed in the Stuart period. Costumes made in matching sets, like those in the account cited above, provided a convenient basis for adaptation to other uniform designs for masks, although there was a limit to such recycling. Although elements of clothing could be recombined–new sleeves, for example, could be added to 'bodies', as the accounts call them–the court audiences could be amused with the reappearance of old costumes for only so long. In a 1560 inventory of Revels costumes a number are noted as having been 'often translated transformed and disguised', and hence are 'so forworne and to muche knowen'.[92] Apart from wear and tear, the stock could be reduced in other ways. Costumes could be given as payment for performance, presumably to those who would have had some professional use for them, while aristocratic performers might take their costumes and properties as souvenirs. Mask costumes appear to have spent the last phase of their useful life as players' dress; the professional actors were at the bottom of the hierarchy of Revels costuming, but any clothing they acquired from playing at court would have had a further career on the public stages. Reporting on the progress of various lengths of crimson damask acquired from the Wardrobe, the Revels clerk writes that they were 'Imployed into ffrockes and priestes gownes *with* wide Sleves translated twise agayne in to torche bearers and vsed by players and to them geven by Composicion .24. and into clokes and Sloppes for torchebearers .16. which was altered agayne for players and to them geven by the *Master* by composicion'.[93]

Not all the costumes the Revels provided for actors at court were hand-me-downs, however. For the nine named plays presented by a variety of companies at Christmas and Shrove 1579–80, the accounts distinguish among productions which required a great deal of new work, those which were 'wholly furnyshed in this offyce with many garmentes newe made manye altered and translated',[94] and those which, while being wholly furnished by the Office, presumably used costumes directly from stock. Altering and translating, although time consuming, were cheaper than making new clothes, so that the Master must have to have been thoroughly convinced of the quality of plays requiring special costuming. One such play was on the subject of Scipio ('Cipio Africanus'), acted by the Paul's children's company. The Revels account gives some slight hints about the conventions of classical costume at this date. The play was 'furnyshed in this Offyce with sondrie garmentes and tryumphant ensignes & banners newe made and their head peeces of white sarcenett scarfes and garters'.[95]

By the turn of the century the professional players were adding in the considerable costs of at least a few new costumes to each fresh production they mounted. Edward Alleyn's inventory of the Admiral's Men's stage dress in 1598 reveals a wide range of items, many of them made from the rich fabrics used at court– silk, velvet, damask, and cloth of gold.[96] From their own resources, the players could rival the kinds of costume originally provided for them by the Revels Office, although they are unlikely ever to have attempted to copy the most lavish of the masque clothing.

The budgets for the most expensive Stuart masques were counted in thousands of pounds, of which a large proportion was spent on elaborately prepared costumes. Several accounts survive for the making of royal costumes, both for Queen Anne and Prince Charles in the Jacobean period, and for Charles when king in the following reign. Antimasque costumes cost considerably less: a list related to *Pan's Anniversary* in 1620 shows that the various characters in the antimasque were dressed for about £11 a head.[97] Expensive cloth and elaborate finishing made the masquers' clothes very costly indeed. Participation in a masque might well involve funding one's own costume; those who could not afford to do so were at the mercy of royal bounty. Expenditure on the masques seems from the start to have been rather *ad hoc*. Advances were issued based on estimated costs, and then supplemented as the expenses climbed. Those who could be expected to afford it might share in being bountiful, perhaps a source of pride, as was one's appearance in the masque itself. There are several early Jacobean portraits of great ladies in their masque dresses, and the costumes were no doubt proudly kept in family wardrobes until they decayed.

Jones was the chief designer of costumes, and the Wardrobe was the central source of fabrics and trim, as well as some of the workmanship, but the costumes were certainly not factory-made under the close supervision of one master tailor. The drawings we can look at are conceptual: the realisation of the clothes must have introduced some changes and individual variations. A few of Jones's sketches contain notes to the tailors on colours and fabrics, but also show that he was not the final arbiter; he might advise on the effect, but his chief patrons had the final word. Two designs for Queen Henrietta Maria's costume as Chloris in *Chloridia* (1631) are deferentially annotated:

> This designe I conceaue to bee fitt for the invention and if it please hir Maijestie to add or alter any thing I desier to receaue hir majesties command and the dessigne againe by this bearer. The collors allso are in hir majesties choise; but my oppinion is that seuerall fresh greenes mix with gould and silver will be most propper.[98]

The gold and silver laid on top of rich fabric was not merely ostentatious in terms of displaying wealth, but had a practical theatrical purpose. While the same effect might have been achieved more cheaply, no cost was spared in the meticulous fashioning of costumes for the royal and noble dancers. For *Tethys' Festival* in 1610, thousands of yards of gold and silver lace, costing over ú1,000, were employed on the dresses. The embroiderer Christopher Shaw sent in a bill for ú55 for embellishing cloth of silver, taffeta, lawn, and tiffany with coloured silk and gold thread, and for decorating the queen's seagreen satin shoes with more gold and silk patterning.[99] The masquers' costumes for *Pleasure Reconciled to Virtue* cost about ú83 each. Once again the basic costume of satin and taffeta was covered with superficial bright decoration, 'thick wrought in divers workes with silver and other laces'.[100] The masquers wore 'headpieces' and 'vizardes', and Prince Charles's head was crowned with a white plume made with 600 egret feathers. Jones's designs for these costumes have not survived. Jonson's 'invention' was that the masquers were 'twelve princes', bred by Virtue on Mount Atlas; for the effect of their appearance we must turn to Busino, who watched them. They were, he tells us,

> dressed as if in livery, six having full hose and breeches with slashes or folds of white silk trimmed with gold and silver, and the other six with their breeches below the knee, their half hose also crimson, and white shoes. Their doublets went well with this, cut in the manner of ancient Roman corslets; and on their heads they had long hair, crowns, and very large white feathers, and on their faces black masks.[101]

The purpose of so much rich surface decoration on the costumes was to make the most of the light. Immemorially the masked entry was a festival of light, and the choreographed movement of twelve sparkling, spangled dancers might have had an entrancing visual effect, accompanied by the aural pleasures of the music. When in 1634 the inns of court collaborated in mounting *The Triumph of Peace*, the performance at Whitehall was preceded in the evening by an elaborate torchlit procession of the masquers and costumed attendants through the streets, beginning in Holborn, and moving down Chancery Lane to the Strand, thence to Charing Cross, and down King Street to the palace. The parade included one hundred mounted gentlemen of the inns, richly dressed. The effect of their appearance was described by Bulstrode Whitelocke, who had helped organise the event:

> Every one of these hundred Gentlemen were in very rich Clothes, scarce anything but Gold and Silver-lace to be seen of them . . . The richness of their Apparel and Furniture glittering by the light of a multitude of torches attending on them, with the motion and stirring of their mettled Horses, and the many and gay liveries of their servants; but especially the personal beauty and gallantry of the handsom young Gentlemen, made the most glorious and splendid shew that ever was beheld in *England*.[102]

Glorious and splendid show was precisely the intention of the masques, and the combination of sparkling costume, movement, music, and light was the chief medium of its expression, for all that Inigo Jones added the delights of perspective scenery and changing views to the Stuart shows. Whitelocke, a stern moralist, notes at the end of his account 'Thus was this earthly Pomp and glory, if not Vanity, soon past over and gone, as it had never been.' It is hard to refrain from moralising about the Stuart masques, but, seen purely as a function of a court proud of its culture and international prestige, they established a style which was at once glorious and not entirely solemn, and was indeed never again beheld in England.

5 Royal audiences

Diagoras. I hope your lordship brings no troop with you; for if you do, I must
return them.
Melantius. None but this lady, sir.
Diagoras. The ladies are all placed above, save those that come in the king's
troop. The best of Rhodes sit there, and there's room.
Melantius. I thank you, sir–When I have seen you placed, madam, I must
attend the king; but, the masque done, I'll wait on you again.
Diagoras. Stand back there!–Room for my lord Melantius!–pray, bear
back–this is no place for such youths and their trulls–let the doors shut
again.–No!–do your heads itch? I'll scratch them for you.
Francis Beaumont and John Fletcher, *The Maid's Tragedy*, 1.2 (London, 1619)

The question of audiences is always one of the trickiest for historians of the
theatre. Audiences have a group life, which is one of the pleasures of theatre-
going, but they break up after an hour or two into their constituent individuals,
with individual impressions and memories. Individuals in modern audiences at
large metropolitan theatres are unlikely to have much contact with each other
beyond their shared time at the play. Friends might discuss the performance over
drinks or a meal, but even such smaller social groups disperse for another few
weeks or months until they meet again for an evening out. Audiences for a
school or college play, or at an amateur production in a small community, are in a
different position. Everyone in such a theatre is likely to have some personal or
social connection with others in the audience, and with the performers. The
theatrical occasion changes or suspends the usual social relationships and perceptions, providing an important part of the pleasure and amusement of the
occasion. Something like these more involved and intimate conditions, we
might imagine, would have obtained among court audiences between 1558 and

1642, particularly for the Stuart masques. Family connections, alliances by marriage, and close friendships between groups of both women and men gave English courts a social cohesion quite unlike that, say, within a modern group of politicians or senior government bureaucrats. To revert to a point made early in this book, the court was a house where important people lived, as well as a virtually public place where official business was done.

In this chapter I will address a few questions which are simple to put but difficult to answer. Who went to court entertainments, beyond the important central figures we can take for granted? How many people saw plays and masques at court? What did they think of what they saw, and how did they behave? To say something about the last point first, our modern expectation about a sixteenth- or seventeenth-century court audience is probably that they would have been, precisely, courtly. The pushing, shoving, and yelling which Beaumont and Fletcher dramatise in the little episode quoted above make the point that the wedding masque for Amintor and Evadne is grimly misplaced, and that the true key of their alliance is discordant. The sketch, however, is perhaps not entirely untrue to life. Writing about what he had heard of the last of the Stuart court masques, *Salmacida Spolia*, Robert Reade, nephew of the Secretary of State, Sir Francis Windebank, had this to say: 'The mask was performed last Tuesday night [21 January 1640], myself being so wise as not to see it. They say it was very good, but I believe the disorder was never so great at any.'[1] 'All that are harsh, all that are rude,' sings the final chorus to the king and queen at the end of the masque, 'Are by your harmony subdued.' Davenant probably did not intend this to apply to the audience, but Reade's comment, taken together with other evidence we shall be considering, is a reminder that even in a court theatre at Whitehall the English could be fractious and unruly.

Court theatres, we have seen, varied in capacity from the largest in the Whitehall Banqueting Houses and Masking Room, and in the halls of Whitehall, Greenwich, Richmond, and Hampton Court, to the small auditoriums in rooms at St James's Palace. Audiences correspondingly varied in size from about 100 people, at a guess, in the smallest places, to many times that number in the largest. The 1605 theatre at Christ Church, Oxford, was calculated to hold about 800 people. It held them in an idiosyncratic layout quite unlike the *Florimène* theatre, which is a surer guide to conversions at court, but the Oxford calculations about the capacity of seating give us a formula which we might apply to other auditoriums, as John Orrell has done in the case of the Globe.[2] The allowances for leg room have already been quoted; those for width are 18 inches per person, a fairly modest space when one thinks of the bulky formal clothing worn by both men and women at the Elizabethan and Stuart courts.

The width formula can be applied, very approximately, to the surviving plans of court theatre spaces. The Cockpit conversion, compactly planned, appears to have been able to hold rather more than 350 people on the ranks of seating shown. Assuming that the upper gallery might have held 100 or so more, we might estimate a total capacity of 500 people for the theatre. The Paved Court Theatre plan shows degrees which would hold about 450 people, and that for *Florimène* in the Hall at Whitehall, with its large scenic stage, shows seating for a fairly modest 400 or so. Stages for the professional players in the Hall must have left more room for degrees, and audiences would have been larger. During the marriage celebrations of Princess Elizabeth and the Elector Palatine in 1613, the Savoy ambassador reported that on 16 February, 'Much expectation was made of a stage play to be acted in the Great Hall by the King's players, where many hundreds of people stood attending the same.'[3] On the dimensions given in the Works accounts, the degrees erected by Ralph Brice in the new Banqueting House early in 1622, however, would have held approximately 1,300 people, a large audience for an indoor theatre space, but certainly corresponding to the numbers reported in other accounts of masque performances. Estimates of the capacity of contemporary playhouses vary, but audiences at the Globe were estimated by contemporaries as including as many as 3,000 people, a figure which has been upheld by modern research, while the indoor playhouses held considerably fewer: the Blackfriars, probably the largest, may have had a capacity of between 600 and 700.[4] Court audiences, then, corresponded more closely in size to those of the London indoor playhouses; the very grandest dramatic occasions at court accommodated about twice that number.

The size of audiences depended, naturally, on the size of the court, so that we should be aware of quite what we may mean by that variable word. 'Under the strictest definition,' R. Malcolm Smuts writes, 'the court consisted of the monarch's immediate entourage and those institutions of the royal household responsible for personal and ceremonial needs. But in an age when all power and government patronage flowed from the king, a much larger social network always formed around this relatively compact group.' 'The court', he concludes, 'was therefore an institution with a distinct nucleus but a vaguely defined periphery.'[5]

All parts of the court expanded after 1603, and the difficulties of controlling it in an orderly fashion, both socially and particularly financially, increased. The 'nucleus' of the household was more concerned with mounting entertainments than attending them, save that the members of the nobility who also served as court officers–the Lord Chamberlain, the Controller of the Household, the Captain of the Guard, and so on–were an important part of the queen's or king's formal entourage, and would have been present. The Lord Chamberlain particularly was directly responsible for supervising the frequently touchy matter of who should sit where, and might not always have found theatrical occasions especially relaxing or enjoyable.

Queen Elizabeth's household servants of all ranks, it has been estimated, numbered about 550.[6] By the time of the wars the combined households of the king, queen, and royal children had expanded to more than three times that figure.[7] Not all of these people would have been present in the court at the same time: duties rotated, except in the very highest posts, both in paid positions and those with an honorific status, like the Maids of Honour. As Grooms of the Chamber, the players after 1603 could technically be summoned to serve in their nominal job, but there is only one record of their being called on to do something other than to act or to swell funeral processions, when in 1604 they served as attendants to the Spanish ambassador;[8] nor did all parts of the household function constantly; the Revels Office, we have seen, was strictly a seasonal operation, with a busy period in the winter months.

An indicator of the extent of what Smuts calls the 'periphery' of the court is the change in the number of the nobility between 1558 and 1642. The feudal power of wealth held in land and represented at the highest level by the peerage of England was shared among 60 people in the Elizabethan period. Over the next forty years, the peerage was increased to over 200 chief nobles, and at the next rank – of knights – the increase was between four and fivefold, from about 500 to over 2,000.[9] The sheer number of people who might have an interest in preserving or furthering their economic and political power, through lobbying at the centre, rose steeply in the early seventeenth century, while struggles over where exactly the centre lay contributed to the governmental crisis.

The membership of the court varied over time; John Guy writes that 'the Court was a hydra, constantly sprouting new heads. It was in a constant state of flux.'[10] Individual members of the nobility held differing views, one from another and at different times in their lives, about the duties and advantages of attending court.[11] At particular periods, however, there were evidently groups of people who might be relied on to form the centre of court gatherings. A list made in about 1598 names 54 'principal gentlemen of value and service that have been and are usually in court' and a further 272 of similar rank 'that dwell usually in their counties'.[12] Any precise count of how large the court may have been in given years, however, seems impossible to arrive at, given the different contemporary definitions of who was and who was not a courtier; of the larger groups who might attend the court in the later Elizabethan years, for example, only relatively few had the privilege of direct access to the queen.[13]

Although court entertainments, to which admission was a sign of favour and privilege, certainly had political significance, their first function was social, as a common gathering point for people who might otherwise have held differing views in the context of the Privy Council, to show common allegiance to the monarch and to uphold national pride. All three courts between 1558 and 1642, even under Elizabeth I, were dominated by men in chief positions of political power, state service, and at the lower level of household operations, but court entertainments were occasions when the women of the court—the wives and daughters of chief nobles and the female companions and maids of honour of the queen—were both visible and prominent. The entire community of interests of the leading families of the realm was represented by the presence of wives, mothers, and daughters, some of whom wielded more actual power and influence than their spouses, and many who were at least as well-read, cultured, talented, and informed as their male companions.[14]

Attendance at plays and masques was also regarded as an appropriate sign of favour and respect to leading foreign visitors of various kinds. Major figures on arranged visits might well have entertainments especially mounted for them, but those who happened to arrive at the right season would be asked to attend Christmas or Shrovetide shows. At least one famous North American visitor watched *The Vision of Delight* in January 1617. John Chamberlain wrote to Sir Dudley Carleton that 'The Virginian woman Poca-huntas, with her father counsaillor hath ben with the King and graciously used, and both she and her assistant well placed at the maske.'[15] The presence of foreign ambassadors at the masques in Stuart times became standard; since ambassadorial parties might be made up of as many as twenty people and, at one time or another, twenty different states sent representatives to the English court (the major European powers regularly and uninterruptedly), a court audience might include a considerable number of foreign observers.

In the Elizabethan period, plays and masks were fairly strictly confined to the festive seasons of Christmas and Shrovetide, with a few special exceptions. These times of the year were periods when the court was on holiday from its more sober and weighty business; particularly at Christmas those who did not attend court regularly might visit and greet the queen, except that the great nobles were also expected to keep Christmas hospitality at their own estates in the shires: there was hence some dispersal as well as gathering together of leading members of the social hierarchy. The ceremony of New Year's gifts, a form of Christmas gift-giving in which presents were delivered to the queen–costly items by the nobility and more modest ones by members of her own domestic entourage–while gifts of money or plate from the royal treasury were returned, was one of the rituals at which monarch and subjects might meet. Christmas was an important religious feast, with services daily in the chapel throughout the twelve days, which all those keeping Christmas with the queen might be expected to attend. The capacity of the royal chapels–frequently as large as the halls–is also a measure of how many people might form audiences for plays in the evenings.

The Elizabethan court, like those that followed it, reflected the alliances and familial connections of the powerful supporters of the crown. Although the queen was nominally head of all the nation, the dynastic history of Henry VIII and his successors had seen powerful nobles taking sides and promoting their own ambitions in the contested matters of royal succession and religious policy. The new queen may have wished to follow a path of studied neutrality after such an unsettled and violent period, which largely she did, but common sense also dictated that she should retain the allegiance of those who had supported her through her difficult childhood and early womanhood. The monarch was a patron, and was expected to reward loyalty tangibly.

Elizabeth's Privy Chamber was an important centre of female power, since the queen appointed as her attendant gentlewomen the partners of her (male) high court officials. Margaret Lady Howard of Effingham was the wife of the first Elizabethan Lord Chamberlain; Elizabeth Lady Clinton was wife of the Lord Admiral, and so on. Pam Wright has described the remarkable prominence of certain noble families among this group.

> [R]ecruitment to the Privy Chamber was virtually a closed shop, with members of the Howard, Carey, Radcliffe, Stafford, Brooke and Knollys families being omnipresent in the department. This means that the Privy Chamber was very much the queen's *familia* in both senses of the word. The Howards, Careys, Radcliffes and Knollys were, as it were, members of the Tudor affinity with a tradition of Privy Chamber service going back at least to early in Henry VIII's reign. And the tradition continued under Elizabeth herself, with daughters following in the mothers' footsteps. These same clans were also part of the queen's family in the modern meaning of the word: her maternal grandmother was a Howard, while the Knollys and Careys were spliced to the Boleyns through Mary, Anne's sister.[16]

Though Elizabeth never married and had children, then, her court had many family characteristics. Chiefly, a remarkably strong and resilient barrier of influential women stood between the queen herself and those male nobles and office-holders–the Earl of Leicester, William Cecil, the Earl of Essex, among others–whose influence on power and the direction of policy was conducted at the level of the Privy Council.

During the first two decades of the reign, up to the time of the establishment of the troupe of players which bore the queen's title in 1583, the patronage of the playing companies which appeared at court might be taken as some guide to the leading members of the audience–those who saw dramatic activity as a way of proclaiming aristocratic magnificence and of supporting their own positions as influential and munificent figures. It should be said that the professional troupes patronised by the nobility were not the only entertainers at court festivals; the boy players of the Chapel Royal and the Chapel at Windsor might be regarded as royal servants. The adult actors of the first half of the reign, however, appeared at court under the sponsorship of leading nobles, chief among them in the early years Lord Robert Dudley, from 1564 Earl of Leicester. His company, in which James Burbage, father of Richard and builder of the Theatre, was a leading player, appeared regularly at court throughout the decade from 1572–73 onwards. His brother, Ambrose Dudley, Earl of Warwick, also patronised a company seen frequently at court in the 1570s.

Noble patrons of other troupes appearing at court in that decade included Thomas Radcliffe, Earl of Sussex (and member of the Radcliffe family referred to above), who in 1572 became Lord Chamberlain: his players are recorded both as the Lord Chamberlain's and Sussex's company. Patronage of an acting troupe by the leading court figure of the Lord Chamberlain continued throughout the queen's reign. Henry Carey, Lord Hunsdon (son of Anne Boleyn's sister, and therefore a cousin of the queen) patronised players from the 1560s onwards, and he became Lord Chamberlain in 1585, when the acting troupe took the name of his title. At his death in 1596, by which time his players were one of the two principal London companies, his son George took over as both Lord Chamberlain and patron of the actors.

The noble incumbents of the leading administrative and military post of Lord Admiral were also consistently patrons of players. Edward Fiennes de Clinton, Lord Clinton, and Earl of Lincoln after 1572, was the first Elizabethan Lord Admiral, followed by Charles Howard, Baron Howard of Effingham, who was served by the famous troupe led by Edward Alleyn at the end of the century. In the 1570s both men patronised players who appeared at court under the names of their current titles. The Earl of Derby, Henry Stanley, Lord Strange, kept a troupe of players from the 1560s, which appeared at court in the early 1580s.

Among the troupes of this period, one is recorded with a noblewoman as patron: the Countess of Essex's company appeared at court at Shrovetide 1578. The Countess was Lettice Knollys, daughter to Lady Catherine Knollys (another cousin of the queen), and like her mother a Gentlewoman of the Privy Chamber, and member of the exclusive group of women surrounding and supporting the queen.[17] Her subsequent secret marriage to the Earl of Leicester would bring her into royal disfavour, but in early 1578 she was a 37-year-old widow who had inherited the players of her late husband, Walter Devereux, Earl of Essex; it is of some interest that she retained them under her own title, and that they were chosen to play at court. Her son Robert, court favourite in the late Elizabethan years, revived the patronage of a troupe under the Earl of Essex's name some years later, but they appear never to have played in London.[18]

Beyond such calculations of the likely leading members of Christmas and Shrove courts in the Elizabethan years it is difficult to say very precisely how the rest of an audience may have been constituted. Younger members of noble families attended court as part of their entrée into adult life (see below), and the social occasions of the festival seasons are likely to have been times when they were present in considerable numbers. Queen Elizabeth's attitude to marriage among her courtiers was rather unpredictable, but, none the less, the court had always been something of a marriage market among the higher nobility, while younger sons of noble families, not in direct line to inherit titles and estates, might hope for court patronage in some post, either directly as a servant of the crown or as a member of the entourage of one of the more wealthy and powerful nobles. Such patronage depended on being introduced and noticed, and any court audience would have included the supporting and aspiring followers of the principal figures.

Although the social group with access to the court was smaller in the sixteenth century than in the seventeenth, there is no evidence that court theatres were more modest or less crowded than in the Stuart years. The large halls were made ready for courtiers to see plays as often as the smaller great chambers, and that they were usually under some pressure from those attempting to gain admittance is implied by John Chamberlain's comment on the unusual Christmas season at Whitehall in 1601–2: 'There has been such a small court this Christmas that the guard were not troubled to keep doors at the plays and pastimes.'[19] The question of who might be admitted to plays and entertainments, raised by this comment, I will turn to shortly.

As is the case in enquiring about the audiences of the Globe or other contemporary playhouses, first-hand information about the court is fuller and more informative in the later years.[20] We know a good deal more about playgoing in the 1630s than in the 1590s, as we know more about the court life of King Charles I than that of Queen Elizabeth. Anecdotal recording–people writing about their own experiences, both mundane and exceptional–increased considerably after 1600, or at least the habit of keeping such writing increased. As a result a wider range of observation about what went on at court is available to us for the entire Stuart period. Lady Ann Clifford, for example, a masquer in *The Masque of Queens* in 1609 (at the age of nineteen), recorded in her diary that she saw John Fletcher's *The Mad Lover* performed at the Christmas court of 1616–17, after supper with Lord and Lady Arundel, leading patrons of the visual arts.[21] Our increased knowledge of later conditions at court might allow us to guess that some practices had remained the same, and therefore to fill out the Elizabethan picture, while others must have changed as court culture changed.

Lady Ann Clifford herself would have been able to assess these changes in her own lifetime. Only thirteen when the old queen died, she had already been seen at court, in preparation for becoming a full member of it. 'In Christmas I used to go much to the Court and sometimes did I lie at my Aunt *Warwick*'s chamber on a pallet, to whom I was much bound for her continual love and care of me, in so much as if Queen *Elizabeth* had lived she intended to prefer me to be of the Privy Chamber.'[22] 'Aunt Warwick' was the widow of Ambrose Dudley, and probably herself a patron of players after his death in 1590;[23] the young girl stayed in her court apartment, no doubt, because they had been up at night watching the Christmas entertainments. The audiences of Elizabethan court plays, then, may have included a number of children, as Stuart court audiences did later. Lady Ann's career as an observer of court revels is likely to have become active once more after her second marriage in 1630 to Philip Herbert, Earl of Pembroke, Lord Chamberlain to the court of King Charles. She watched theatre at court in the reigns of three monarchs, over the course of forty years.

From 1603 onwards, a gathering of the entire court entailed three distinct royal entourages, of a different character from those with which Queen Elizabeth had surrounded herself. The court of King James has suffered from a fairly hostile press from his own day until relatively recently, when a more sympathetic examination has been made of his conscious attempt to change the manner of royal government, and to combine two kingdoms in one, both of which enterprises generated local animus in Whitehall. James's style was participatory rather than reclusive. Though cautious of his safety, with some personal justification, he surrounded himself with a trusted group of favourites intended to act as a conduit rather than a barrier to royal favour. It was through this circle that

Robert Carr and George Villiers, Duke of Buckingham, rose to prominence. Both these men were active patrons of the arts, and Buckingham particularly was an enthusiastic participant in the masques.[24]

The existing family groups of English aristocracy were joined by those of the Scottish nobility, of whom Carr was one; some of the new arrivals were family relations of the king. The Elizabethan structure of a group of powerful and influential women surrounding the queen was continued in the court of Queen Anne; many of them joined her as costumed dancers in the masques, among them Alathea Talbot, Countess of Arundel; her sister Mary, married in 1604 to William Herbert, third Earl of Pembroke and Lord Chamberlain after 1615; and Lucy Harrington, Countess of Bedford. The courts of the Prince of Wales, although that of Henry has been characterised as a rival to his father's, really had complementary and overlapping membership, as did the entourages of the king and queen. Thomas Howard, Earl of Arundel, took a particular interest in Prince Henry, but he was also a leading member of the king's court, dancing in the masques as well as holding high office, becoming Earl Marshal in 1621. The Duke of Buckingham's rise as Gentleman of the Bedchamber in the court of King James led to a very close relationship with Prince Charles, in whose court, after he became king, Buckingham was a leading figure until his assassination in 1628.

Although the court grew in size, then, the links connecting its parts could be strong. It appears to have been James's deliberate policy to widen the network of patronage and support emanating from the court, in contrast to that of the rather restricted and controlled Elizabethan system. It would be naive to read his encouragement of favourites as merely lazy infatuation, and to discount their function as symbolic creations of a new kind of royal power. At least at the start of his reign, James took more direct interest in the running of his court than had his predecessor; he was more active, more visible, and more likely to incur criticism. As to the courtiers, their desire to be seen within this new court world, and to gain or maintain influence within it no doubt ensured that the festive occasions of the year were well attended.

The masques particularly gathered crowds, partly for their cachet and partly because they were regularly performed on Twelfth Night, the culmination of the Christmas festival. While Busino waited to watch *Pleasure Reconciled to Virtue*, he and his companions admired the assembled women in the audience, whom he estimated to number 600; he makes no guess at the total size of the crowd, but he and his party 'were so crowded and uncomfortable that had it not been for our curiosity we would have given up or expired'.[25] The Banqueting House was packed, and full for two hours before the king arrived and the performance began. If at least as many men as women were present the audience numbered somewhere between 1,000 and 1,500 people, which seems in line with my earlier estimate of the capacity of the seats in the Banqueting House in 1622.

Women, Busino suggests, sat together, as they did in the Oxford theatre in 1605, in the more comfortable seating near the stage. Although there was no strictly enforced segregation, other incidental indications suggest that in a masque theatre a whole bank of degrees nearest the dancing area was the preserve of female spectators, for all that in *The Maid's Tragedy* they are 'all placed above'. Sir John Finet speaks of 'the ladyes syde at the lefte hande of the queene' for *Albion's Triumph* in 1632, and elsewhere of separate ranks of seating for *Albion's Triumph* in 1632, and elsewhere of separate ranks of seating for lords and ladies.[26] Leading members of the court might have boxes or partitions reserved for their own use, to which they could invite particular guests. The *Florimène* plan shows this to have been the practice at plays also: the Countess of Arundel, a prominent senior figure at the Caroline court, had a large square area containing five levels of degrees partitioned and reserved, to the right and rear of the royal state. Yet even in a box, and even if one were a reasonably prominent noblewoman, one might not have been able to sit down. In the year before Busino watched the English court ladies, Lady Ann Clifford, at that date Countess of Dorset, attended the Twelfth Night masque in the Banqueting House, *The Vision of Delight* (1617). 'We *stood* to see the Masque in the box with my Lady *Ruthven*', she records in her diary.[27]

The management of large audiences at court can never have been easy. The Countess of Arundel and others of her rank would have expected to have been recognised and admitted without fuss; those attempting to ensure that the proper hierarchies and priorities of seating were respected would have had more trouble with the middling sort, the indefinable number of minor associates and followers of great figures who might have laid claim to being admissible, and particularly when they came as a 'troop', as Diagoras calls it. The pushy and the curious might well have inveigled their way into a masque by hanging around the doors and slipping in with a large party. The royal guards, who provided one level of security at the entrances to the theatre, could hardly have been expected to distinguish by sight those authorised to attend from those who thought it might be worth trying to get in. Unlike the playhouses, royal theatres did not use the collection box as a criterion of entry.

Officially, those at royal entertainments had been invited by the monarch, or by the other royal figure sponsoring the occasion. By the time Busino attended court, tickets of admission to the masques were being issued, as they continued to be in the Caroline period. The tickets were the responsibility of the Lord Chamberlain and his deputies, to whom all disputes about entry and seating were referred. Large parties might be asked to confine themselves to a stipulated number, with a checklist of those in the group to be submitted in advance.[28] The ticket system, Busino suggests, was not entirely watertight, however: 'though they claim to admit only those favoured with invitations', he says, the theatre was uncomfortably packed.[29] Since the Works knew how to calculate the capacity of the theatres they built, the responsibility for crowding lay somewhere else: control at the doors was lax, or the invitations were not strictly limited to the number of places.

As in the Elizabethan years, the level of attendance at the Christmas court was partly a matter of chance. In Christmas 1607–8 John Chamberlain wrote to Dudley Carleton that 'All the holy-dayes there were playes, but with so litle concourse of straungers, that they say they wanted companie.'[30] '[S]traungers' might generally mean those not normally resident at court, but in the early years of the new reign it could also mean the Scots lords, who were perhaps not used to the cultural habits of the English court. Later in the same letter, Chamberlain relates a sumptuous banquet given by the king, who, he surmises, 'wold shew himself in glory to certain Scottes that were never here before, as they say there be many lately come, and that the court is full of new and straunge faces'[31] – faces which did not show themselves at plays, it appears.

The weather could also influence attendance. The court festivals took place at the coldest time of year, and though chambers may have been aired by heating in advance, and the occasion itself created a certain amount of heat from the open flames of the lighting and the breathing human bodies packed into the room, some places were simply too exposed or draughty for the very coldest conditions. The Revels consistently supplied earthenware pans 'for fier'–presumably char-coal heaters–which seem to have been for the actors' use, in the tiring houses.[32] The first production in the new wooden Masquing House, perhaps not quite finished at the time of the show, was *Britannia Triumphans*, on 7 January 1638. As George Garrard wrote in a letter, the temperature was far too low for everyone to endure several hours of confinement, even if seated: 'It was performed on a Sunday Night, the Day after Twelfth-night, in very cold weather, so that the House was not filled according to Expectation.'[33]

A further suggestion of Busino's account is that the seating at the masques, tickets or no, was not entirely reserved in advance. During the run of especially popular plays in seventeenth-century London, one had to be prepared to go to the playhouse well before performance time in order to be sure of a seat or a good standing. That prominent people were prepared to wait two hours in a court theatre suggests a similar competition for space; holding an invitation may not have counted for much if one arrived at the last minute. Equally, waiting around at the door may occasionally have paid off. If there was anything like a 'general admission' area in the court theatres it may have been opened up when the press of invited audience was less, to avoid the embarrassment of empty seats. In 1622, James revived the ordinance requiring noble landowners to return to their own estates for Christmas and to keep local hospitality; Chamberlain wrote to Carleton that the proclamation 'comes yll to passe for divers of all sorts that were come up with theire wives and families to nestle here, and are now faine to packe away againe'. The edict was so effective that 'to prevent that the court be not too thin and bare by the absence of so much nobilitie and gentrie, there is order given that (besides the Lordes of the Counsaile and others that attend about the Kings and Princes persons) all the gentlemen of the privie chamber and Pensioners shall waite and geve ordinarie attendance all the holy-dayes'.[34] The balance between an overcrowded and an embarrassingly deserted court may have been hard to strike, and, in years when the latter situation had to be dealt with, court audiences for plays and masques may have been somewhat padded with those who would not otherwise have been let in.

How accessible Whitehall may have been at festival times in the Jacobean years is difficult to say, but for the marriage of his daughter Elizabeth at Shrovetide 1613 James appears to have thrown the court open to a wide range of 'people of fashion, as well Citizens as others, and few came thither that departed without kind entertainement; for liberallitie, with spredding armes, kept open household'. Tournaments in the Tiltyard were witnessed by 'many thousands'. The other side of the coin was increased security: a watch of several hundred musketeers guarded the court at night, access to the Chapel was very restricted for the marriage ceremony itself, and a close eye was kept on 'the too forward unruliness of many disordered people' who watched the various entertainments.[35]

Ben Jonson's masques include a number of situational jokes about the wrong kind of people gaining access to the court if they happen to be determined or lucky enough. *Christmas his Masque* (1616) begins with members of the guard entering the performance area in an attempt to eject Christmas himself, a disreputable figure of Falstaffian appearance, supposed to have pushed his way inappropriately into the theatre. His fellow performers are similarly humble or marginal figures from the city, rather awed by their luck in penetrating high society at the palace. Even the usual characters of the masques, allegorical abstractions and mythical figures, are parodied in the action. Venus, great goddess of love, appears as a broken-down backstage figure, a dresser or wardrobe-woman, who is determined to see her son Cupid perform in the entertainment: 'he is prentice in Love Lane with a bugle maker'. Like the opening of the masque, her entry mimics a disorderly gatecrashing, even – the text seems to suggest – through the audience rather than from a stage entry.

> *Enter Venus, a deaf tirewoman.*
>
> *Venus.* Now all the lords bless me, where am I, tro? Where is Cupid? Serve the king? they may serve the cobbler well enough, some of 'em, for any courtesy they have, iwis; they ha' need o' mending. Unrude people they are, your courtiers; here was thrust upon thrust indeed! Was it ever so hard to get in before, tro?
>
> *Christmas.* How now? what's the matter?
>
> *Venus.* A place, forsooth, I do want a place; I would have a good place to see my child act in before the king and queen's majesties, God bless 'em, tonight.

Similarly at the opening of *Love Restored*, in the previous Christmas season of 1615–16, Robin Goodfellow delivers a long account of his various efforts to get into the court, finally to prevail 'disguised' as himself, and by announcing he was in costume for the masque.

Any entertainment at court might be subject to the press for admission commonly experienced at the masques. Even the tediously long play *The Shepherd's Paradise*, acted by the queen and her ladies in the Paved Court Theatre at Somerset House early in 1633, evidently drew much attention. A letter to Sir Thomas Puckering in the first week of January informed him that:

> On Wednesday next, the queen's pastoral is to be acted in the lower court of Denmark House, and my Lord Chamberlain saith that no chambermaid shall enter, unless she will sit cross-legged on the top of a bulk [timber support]. No great lady shall be kept out, though she have but mean apparel, and a worse face, and no inferior lady or woman shall be let in, but such as have extreme brave apparel and better faces.[36]

This is fairly evidently facetious, and is probably meant to hint at the reputation of Philip Herbert, Earl of Pembroke, the incumbent Lord Chamberlain. None the less, it does suggest that a range of social ranks at least aspired to be present, and on occasion they probably succeeded.

To prevent too many gatecrashers, turnstiles were set up at the entries to court theatres in the later Stuart years, and may have been used earlier.[37] A 'turning dore' was erected at the entrance to the Banqueting House for *The Temple of Love* in 1635. It was lined with cloth, and thus was probably a revolving door at full height, made in four panels.[38] Similar entry-points were made at Merchant Tailors' Hall for the second performance of *The Triumph of Peace* in February 1634, where a section of the audience was made up of citizens and their wives, admitted at a 'tourning door by tykett', and also at Middle Temple Hall for *The Triumphs of the Prince d'Amour* at Shrovetide 1636.[39] From Elizabethan times onwards, members of the royal guard, intimidatingly armed, were the principal means of security at the entries to the theatres, and no doubt some of them were on duty inside the auditorium also. Chief court officers were also present, however, as ushers and as supervisors of order. In the Stuart years, the Master of Ceremonies and his assistant greeted important guests and showed them to their seats, but they were also supported by the Lord Chamberlain himself in the case of any difficulty.

The Lord Chamberlain's responsibilities included not only the overseeing of the relatively ordered process of admitting and seating the audience, but also that of settling them down after the monarch's arrival, which was not necessarily the signal for everyone to lapse into attitudes of quiet attention. Perhaps they did so more readily at plays, but at *Pleasure Reconciled to Virtue* Busino watched as the king came in to a fanfare, following which people who were evidently milling around the floor had to be persuaded to move back to their seats. 'After his majesty had been seated under the canopy alone . . . he had the ambassadors [of Spain and Venice] sit on two stools, and the great officers and magistrates sat on benches. The Lord Chamberlain then had the way cleared, and in the middle of the room appeared a fine and spacious area all covered with green cloth.'[40] That is to say that the entire dancing floor between the stage and the state had previously been completely out of view, and covered with people standing. Similarly aimless and chaotic moving about marked the masque at the Middle Temple in 1636 attended by the Palsgrave, Prince Charles Louis, Count Palatine of the Rhine, and his brother Prince Rupert, King Charles's nephews.[41] The masque was sponsored by a mock lord, the 'Prince d'Amour', who held a court with all the appurtenances of the real thing. Sir John Finet, who kept a careful official eye on the lawyers' revels, reports that when the royal party arrived at the Middle Temple they had to wait in an antechamber before being seated, 'The hall appointed to dance in, being in the mean tyme with much ado cleared of the pressing number of both sexes.'[42]

Even at events which one might expect to have been strictly controlled and policed, those admitted were given to moving about, and clustering into crowds in inappropriate places. The Works account of the theatre made in the Hall at Woodstock in 1621 speaks of formidable barriers 'to keepe the people from

175

pressing into the middle Isle of the Hall'[43]–that is between the king and the stage, as at the beginning of *Pleasure Reconciled to Virtue*. Similar disorderliness could upset the dignity of other court ceremonies. At the reception of a Spanish ambassador by the king and queen in the Banqueting House in April 1640, a central aisle 20 feet wide was ineffectually defined by rails – crash barriers, in modern terms – 'to keep off the intruding multitude'. Quite how intruders might have got in to such an important state ceremony is hard to understand, but get in they did, and 'such was the confusion grown from the excessive number of intruders of all sortes...as all that could possibly be effected by the lord chamberlin, wyth the earl marshall and gentleman Ushers, was but to make a lane of prospect and of march for the ambassador between the lord chamberlin and the lord conductor up to theyr majestyes seates'.[44] Like modern celebrities with an escort of bodyguards, the ambassador and his attendants were squeezed with difficulty through a crowd of standing people, who once in position would have been very difficult to move.

Having 'the way cleared' at a masque, therefore, would have taken some time, particularly if hopefuls without seats had to be shown, or unceremoniously shoved, out. Physical violence–itself a symptom of unrestrained behaviour on the part of the crowd–may have been a last resort, but it was certainly used. The Polonius-like Calianax, the Lord Chamberlain of the court in *The Maid's Tragedy*, is a testy and senile character whose methods of crowd control seem to detract from the dignity of his position. Diagoras, despairing of his own ability to keep the door, wishes for his master's help: 'would he were here; he would run raging amongst them, and break a dozen wiser heads than his own in the twinkling of an eye'.

That this picture might be rather less of a caricature of real conditions at the English court than we might think is indicated by a letter from John Chamberlain written in early 1617. His friend Sir Thomas Edmonds had recently been appointed to the post of Controller of the Household, an official whose duties clearly included keeping order at royal entertainments. Edmonds's zeal was apparent in his wielding of the ceremonial long white staff carried by leading court officers. (Such staffs may be seen in a number of portraits of Tudor and Stuart nobles; a figure at bottom left of Plate 10 carries one.)

> Sir Thomas Edmonds was made controller, and had the white staffe delivered him the first howre he saw the King, and dothe execute the place with courage and authoritie enough but they say he doth somewhat too much flourish and fence with his staves, whereof he hath broken two alredy (not at tilt) but stickling at the playes this Christmas.[45]

Although once again a facetious and amusing account it is likely to reflect the actual conditions of court gatherings. Clearing the way in a royal theatre relied on a certain amount of brute force, executed not only by the burly members of the royal guard but also by those with executive rather than physical power–Edmonds was a famously short man.

He was certainly not alone, however, in wielding his staff of office as a weapon. Another of Jonson's jokes about unauthorised invasions of the court occurs at the start of *The Irish Masque at Court*, performed at Whitehall twice in the Christmas of 1613–14. The action begins with a noisy group of enthusiastic but unsophisticated Irishmen, come to greet the king, one of whom regards himself, ludicrously, as an ambassador, and whose dignity has been offended by the rough treatment he has received while getting in: 'Ish it te fashion to beat te imbashators here, ant knock 'em o' te heads phit te phoit [white] stick?' The Lord Chamberlain himself could, like Calianax, be active in clearing the crowd. The poet and minor dramatist, Thomas May, ran afoul of Philip Herbert, Earl of Pembroke and Montgomery, during the preparations for *The Triumph of Peace* in February 1634, as a contemporary letter relates. The assembly of both audience and performers must have been unusually difficult, because the masquers and their attendants–members of the various inns of court–arrived in the procession referred to in chapter 4, and first rode around the Tiltyard at Whitehall while they were watched by the king and queen from the gallery above. Despite the formidable organisational problems all went well, 'only this one Accident fell, Mr *May* of *Gray's Inn*, a fine Poet, he who translated *Lucan*, came athwart my Lord Chamberlain in the Banquetting House, and he broke his Staff over his Shoulders, not knowing who he was'.[46]

Audiences at masques were also given to unruly behaviour following the performance itself. The 'disorder' Robert Reade had heard about at *Salmacida Spolia* in 1640 was in the line of a long tradition in court life. More than a hundred years earlier, the costumes and properties of shows in which King Henry VIII himself had taken part were rifled and taken away by the assembled crowd, and similar destruction and pilfering continues to be recorded in the Revels records thereafter.[47] Partly such behaviour was similar to that of excited crowds today, eager to snatch a tangible memento of their encounters with famous footballers or rock musicians, and partly it seems to have been similar to rituals of 'ragging' at schools and universities, in which destructive disorder is let loose for a recognised period, while not being exactly sanctioned. Since few members of a court audience would have had anything to gain materially from such behaviour, it appears rather to have had the character of a somewhat boisterous game. The masques, performed at Christmas and Shrovetide, occurred at periods when festive misrule had habitually been given some recognition, and the behaviour of audiences following the shows perhaps expressed its spirit. In 1618 an uproar broke out at the banquet which was served to guests and performers after the show. Once the king had escorted the ambassadors to the chamber containing the refreshments he retired for the night, and mayhem followed:

> at once like so many harpies the company fell on their prey. The table was almost entirely covered with sweetmeats, with all kind of sugar confections. There were some large figures, but they were of painted cardboard, for decoration. The meal was served in bowls or plates of glass; the first assault threw the table to the ground, and the crash of glass platters reminded me exactly of the windows breaking in a great midsummer storm. The story ended two hours after midnight, and half disgusted and exhausted we returned home.[48]

Busino's account of conditions in 1618 is corroborated by an observer of the performance of *Oberon* in 1611. 'The masques being laid aside, the king and queen with the ladies and gentlemen of the masque proceeded to the banqueting hall, going out after they had looked about and taken a turn round the table; and in a moment everything was thrown down with furious haste, according to the strange custom of the country.'[49] Another foreign observer at the Twelfth Night masque of 1619 regarded the spoliation of the banquet as 'according to the custom of great courts' rather than anything peculiarly English,[50] as if royal and aristocratic magnificence might be expressed in a certain amount of wanton destructiveness; Busino, 'disgusted' by the end of the night, hardly thought so.

On festive occasions, audiences were hence quite capable of turning their excitement and high spirits into a kind of hooliganism. There must have been something of an edge to the atmosphere of gaiety among the large gatherings of people at the Stuart masques, although there are no surviving accounts of disorder during a performance. King James himself, calling out impatiently at a break in the dancing during *Pleasure Reconciled to Virtue*, committed the worst breach of etiquette we know of. He would not have been amused by others following his example, and his son had sterner views about modest and respectful behaviour. It was, significantly, once the monarch had left that disorder was released; nor were the masquers themselves always models of sobriety. The late arrival of the revellers from Middle Temple and Lincoln's Inn for their scheduled entertainment in February 1613 was partly due to an adverse tide which slowed down their boats from the city, and partly to the 'very unruly' conduct of the passengers.[51]

The atmosphere at court plays was probably rather different. Theatres for plays were generally smaller, and there was less room, in an auditorium without a dancing floor, for circulating before the show, although 'stickling' was still required to maintain order. Since the performance was entirely self-contained—the performers were not members of court society and did not mix with the audience after the show—the audience would have dispersed directly it was over. Plays at festival seasons, like masques, were no doubt open to anyone with a valid claim to being connected to the court and who was of suitably high rank. Sir Humphrey Mildmay, who attended performances at court on a number of occasions, took his chance at arriving late at a play in February 1638 after having had supper at Whitehall with Sir John Coke, Secretary of State, and was disappointed, as he recorded in his diary: 'Came home durty & weary / the playe beinge full.'[52] Other occasions could be restricted by design rather than chance. The queen's performance in *Artenice* at Somerset House in 1626 was watched, according to the Florentine ambassador, by a selected audience of 'a few of the nobility, expressly invited, no others being admitted', and the Venetian ambassador confirms that the spectators were 'picked and selected'.[53]

Similarly 'private' entertainment might be commissioned by leading court figures as well as by members of the royal family. At the departure of the French ambassador, La Trémoille, in May 1619 the diplomatic party was entertained twice, first by a supper, play, and banquet at the house of the Earl of Dorset,[54] and in the following week by a similar party at Whitehall, hosted by the Duke of Lennox, Lord Steward of the Household, at which the King's Men acted *Pericles*. The Lord Chamberlain, the Earl of Pembroke, absented himself, because, he explained in a letter, he found himself unable to watch the actors so soon after the death of Richard Burbage. The entertainment was evidently a lavish affair, and it used two of the larger chambers in the palace. John Chamberlain reported that it cost ú400, wryly adding that it 'wold have cost another the double, but that he is Lord Steward'.[55] Sir Gerrard Herbert, writing to Sir Dudley Carleton, gave this account of it:

> The Marquise Trenell on Thursday last tooke leaue of the Kinge: that night was feasted at White Hall, by the Duke of Lennox in the Queenes greate chamber . . . In the kinges greate Chamber they went to see the play of Pirrocles, Prince of Tyre, which lasted till 2 aclocke. After two actes, the players ceased till the French all refreshed them with sweetmeates brought on Chiney voiders, & wyne & ale in bottells, after the players began anewe.[56]

Although this has sometimes been read to mean that the French kindly treated the players to drinks, I think it far more likely that 'refreshed them' is reflexive rather than transitive: the guests of honour were entertained by the banquet (the seventeenth-century term for such portable restoratives) during an interval. The more usual order of things was for the banquet to follow the entertainment, as at the masques, and at the Earl of Dorset's party of the preceding week, but a similar interval banquet was offered to the royal visitors at *The Triumphs of the Prince d'Amour* in 1636,[57] and it may have been a feature of royal entertainments at which particular guests were to be honoured.

The leisurely pace of the evening's amusements for the French in 1619 is of considerable interest, while the entire event was of a large scale, in cost and physical appointments. The theatre was made in the Great Chamber, and though the play was a private occasion it is likely to have attracted a prominent invited group of some size in order to bestow honour on the chief guest. '[A] great many of Lords and Ladies' had attended the Earl of Dorset's evening, his wife noted.[58] By the later Jacobean years the leading figures of the court were perhaps acting in the place of the increasingly sick and withdrawn King James; equally, in a culture in which women held an important place, the court lacked a symbolic female leader between Queen Anne falling sick in 1618 and the arrival of the new Queen Henrietta Maria later in 1625. In January of 1624 the Duchess of Richmond, wife of the Lord Steward, was the nominal sponsor, 'in the kings absence', of another appearance at Whitehall by the King's Men, who on this occasion acted *The Winter's Tale*, which had been revived in their repertory the preceding August.[59] This was possibly another more private celebration, but it fell in a period when the court was assembled for Christmas, when the Twelfth Night masque had been cancelled, and when the king 'hath ben of late so troubled with paine and weaknes in his feet that he lookt litle abroad'.[60] The communal celebrations of the season may then have been taken up by the court itself, as it were.

A similar internal demand might be read into a performance sponsored by the Lord Chamberlain himself, in November 1624, of Fletcher's *Rule a Wife and Have a Wife* by the King's Men, 'at court for the ladies'.[61] An audience entirely composed of the leading noblewomen and their attendants is one possible kind of gathering at court entertainments, then; if it were not entirely so composed, this particular occasion yet demonstrates the influence of female taste and patronage on court culture, even before the arrival of the new queen. At court theatres, women and men met as equally important participants in a communal occasion. The judgement of female spectators and patrons must have governed that of the male figures who nominally controlled what was seen at court: the Master of the Revels and the Lord Chamberlain.

People's opinions about what they saw at court were certainly listened to if they were regarded as important enough, and occasionally they were recorded, even though the comments are mostly brief and general. Busino's account, written as a dispatch to his superiors in Venice, is unusual in its length and rich detail, and in its individuality of observation: we gain some sense of his taste and judgement through what he notices and how he writes. Though ambassadors frequently went to plays and masques, most written accounts in dispatches tend to record, first, that the ambassador was invited to be there (and therefore that national honour had been upheld), and given such and such a prominent seat, better than the seat of such and such another ambassador. Pecking order comes first, and comments about the shows tend to be confined to who was in it, if it featured royal masquers or actors, and observations that the general effect was splendid and magnificent. Adversely critical comments which might impugn the hosts are few, and personal perceptions suppressed in favour, appropriately, of diplomatic language, sometimes amusingly divergent from franker opinions. Where the Venetian ambassador at *The Temple of Love* in 1635 reported 'pleasant diversions' with 'most stately scenery, machines and dresses', Sir Thomas Roe thought that the masque was 'performed with much trouble and wearisomeness'.[62]

Lady Ann Clifford unfortunately did not see fit to record in her diary what she thought of *The Mad Lover* in 1617–either of the play itself or of its performance by the King's Men, at that date still including the renowned Burbage. Yet it seems certain that she would have discussed it with her companions, the Earl and Countess of Arundel, and that such conversations were a common part of court culture, and had been for some time. Late in the Elizabethan years, the queen was observed by Dudley Carleton at a private performance of a play at the Lord Chamberlain's house 'with all her *candidae auditrices*'.[63] His Latin adjective for the queen's ladies-in-waiting simultaneously describes their appearance–splendid, beautiful–and their qualities of mind and character: sincere, fair, and frank. The fair listeners must have engaged in shrewd discussion once the performance was over, in which the queen undoubtedly joined.

Yet we have little recorded information about what Queen Elizabeth thought about entertainments presented to her. She made her displeasure clear early in her reign about a court show caricaturing Catholics, and, thereafter, contentious material was no doubt avoided. There are a few more direct and oblique indications about King James's opinions. At Shrovetide in 1605 he called for a repeat performance of *The Merchant of Venice* at court; the King's Men had presented the decade-old play on Shrove Sunday, and did so again, 'Comanded

By the Kings Matie', on Shrove Tuesday, presumably cancelling the show scheduled for that day.[64] Other multiple court performances of the same play, then, may also be a sign of royal approval: Fletcher's *The Maid of the Mill*, for example, was played at court three times in 1623. Yet in the more complex Stuart court one show could be presented to various distinct groups, and the king saw neither performance of *Rule a Wife and Have a Wife* in the 1623–24 court season, for example.

James was perhaps particularly intrigued by the great courtroom scene in *The Merchant*, but his monarchical forbearance through tedious performances was liable to snap. After several days of celebrations for Princess Elizabeth's wedding in 1613, the late arrival of Sir Francis Bacon with his masquers from the Middle Temple and Lincoln's Inn was too much for the king, who 'was so wearied and sleepie with sitting up almost two whole nights before, that he had no edge to yt, whereupon Sir Fra Bacon adventured to intreat his Majestie, that by this disgrace he wold not as it were bury them quicke: and I heare the King shold aunswer, that then they must burie him quicke for he could last no longer'.[65] Busino records his memorable eruption at the masque in 1618, but he had worse to suffer a few years later. The entertainment provided for him at Woodstock in 1621 by visiting academic actors from Oxford, *Technogamia*, was a notable disaster. It probably suffered by contrast with two performances the king had recently seen and enjoyed, of Jonson's witty, lively entertainment, *The Gypsies Metamorphosed*, offered by the Duke of Buckingham as part of the reception of James at his country home, Burley-on-the-Hill. The Latin comedy from Oxford was another matter, 'being too grave for the king, and too scholastic for the auditory, (or as some have said, that the actors had taken too much wine before they began)'. Anthony à Wood records that James was ready to abandon the theatre: 'his majesty after two acts, offr'd several times to withdraw. At length being persuaded by some of those that were near to him, to have patience till it was ended, least the young men should be discouraged, sate down, tho' much against his will.' A satirical verse on the occasion even adds that 'Jn despayre hee fell in a slumber' – nominally present, if unconscious.[66]

If James had not been talked down, not only would the young men on stage have been discouraged (if they were sober enough to notice). Once the monarch retired, the focus of a court audience was no longer there, and the king's removal was a sign for everyone else to disperse, just as when for one reason or another he did not arrive for a scheduled entertainment, it did not proceed. For the king to leave the theatre amounted to cancelling the performance, which was avoided only by a hairs-breadth in August 1621. The audience on this occasion was probably a large one, formed partly by those courtiers travelling with the king on progress, perhaps partly by local noble Oxfordshire families, and partly by Oxford students and dignitaries come with the actors to honour their ruler. The Works preparations show every sign of expectation of a large crowd; the 'partitions' running the full length of the Hall to keep people out of the central area have been referred to above; they were, the account says 'xij foote highe'. Rather than being forbidding walls, however, I think that the partitions must have been part of the construction which included the 'fitting and making of Seates'[67]–degrees, rising to 12 feet in height, and with a barrier rail in front, running down the side aisles of the Hall, perhaps for most of the 118 feet of its length, and thus creating a theatre of considerable capacity.

Royal opinions are most fully recorded in the final decade of court theatre. In the early 1630s Sir Henry Herbert suddenly began to jot down brief notes in his Office Book on the reception of plays mounted for the king and queen by the Revels Office. These are frequently only one or two words in length, and indicate whether the play was 'liked' or, more rarely, 'not liked'; Jonson's *Tale of a Tub* in January 1634 fell into the latter category. Degrees of modification seem to record the strength with which royal pleasure was expressed. *The Taming of the Shrew* was 'Likt', whereas its companion piece, *The Tamer Tamed*, performed two days later, was 'Very well likt'; *Cymbeline* was 'Well likte by the kinge', the queen perhaps having had other views.[68] The first performance of a visiting French troupe at the Cockpit at Whitehall in 1635 was received 'with good approbation'; when they played *Le Trompeur Puni* in April the show was greeted 'with better approbation than the other'.[69] Occasionally more complex judgements are recorded. Davenant's new play of 1634, *The Wits*, which had been the subject of discussion between Sir Henry and the king himself regarding the revisions required for licensing, was performed at court on 28 January. Herbert records that 'the kinge commended the language, but dislikt the plot and characters'. Charles himself had a hand in the composition of James Shirley's play *The Gamester*, presented at court in the following week, and was more satisfied with its construction: 'The Gamester was acted at Court, made by Sherley, out of a plot of the king's, given him [Shirley] by mee; and well likte. The king sayd it was the best play he had seen for seven years.'[70]

The king was interested in the structure and the style of drama, then; comments on the art of the performers themselves are rarer, but tend to be expressed when success might have been in some doubt–when the actors were not professionals. Thus Habington's play *Cleodora*, acted at Whitehall in April 1640 by the family and servants of the Lord Chamberlain, drew particular notice. Herbert wrote that 'The king and queen commended the generall entertaynment, as very well acted, and well set out',[71] and they must have been sincere enough in their praises since they called for a second performance, which they attended.

Royal enthusiasms tended to spread and to create fads, although royal taste sometimes caught up with that of the town. The queen first saw Lodowick Carlell's play *Arviragus and Philicia*, 'w[ch] is hugely liked of every one',[72] at the Blackfriars playhouse. Thereafter, the two-part play was seen numerous times at court in 1636 'with great approbation of K. and Queene'.[73] Another sensation of the same year was Cartwright's *The Royal Slave*, first performed by amateur actors at Oxford for a royal visit in August and early September, and evidently a far better performance than the dreary *Technogamia* of 1621. Archbishop Laud, then Chancellor of the university, recalled that 'all men came forth from it very well satisfied. And the Queen liked it so well, that she afterwards sent to me to have the apparel sent to Hampton Court, that she might see her own players act it over again.' Another observer reported that the play was 'generally liked, and the Lord Chamberlain so transported with it, that he swore mainly he never saw such a play before'. The professional performance at the court in January 1637, by the King's Men, did not live up to the high expectations; Laud smugly noted that 'by all men's confession, the players came short of the university actors',[74] although at some months' distance the true appeal of the play perhaps also came short of gilded memories.

Sir Henry Herbert's own opinions were largely confined to the written texts he vetted for the stage. He was particularly concerned about touchy political material and bad language, and his recorded praise of a newly written play by Shirley in 1633 succeeds in making it sound rather dull: 'The comedy called The Young Admirall, being free from oaths, prophaness or obscenes, hath given me much delight and satisfaction in the readinge.' He writes of its virtues, he says, that it might serve as a model to other dramatists, and subsequently he must have been pleased to note that the court performance of the play was 'likt by the K. and Queen'.[75] Of performances he regularly records only the reactions of his master, save once when strong feeling evidently overcame him, and which incidentally demonstrates that, as we would expect, he too was in the audience during royal entertainments. On Twelfth Night in 1624 the scheduled masque, *Neptune's Triumph*, was cancelled, and Middleton's *More Dissemblers Besides Women* was acted by the King's Men at Whitehall, 'the prince only being there'. Herbert does not record what Charles thought of the performance, but was moved to write in the margin 'The worst play that ere I saw.'[76] The terse eloquence of these few words tells of the hours of tedium the Master had to endure in fulfilling his duties, although, if he was thorough about the audition process, court audiences should not have shared them. Perhaps *Dissemblers* was the best the actors could provide at short notice.

The masques were much talked about in the Stuart court; gossip and 'buzz' to a certain extent directed opinion, since no one wished to be out of step with what leading figures thought. When a number of distinct comments about an occasion survive, we normally have an indication that it was a hit, whether it was a genuinely striking performance or simply became 'cried up', gathering a reputation by means of the snowballing effect of gossip. *Pleasure Reconciled to Virtue* is unusual in having been generally regarded as disappointing, while having generated a good deal of notice, perhaps because it was Charles's entrée as Prince of Wales. Sir Edward Harwood records the general opinion that the masque 'was not well liked: the Conceite good, the poetry not so'. Edward Sherburn thought that 'a poorer was never seen', laying the blame at Jones's door; John Chamberlain that 'the invention proved dull', a phrase which damns both poet and designer; Nathaniel Brent squarely blamed Jonson: 'The maske on 12th night is not commended of any the poët is growen so dull that his devise is not worthy the relating, much lesse the copiing. Divers thinke fit he should retourne to his ould trade of bricke laying againe.'[77]

How many of these men had actually been in the Banqueting House and seen and heard the performance for themselves, as Busino had, is a nice question. Chamberlain particularly was not a participant in so much as an observer of the court, and he represents an entire class or category of contemporary London society: comfortably off men of middle rank who kept an attentive eye on what went on around them. He had friends who were important figures at court and in the diplomatic service, and he kept up with the latest political and social events in the capital, evidently by spending a good deal of his time in conversation. His letters were sent principally to Sir Dudley Carleton, English ambassador in France and the Netherlands, to keep him informed, before the days of news-papers, of current London affairs of all kinds, from the momentous to the trivial. In some respects, then, he can be seen as a version of that modern figure, the journalist, who kept a journalist's eye on the court. He made no pretensions to be personally *au fait* with court circles, and made a shrewd critique of the reliability of others' reports: 'I am a meere straunger to the court and court busines, more then by hearsay, which is as uncertain and varies as often as the severall humors and affections of the parties I meet with.' None the less he visited court when he felt like it, as he did to see Princess Elizabeth and her fiancé, the Elector Palatine, just before their marriage in February 1613.[78]

He did not attend masques, however, and what he relates about them he had entirely heard from others, and on occasion he heard more than one kind of opinion. Chamberlain reported the remounting, a month later, of an altered version of *Pleasure*, as *For the Honour of Wales*, to Carleton on 21 February as having been 'little bettered', despite the changes and additions. A day later he had heard otherwise, and wrote that 'it was much better liked than twelveth night; by reason of the newe Conceites and antemasks, and pleasant merry speeches'.[79] His comments on the Twelfth Night masque of the preceding year (1617), *The Vision of Delight*, which was performed again on 19 January, demonstrate that he relied on what he picked up from talking: 'I have heard no great speach nor commendations of the maske neither before nor since, but yt is apointed to be represented again to morow at night.'[80] Aware of the court calendar, he had not been able to discover its rationale. Robert Reade also went on what he had heard about *Salmacida Spolia*. Many of our reports about court performances are given at second hand, but at least are a register of 'the several humours and affections' of the time.

Chamberlain might be compared with Sir Humphrey Mildmay, who was rather younger and of rather higher rank, and from a family with a tradition of court service. Two of his brothers had court positions, which helped his access to Whitehall, and he was acquainted with Sir John Coke, Secretary of State, and his wife. Though he attended several court plays, with his brother Anthony and others, including a performance of Jonson's *Catiline* on 9 November 1634, he saw only one masque, when he went as the companion to a lady higher in the hierarchy of court society; he recorded that he 'wayted on My Lady Cooke [Joan, wife of Sir John Coke] to a pretty Masque of Ladyes':[81] *The Temple of Love*, performed at Shrovetide 1635. Mildmay's experiences rather suggest that the masques were harder to get into than were plays, and that the barrier of rank was higher.[82]

Chamberlain's reference to discussion of the masque *before* its performance also reminds us that leading court figures were directly involved in rehearsing dances, being fitted with elaborate costumes, and finally in dress rehearsals with the orchestra and scenery in the completed theatre during the days before the show itself. The Banqueting House or Masquing House became a theatre in rehearsal, with all the comings and goings and waiting around that rehearsals entail. The temporary seating, stage, and scenery filled the chamber, and strains of music could be heard in the rooms and corridors adjoining it. The masques involved the assembled Christmas and Shrovetide courts in a way that plays did not, and the anticipation and excitement generated by the preparations partly account for

why *Pleasure* was such a disappointment when it 'came far short of thexpec-
tacion'.[83] Privileged peeps at the scenery could probably be arranged if one knew
the right person to ask, and at least once an 'open' dress rehearsal was held, for
Salmacida Spolia, when the French ambassador was departing before the scheduled date of performance, 21 January 1640. He and his wife sat in the Arundels'
box, and were 'honoured with a sight of the practice of the dances and of the
motions of the scene, three or four dayes before the maske was to be completely
acted'.[84] On this occasion both the king and queen were called for rehearsal.

The Triumph of Peace, brought to court with great splendour and ceremony
from the legal inns in 1634, also elicited much comment. It too was at least partly
rehearsed within the court, since it was first staged in the Banqueting House,
prepared by the Works, and with Inigo Jones's scenery.[85] Herbert notes that the
young lawyers 'performed it very well', Finet that it was 'so well performed and
well lyked' that the king and queen determined to attend a second performance,
at Merchant Tailors' Hall. The Venetian ambassador mentioned the masque in
his dispatch, noting that it 'afforded particular gratification to their Majesties'.[86]
Two accounts by the participants also survive, the more substantial being the
lengthy and informative description by Bulstrode Whitelocke of his part in the
preparations, and of the procession and performance. His description of the
evening is worth some extended quotation. The audience, he tells us, was a large
one: 'the Banquetting-house at *Whitehall* was so crouded with fair Ladies,
glittering with their rich Cloths and richer Jewels, and with Lords and Gentlemen of great quality, that there was scarce room for the King and Queen to enter
in'. He does not recount Thomas May's misadventure with the Lord Chamberlain, a consequence of the crowding, but passes on to the show itself, which 'was
incomparably performed in the Dancing, Speeches, Musick and Scenes; the
Dances, Figures, Properties, the Voices, Instruments, Songs, Airs, Composures,
the Words and Actions, were all of them exact, and none failed in their Parts of
them, and the Scenes were most curious and costly'. Following the formal
dancing, the masquers invited members of the audience onto the floor. 'The
Queen did the honour to some of the Masquers to dance with them her self, and
to judge them as good dancers as ever she saw, and the great Ladies were very free
and civil in dancing with all the Masquers, as they were taken out by them.'[87]

A letter from Justinian Paget, a participant in the procession, adds that the
masque was received 'with much applause and commendation from the K and
Queene and all the Spectators', and that 'Sir Henry Vayne, and other great
Travellers say they never saw such a sight in any part of the world'.[88] The masque
was partly to celebrate the birth of Charles's second son, James Duke of York,

but was partly advertised as a declaration of loyalty in opposition to the anti-theatrical polemic *Histriomastix*, by lawyer William Prynne, published in 1632, and under prosecution at the time of the performance. Some thought, Whitelocke recounts, that 'this action would manifest the difference of their opinion, from Mr *Prynne*'s new learning, and serve to confute his *Histrio Mastix* against enterludes'.[89] There can rarely have been so splendid a confutation of a long, pedantic book, though it did not deflect the vindictive punishment of the unfortunate Prynne himself.

For Sir Henry Herbert the success of this occasion was outdone by the Shrovetide masque, *Coelum Britannicum*, which followed it two weeks later and which used the same stage structure as *The Triumph of Peace*, left standing within the Banqueting House. 'It was the noblest masque of my time to this day,' he writes, 'the best poetrye, best scenes, and the best habitts. The kinge and queene were very well pleasd with my service, and the Q. was pleasd to tell mee before the king, "Pour les habits, elle n'avoit jamais rien vue de si brave!"'[90]

The spectacle of the masques sought to draw superlatives from audiences; the less showy art of the players, at least in the tradition inherited from the sixteenth century, called on different kinds of attention and engagement, which could be exercised as well at the playhouses as at the theatres at court. Court figures, including the queen herself, were increasingly seen at the Blackfriars Theatre in the Caroline years, so that royal presence at the London theatres, a characteristic of post-Restoration city culture, can be said to have begun before the wars. The sharp distinction of the Elizabethan years, between the select audience for plays at court and the mixed, demotic audiences of the commercial playhouses, had been replaced by a series of distinctions in the social level and taste of audiences at particular seventeenth-century theatres, and by 1640 one might have observed that court audiences and those at the Blackfriars overlapped somewhat. Certainly the men who mounted *The Triumph of Peace* were regular playgoers at Blackfriars. The appeal of what the actors offered, for all that contemporaries wrote so little about what they saw and heard at plays, is amply demonstrated by the frequency of the visits of playing troupes, especially the King's Men, to the court, and by the wide variety of plays they offered, including those several decades old. The Caroline court saw a wide repertory of famous plays. The last, probably, to be performed at Whitehall was a sprightly old Beaumont and Fletcher comedy revived by the King's Men, to amuse an eleven-year-old boy in a gloomy season: 'On Twelfe Night, 1641 [= 1642], the prince had a play called *The Scornful Lady*, at the Cockpitt, but the king and queene were not there; and it was the only play acted at Courte in the whole Christmas.'[91]

6   Royal occasions

This day the court doth measure
Her joy in state and pleasure,
And with a reverend fear
The revels and the play
Sum up this crownèd day
Her two and twentieth year!
Ben Jonson, 'An Ode, or Song, by all the Muses, in Celebration of Her
Majesty's Birth-Day, 1630' (London, 1640)

If there was indeed a play performed at court for the birthday of Queen Henrietta
Maria on 15 November 1630, it is likely to have been presented in the recently
converted Whitehall Cockpit Theatre, which had been opened only ten days
earlier. Royal birthdays (and other anniversaries) were marked by similar celebrations in other years. A masque had been performed at Somerset House for
the queen's birthday in 1626. The king's birthday fell four days later, on 19
November, and plays were presented on that night in 1630 (Jonson's *Volpone*, in
the Cockpit), 1633, 1634, and 1636. A play given for Prince Charles at Richmond in 1639 was 'vpon the Duke of yorkes birth day' (14 October). It was
James's sixth birthday; Charles was nine.[1] Although we have no court records to
confirm Jonson's poem it seems probable that the Queen's company, which
presented sixteen plays at court on unspecified dates between mid October 1630
and the following February, were, appropriately, the entertainers. The leading
dramatist writing for the troupe at this period was James Shirley, and we might
imagine that one of his earlier comedies would have contributed suitably to the
'pleasure' of the evening.

In this final chapter I concentrate solely on 'the play' as a court entertainment,
and attempt to place a number in the context of their performance at court,

choosing where I can plays still reasonably well known to readers, without allowing Shakespeare's plays to be disproportionately represented. To understand the performance conditions of Tudor and Stuart plays we need to think not only of contemporary playhouses and the playing places visited in the provinces but also of the theatres at court, where the players fulfilled their function as entertainers to the monarch. Although such descriptions of actors in their licences are frequently characterised by modern commentators as a legal fiction which allowed them to pursue commercial playing, in fact royal demands on playing companies grew as time went on: all the major playing troupes in London performed at court far more frequently in the later period, when they had firmly established themselves as a part of city culture. As in the earlier chapters my principle is to give roughly equal attention to the three reigns, and in order to do so I will focus on three decades: the 1580s, the first ten years of King James's reign, up to and including the marriage celebrations for his daughter Elizabeth, and finally the 1630s.

If we add up the surviving information about court revels in the 1580s there are a number of occasions when plays we can still read (and act) can be placed in a temporal and physical context. *The Misfortunes of Arthur*, performed in the Hall at Greenwich in late February 1588, and to which I have given some attention in chapter 3, is one such, although it is unusual, like the earlier *Gorboduc*, in having been an amateur production: it had no stage career beyond the single court performance (which in this case can hardly be lamented). Many of the titles of plays from the commercial theatre in the Revels records—*The Duke of Milan and the Marquis of Mantua*, *The Game of Cards*, *Ferrar*, and so on—are now no more than titles, but 'A Historie of Loue and ffortune', acted at court on 20 December 1582 by the Earl of Derby's Men, was published five years later as *The Rare Triumphs of Love and Fortune*, with the claim on its title-page that it had been 'Plaide before the Queenes most / excellent Maiestie'. The Revels Office provided scenery for the play—'one Citty and one Battlement of Canvas iij Ells of sarcenet [silk] A . . . of canvas'[2]—although unlike *The Misfortunes of Arthur* the text itself makes no mention of 'houses'. The Revels also distributed the habitual honorific gift of '8 pairs of gloves' to the players, which were presumably worn during the performance. Eight was probably the number of leading actors in the troupe, to which apprentices and supernumeraries must have been added: the opening scene of *The Rare Triumphs* calls immediately for ten performers, who are subsequently joined by five or six more.

The Christmas season of 1582–83 was one of the few held at Windsor Castle by Queen Elizabeth, and after this year no other royal Christmas was kept there before 1642, the Stuarts favouring Hampton Court as a rural alternative to the London palaces. The unusual location did not restrict the entertainments: four plays and a mask were presented to the court, a number similar to those of other Christmas courts of the 1580s held at Whitehall, Greenwich, and Richmond. The theatre at Windsor, as at the other palaces, is likely to have been set up in either the Hall or the Great Chamber (see chapter 2), with the usual provisions of degrees set against the walls, and a centrally placed state facing the stage. The queen looked at a painted city and battlement lying behind the stage platform, but as the action of the play unfolded the actors would not have made much reference to them. The text of the play makes little mention of these locations, and demands other stage facilities not described in the Revels accounts.

The stage platform must, for example, have been equipped with a trap if the play was performed in the version printed, and so must have been sufficiently high from the floor to allow for a practical stage cellar. The actor playing the fury Tisiphone, who 'riseth' in a preliminary show, would have made his way under the stage to begin the performance; the closing lines of his speech describe a descent to the cellar once again, with a built-in cue to the stage-hands below: 'Give place thou aire, open thou earth, gape hollow hell belowe, / and vnto all that live and breathe, I wishe a worlde of woe' (ll. 62–63). This spectacle is matched elsewhere in the play by effects produced on stage by the actors, chiefly in the 'triumphs' or musical processions of the contesting Venus and Fortune, which conclude three of the five acts.

The connection between the action of the play and the painted canvas locations of the Revels accounts does not at first sight seem very close. The human figures of the central plot of the play, subjects of the contest between Love (represented by Venus) and Fortune, are ruled over by a monarch called King Phizantius, whose kingdom the painted 'Citty' might rather generally represent, but a good deal of the action takes place in the woods, around a 'cave' or 'darksome cell' (l. 609), perhaps the missing item left blank in the Revels list, which is used as a practical point of entry and exit in act 3. The contrast between the corrupt, repressive court and the honest, if primitive, country–that of much pastoral drama, including *As You Like It*–may therefore have been embodied on stage at Windsor by symbolically opposite houses, the city and the cave, perhaps with a sarcenet curtain between them which might be used for the entries and exits of the choric gods. The 'Battlement' would appear to have been a redundant detail, merely decorative in effect. No action is required to take place in an area above the stage, and the play has no military scenes.[3] Unlike *The Knight in the Burning Rock*, *The Rare Triumphs* was calculated to be confined within the limits of a platform stage, and is entirely suited for playing elsewhere, on playhouse or temporary stages, the initial trap scene presenting the only technical challenge. The costumes in the play could have been quite elaborate, however, and at court the actors are likely to have drawn on the resources of the Revels Office wardrobe store. A large number of classical and mythological figures, frequently represented in masks and allegorical shows, and with a well-established iconography in paintings and prints, take part, however briefly, in the action: Mercury, Vulcan, Venus, Fortune, Tisiphone, Jupiter, Juno, Minerva, Mars, Saturn, Troilus and Cressida, Alexander, Dido, Caesar and Pompey, and Hero and Leander. All of these appear either concurrently or in fairly rapid succession in act 1, and such a parade may have taxed the regular theatrical wardrobe of Derby's Men. For their Christmas performance, they no doubt borrowed Revels costumes which may have been seen in other court shows on previous occasions.

The text of *The Rare Triumphs of Love and Fortune* gives an intriguing glimpse into the repertory of adult professional players in the earlier 1580s, a matter about which we otherwise know very little. Entertainers at court in the 1580s were divided fairly equally between the adult troupes–Derby's Men and similar groups–and the children's companies connected nominally with the Chapel Royal and with the choir school of St Paul's cathedral but in fact being managed as commercial enterprises by then. One of the entrepreneurs in these ventures was the writer John Lyly, who provided his own plays for performance by the young actors. The principal plays of Lyly, still read today and very influential in their own time–both Shakespeare and Jonson learned much from them–were all performed at court. The Revels accounts for the 1580s have recorded the titles of court plays rather patchily, so they cannot confirm the precise dates of Lyly's *Campaspe*–printed in 1584 with the information on the title-page that it was 'Played beefore the / *Queenes Maiestie on* / newyeares day at night' by a combined company of the Chapel and Paul's children–nor of his *Sappho and Phao* published in the same year with a similar title-page announcement: it was '*Played beefore the* / Queenes Maiestie on Shroue- / tewsday' by the same group of actors. Modern scholars believe that the plays were performed in the same year as their printing, given that we know that the acting troupe in question was at court both on 1 January and 3 March (Shrove Tuesday) in 1584.[4]

At both Christmas 1583–84 and Shrovetide 1584 court was kept at Whitehall, and the Works prepared the Great Chamber for revels with degrees, standings, and a state for the queen. The room was used for 'Dauncinge', probably at Christmas, but at Candlemas (2 February) it was quite specifically prepared 'for the playes'.[5] The entertainers on the latter occasion were the Children of the

Chapel alone, and it seems quite likely that at least part of what they offered (if the plural 'playes' is to be trusted) was George Peele's surviving play, *The Arraignment of Paris*, also printed in 1584 with the temporally vague information on the title-page that it had been 'Presented before the Queenes / Maiestie'. One cannot be quite as confident in identifying 2 February as the date of this performance;[6] if *The Arraignment* was indeed acted then, as I shall assume here, the first eleven weeks of 1584 constituted a quite remarkable season of court theatre.

All three plays are likely to have been acted in the same theatrical space, then, on a stage platform of similar size from occasion to occasion, and to a similar size of audience. Lyly's plays, in which elaborate and brilliant verbal delivery is so important, can only have been helped by the dimensions of the Great Chamber and by the consequently more intimate acoustics in which the boys' voices could operate. The Revels Office, we have noted, continued to supply the players with 'houses' for their performances, although in the case of all three of these plays there are no corresponding notes on precisely what was made. In general terms the plays make very little internal reference to specific localities, so that if they were all written, as seems likely, with an eye to performance at court, it is of interest that they make no special dramaturgical demands on the Revels system. *Campaspe* is rather different from the other two in this regard, in that the philosopher Diogenes famously inhabits a 'tub', the theatrical embodiment of which must be one of the physical points of interest on the stage: 'see where his tub is', Alexander remarks.[7] It was no doubt treated as a 'house', although something like a three-dimensional cylinder would have proved more amusing than a painted canvas surface.

The ubiquitous 'city' might also have been provided for the play, which takes place in Athens, and possibly the shop of Apelles, the painter, was represented as a distinct place, although it would simply have served as a point of entry and exit. The costuming for the play is likely to have been supported by the Revels Office. A central character is Alexander the Great, a favourite 'worthy' in plays and pageants; he makes a brief appearance in a show within *The Rare Triumphs of Love and Fortune*. Costumes from the Revels stock, however, would have to have fitted the smaller stature of the boys without looking ludicrous; since boy players frequently appeared at court in the earlier Elizabethan period, the Revels perhaps kept common costume items in a range of sizes. How classicised the costumes may have appeared is an open question. On the whole it seems unlikely that the performers looked very archaeologically 'Greek'; quite what expectations educated Elizabethans might have had about the appearance of Plato and

Aristotle, both characters in the play, is hard to tell, but they were no doubt taken into account both by the classically educated Lyly, who was connected with the production of his own play, and by Edmund Tilney.

The Arraignment of Paris is not a self-enclosed play, like *The Rare Triumphs* and *Endymion*, which might easily have been played in a playhouse without any changes. Its 'conceit', to use an Elizabethan word, is that in the beauty contest of the goddesses which launched the Trojan war the prize of the golden apple was wrongly awarded, and that in 1584 it should rightly be given to the great queen of England, as indeed it was at the end of the performance. The queen's presence is necessary to make the combined dénouement and compliment work, and thus the play as it was published is a court play like no other, especially designed in the writing to connect the performance with the central member of the audience. At the conclusion of the play the assembled court watched as the queen became an actor–silent, but through her sheer presence superseding the lesser charms of the play. As a delightful surprise, as it was probably intended to be, it can only have worked once: it is indeed an occasional play in a thorough sense. The staging of the play resembles the unique, particular character of the Stuart masques; at the end the actors playing the Fates and gods stepped down from the stage platform and crossed the floor of the Great Chamber to the state, where in resignation to her power the Fates '*lay down their properties at the Queenes feete*' and the goddess Diana '*delivereth the ball of golde to the Queenes owne hands*' (l. 1241).

Once again the costuming of the play is classical and mythological, with characters whose conventional visual forms would have been familiar from graphic representations, and from decorations of textiles and ceramics. As to setting, there is only one precise indication of the kind of location habitually represented by the Revels houses. The general place is Mount Ida, for which some kind of pastoral painting may have served, and there are internal references to a '*tree*' and to '*Dianas bowre*'. The first seems incidental to the action, but the second was evidently some special stage structure, likely to have been one of the houses prepared for the performance. In act 4 eleven actors sit within it at the trial of Paris, like magistrates on the bench. In other respects the play calls on stage effects of considerable elaboration which would have required careful physical preparation by the Revels, or perhaps by the Works, since they involved construction within the stage platform. The stage included a trap, like that for *The Rare Triumphs*, but, for *The Arraignment*, with a mechanism capable of lifting a seated actor from the stage cellar into view on the stage above: '*Pluto ascendeth from below in his chaire*' in act 4, scene 3. Earlier in the play, as part of a series of shows put on to impress Paris, Juno makes a golden tree '*laden with Diadems and*

Crownes of golde' rise from the stage; after a few lines it 'sinketh' (l. 457). This effect used the same machinery, which would have been built on the mechanical principles used in earlier court shows like *The Knight in the Burning Rock*. If the text truly represents the performance, the court staging of *The Arraignment of Paris* was a notable, unique event.

One of the two Shrovetide plays in 1584 was *Sappho and Phao*; the Queen's Men performed a second of which we do not know the title. Lyly's prologue to his play apologises to the queen for 'plainness'; her eyes 'variety hath filled with fair shows', and what she is about to see cannot compare, perhaps, with *The Arraignment of Paris*. The physical requirements of the play *are* relatively simple, but the text of *Sappho and Phao* gives the clearest notion of what the Revels must have supplied in the way of houses in 1584. Two distinct locations are required: a 'cave' for Sibylla (which really need not have been much more than a point of entry) and a bed for Sappho, which must be curtained, and capable of being concealed. The play's most recent editor, David Bevington, has suggested that these two houses were set in symmetrical opposition at the rear of the platform. This seems quite likely. We have noticed that Revels houses were frequently listed as pairs, and Lyly, fond of antithetical structures, in this play capitalised on one physical form of court stages.[8] A third location, Vulcan's forge, may have been accommodated in a distinct house, although it is not clearly required as a physical feature of the stage.

As with *Campaspe*, much of the play's appeal is aural; the crisp and agile delivery of the witty arabesques of the intricately constructed speeches must have been the chief concern of the director of the children in rehearsals, perhaps Lyly himself. Like *Campaspe* and *The Arraignment* the play has a classical-mythological setting, calling for costuming similar to that in the earlier productions. Venus and Vulcan, both characters in *Sappho*, had recently appeared on stage in *The Arraignment*, and their costumes would have been given a second showing.

Classical legends and myths, then, were leading themes of court entertainment in the earlier 1580s. Two court performances of later plays by Lyly which continue to work the same vein can also be precisely dated, once again within a short period of time. *Gallathea*, published in 1592, 'was playde before / the Queenes Maiestie at / Greene-wiche, on Newyeeres / day at Night' by the Paul's Boys company; *Endymion* was printed in 1591 with the information on the title-page that it was also acted at Greenwich 'on Candlemas day / at night' by the same actors. Given what we know of the visits of this troupe to the court, these performances must both have fallen early in 1588: *Gallathea* on 1 January, and *Endymion* a month later, on 2 February.

Greenwich Palace was favoured as the location for Christmas and Shrove courts for four consecutive years beginning in 1584–85. The Christmas court there in 1587–88 included revels in the Hall and Great Chamber, which were prepared by the Works 'for playes and daunsinge'. Three plays, including *Gallathea*, were presented: the Queen's Men played on 26 December 1587 and again on Twelfth Night, 6 January 1588, for which the Works made further preparations, 'settinge vp degrees'.[9] We might guess that the Hall was used for the play on Twelfth Night, with extra accommodation for the larger crowd which might be expected, and that *Gallathea* was played in the Great Chamber, but this is no more than a guess, and it is possible that the boy actors had to contend with the large theatre space within the Hall.

Gallathea is set in a pastoral never-never land, nominally in Lincolnshire, but featuring Neptune, Venus, Cupid, and Diana as characters, as well as shepherds called Tityrus and Melibœus. An oak tree, referred to in the first few lines of the play, is the chief physical location in an action which otherwise makes very little reference indeed to the kinds of location which the Revels houses traditionally represented. A general painted background ('a wood') may have been provided on the frameworks at the rear of the stage, with the oak tree featured prominently, or else perhaps painted on a free-standing piece of scenery. *Gallathea* could very easily have been played on an entirely unlocalised stage, however, and its freedom in this respect could be taken as a sign of changing stage practice. When Phyllida invites Gallathea to 'wander in these groves' there is no more need to embody the location than there is to realise 'this wood' in *A Midsummer Night's Dream*, a play written and performed about eight years later. Once again, traditional costuming seems called for in the case of the divine figures in *Gallathea*, although the pastoral costumes would have been open to a variety of treatments. The play also includes a comic trio of boys, Rafe, Robin, and Dick, who encounter a caricatured alchemist and an astronomer, both of them likely to have been costumed with exaggerated absurdity, in the style of the antimasques. The charming, tongue-in-cheek character of the play, which would have been sustained by the skill of the actors, is contained within a fairly simple theatrical framework.

Endymion, a longer and more ambitious play, also calls more frequently on localised stage space: the bank where Endymion endures his long sleep; the hermitage of Geron, with a magic fountain; a tree, a castle, and the palace of Cynthia. Preparations for the performance at Greenwich are not mentioned in the Works accounts, unlike those for *The Misfortunes of Arthur*, performed at the end of the same month, when 'a greate Scaffolde with degrees and pticons' was set up, no doubt in the Hall.[10] This *may*, but need not, indicate that the Candlemas and Shrove plays were more modestly mounted in the Great Chamber.

The Revels stage provisions would have included houses representing at least some of the locations mentioned, of which by far the most important from a practical point of view is Endymion's lunary-bank.[11] While this could have been as simple as a canvas-covered box on which the actor reclined, it may possibly have been set within a recessed booth, allowing the sleeping figure to have been concealed during the considerable length of the play when the action does not refer to him directly. On the other hand his continued presence in the view of spectators, like a statue or an emblem, between his falling asleep towards the end of the second act and his being awakened at the start of the fifth would not have seemed inappropriate, theatrically or thematically.

Although some of the characters bear classical names, the play is more truly romantic than mythic, and might have been costumed in any style roughly appropriate to a court of high-born ladies and their gentleman lovers. Some of the characters are grotesques, and would have required suitably exaggerated dress: Dipsas, the crone–sorceress; Sir Tophas, the bombastic soldier; some comic watchmen; and fairies. None of this costuming seems particularly out of the ordinary, however, and if by 1588 the Revels had reduced their wardrobe supplies for actors, then the Paul's troupe had its own costumes for use in its playhouse. Indeed, *Endymion* could partly have been dressed in the costumes earlier used for *Gallathea*.

By 1603, playhouse practice and royal economy had changed the appearance of plays at court. Court audiences no longer looked at painted houses, nor would they have recognised familiar items of Revels costumes and properties returning from play to play and year to year. The records of the first decade of the Jacobean court enable us to connect a great many more surviving plays with particular occasions and physical locations, although the information remains very patchy. In six of the ten seasons between 1603–4 and 1612–13, when plays presented between October and the following summer numbered between fifteen and twenty-six per year, we have either no play titles or only a single one, and frequently no precise date of performance. In 1612–13, by contrast, most of the titles of the numerous plays presented at court have survived. Generally the King's Men were a favoured playing troupe, performing more often at court than any other company. The plays we know them to have acted there included their recent and up-to-date repertory–*Othello* in November 1604, and both *The Tempest* and *The Winter's Tale* in November 1611–as well as older comedies, ten or more years old. Fourteen plays by Shakespeare are known to have been presented in this decade, some of them more than once, and we can probably venture that several more (*Twelfth Night*, *As You Like It*, *Hamlet*, and *Macbeth*, for example) were among those court performances which remain unnamed. The King's Men also presented several plays by Jonson – at a time when that poet was establishing himself as the principal writer of the texts of the masques – and by Beaumont and Fletcher.

Their performances, however, also included plays not at all known today. The first Christmas court of the new king, held at Hampton Court because of widespread plague in London, is not particularly thoroughly documented in terms of theatrical activity. The King's Men gave five performances in the Hall, consecutively on the nights of 26 to 30 December 1603, and then again on 1 January 1604;[12] they gave one more performance at Hampton Court at Candlemas, 2 February 1604. In a letter, Dudley Carleton reported that, on the night of New Year's Day, 'we had a play of Robin goode-fellow', which seems likely to have been *A Midsummer Night's Dream*.[13] No play titles were recorded elsewhere, but in February 1605 the anonymous play *The Fair Maid of Bristow* was entered for printing in the Stationers' Register, and described as having been 'played at Hampton Court by his Maiesties players'; it was subsequently published by Thomas Pavier.[14] *The Fair Maid* is an undistinguished melodrama with a rather old-fashioned air, but with some similarities to *Measure for Measure*; its writer is certainly in Shakespeare's debt in borrowing from *Romeo and Juliet*, but Shakespeare himself perhaps drew some suggestions from the lesser play he acted in at court in 1603–4.

All the companies playing at court during the first Jacobean Christmas were at the disadvantage of not having performed their plays in the theatres for the preceding nine months. A severe outbreak of plague had coincided with the death of Queen Elizabeth, and it remained virulent throughout 1603; the playhouses were closed to prevent the spread of infection. The actors may have done some touring, but since the infection was widespread in England they had probably not been allowed to give many performances. Since they had not been producing new plays for public audiences, then, for the Christmas court shows they must have relied on older plays from their repertory or have produced specially rehearsed new ones, which would then have been seen in the playhouses once they reopened, later in 1604. *A Midsummer Night's Dream*, seven or eight years old, was a revival, and *The Fair Maid of Bristow* generally has the air of an older play.

Neither would have required any theatrical provisions beyond those of a platform stage and a tiring house, set within the ample space of Hampton Court Hall. *A Midsummer Night's Dream* seems a particularly appropriate choice for a festive occasion, and the new monarch and his family would not have seen it before. The energy it requires of its performers is perhaps reflected in Carleton's invented title: the memorable actor of Puck, who closes the play with an epilogue as well suited to a performance at court as to one in a playhouse, had set his seal on the whole entertainment. The play's own parody of entertainment for the court – the play of Pyramus and Thisbe by Bottom and Quince, and the schedule of attractions read out by Philostrate to Duke Theseus – is interestingly similar to some of Jonson's jokes in his later masques, and it may have appealed to the same vein of humour in the king. The physical demands of the play, beyond those of costumes and properties, are quite simple, for all that it has often been elaborately produced during the 400 years of its career on the stage, and there is little reason to think that the Jacobean court performance was substantially different from earlier stagings of the play in the playhouses.

Titania's 'flow'ry bed', in acts 2 and 3, *may* require some special structure to be set on the stage, or within a recess of the tiring house, but Titania and Bottom *can* sleep as simply as the lovers do, merely by lying down on the surface of the stage. The first printed text of the play (1600) includes directions which speak of the stage management at contemporary playhouses: '*Enter the King of Fairies, at one doore, with his traine; and the Queene, at another, with hers.*' Although actual doorways seem less likely than curtained entries in the kind of tiring house built by the Revels and the Works for the court staging of this moment (2.1), the actors would have treated the space at court in the same way as that in the playhouse: the theatrical requirements are symmetrically opposed points of entry for a simultaneous appearance of two groups, who converge for a confrontation down centre. The same two doors or entries, with the platform stage in front, constitute all the physical facilities required to mount the play.

The Fair Maid of Bristow is equally modest in its physical demands. The dramatic and literary qualities of the play are far below those of *A Midsummer Night's Dream*, but its appeal, like that of *Measure for Measure* and *The Merchant of Venice*, both subsequently staged at court, may have been calculated on the king's likely interest in the elaborate final trial sequence, presided over by King Richard. The play begins with dancing and a duel, both echoes of *Romeo and Juliet*, and these scenes provide immediate spectacular attraction. There are frequent disguise tricks through the course of the play, but they rely on stock costumes from the actors' wardrobe store; as in *Measure for Measure* dénouement is effected by a disguised friar removing his hood. Like *A Midsummer Night's*

Dream the play is composed for a stage with two entries, as the following direction indicates: 'Enter at one doore, Anabell disguised like a man, and at another Challener'. Altogether the play seems like modest playhouse fare, although its distinguished cast no doubt did their best to give it some character: weaker texts are sometimes supported by memorable performances. That Shakespeare probably played in it is an instructive reminder of his working conditions, going 'here and there' with his fellows, and breathing life into mediocre plays for eminent audiences.

All the plays of the first Jacobean Christmas were acted in the large space of Hampton Court Hall. In the following year, 1604–5, court was held at Whitehall, as it continued to be for the next twenty years. In a remarkable season, six of Shakespeare's plays were seen at court between November and February, two of them newly composed; the actors had been allowed to reopen their theatres in 1604 after a year of enforced closure due to the plague. Once again all the court plays were presented in large chambers, the Banqueting House and the Hall, before large audiences. *Othello*, a play only recently produced at the Globe, began the season at the Banqueting House on 1 November 1604. This building was Elizabethan, reportedly in a rather decrepit state, but possibly as large in floor area as the new building which replaced it in 1606–7, and hence capable of holding an audience as large as 1,000 people or more. The stage placed within it could easily have matched that at the Globe in area. The tiring house provided for *Othello* would have required a practicable second level, used in the opening scene of the play for Brabantio's appearance at the window of his house, having been awakened by Iago. The upper level is used only once, but the episode of 'rough music' awakening a sleeping household is an important effect for the play as a whole, and the players are likely to have insisted on the physical conditions to stage it, if by the early seventeenth century tiring houses made by the Revels and the Works were not regularly structures built in two storeys. Two other fictional locations require specific theatrical provision: the assembled Venetian senate in the third scene, and the bed in the last act. The first of these is simply a hierarchical group of seats, perhaps placed around a long table: such furniture was commonly required in plays, and was probably borrowed from court stores rather than carried from the Globe. The same may have been true of the bed, although if the actors calculated their effects on a bed of a certain size and shape–a canopied bed with curtains seems to be called for by the text of the play–then it would have made the trip by boat from Bankside to Whitehall Stairs.

The play's imagined darkness–it opens and closes with scenes set at night–would have appeared rather differently at court from daylit performances at the Globe; as I pointed out above, the yellow shimmer of candles hung above the auditorium would have illuminated Othello's entry with the hand-held candle before the murder, as in the previous year it shone on the 'moonlight' meeting of Oberon and Titania. Above the bright suspended candles in the Banqueting House the painted clouds of the canvas ceiling might have been made out, providing a further layer of illusion to the theatrical moment. In the relatively dimmer light indoors, however, any practical lighting on the stage must have created more of an accent than in stagings at the Globe. The title character's own darkness—a chief visual interest of the play—was interestingly matched later in the same court season by the queen's masque, *Blackness*, presented on 6 January 1605 in the same space, the Banqueting House, with the queen and her leading ladies-in-waiting wearing dark make-up as 'moors'.

Othello was not presented, however, during the immediate Christmas period, for which its bleak emotional power does not seem particularly suited. Christmas plays were not simply jolly comedies, however. On St Stephen's Night (modern Boxing Day, 26 December), *Measure for Measure* was the play chosen to entertain the king and court in 1604, and two years later, on the same date, *King Lear*. *Measure for Measure* was played in the Hall at Whitehall, as were the other Christmas plays of 1604–5, which included *The Comedy of Errors* and *Henry V*. For the Cambridge edition of *Measure for Measure* published in 1991, C. Walter Hodges drew a representation of the Christmas court performance, showing the scene with Barnadine in the prison (4.3) being acted before the king and queen, seated side by side on a raised platform. Hodges's version of the staging is influenced by Southern (see chapter 3): the actors perform on the Hall floor directly in front of the screen, the two doors in which serve the actors as stage doors, with the screens passage as a tiring house. For reasons I have explained in chapter 3 of this book, I regard this arrangement as unlikely, but there is nothing in the play itself which would be impossible to realise in such simple conditions. Hodges shows a convincing representation of the Revels lighting, with some candelabra fixed over the screen itself. Part of the audience is shown seated on four ranks of degrees against the wall on the king's left, and also in the gallery above the screen, a position which no surviving evidence about court seating can confirm. The drawing is therefore valuably suggestive about the atmosphere of court theatre, but questionable in its details.

Measure for Measure is economical in its calls on stage space, although stage space itself, on which the actors are disposed in significant relationships and groupings, is particularly important in visualising the play's intellectual and emotional tensions. Its most powerful scenes in the first half of the play involve only a small number of actors: the largest assembly is for the long final scene of dénouement, from which only the comic grotesque characters (Pompey, Elbow, and Overdone) are excluded. The play's staging at the Globe would have required no adaptation for the Whitehall performance. Lucio's admittance to the nunnery ('Turn you the key'; 1.4.8) would have employed a door where one was available, but the effect of offstage calling and formal admission could easily have been made to yield theatrical sense in performance before a curtained façade. The only other physical feature the play absolutely requires, in the last scene, is seats, to serve as judges' chairs–they may also have been used in the earlier scenes of judgement in the play. Since their significance is symbolic practically any seat might have served the actors, and no doubt stools or chairs were borrowed from the considerable supply at court. The prison scenes at the centre of the play, whether at court or in the playhouse, would have been represented largely by the verbal context rather than by any scene dressing. Claudio, Barnadine, and Pompey may have worn fetters to signal their condition (as Hodges's Abhorson wears a large ring of keys at his belt), but neither spoken text nor stage directions make any clear reference to such properties. The chief visual effects of the play, which are central to its plot, are those connected with the perennial theatrical favourite, disguise. The friar's costume worn by the Duke came from the King's Men's wardrobe store, and had been seen at court the previous year in the performance of *The Fair Maid of Bristow*.

The first Jacobean decade, so fertile for theatre at court, closed with its own combination of comedy and tragedy. In the middle of October 1612, the German prince chosen as bridegroom for James's sixteen-year-old daughter Elizabeth–Frederick, Count and Elector Palatine of the Rhine (also known as the Palsgrave)–arrived in England. The preparations for their marriage were almost immediately interrupted by the sickness and subsequent death, on 6 November, of the heir to the throne, Prince Henry. The king decreed a long period of official mourning, and the wedding was put off until May, but in the event the formal engagement ceremony took place at Christmas, and the marriage on Shrove Sunday, 14 February 1613. The Shrovetide court was thus extraordinarily active: three distinct masques were presented within the period of a week. Before the wedding, Frederick was installed as a Knight of the Garter at Windsor with the customary processional ceremony, and the whole court was entertained by a naval show on the stretch of the Thames by Whitehall, and by a firework display over the water. On Shrove Tuesday there was a tournament in the Tiltyard before a large public audience, in which James himself took part in running at the ring (in which a rider attempts to catch a small target on the point of a lance). From the time of Frederick's arrival until the departure for Germany of the married couple in April, plays were frequently presented at court by a number of companies; the King's Men gave twenty performances in this period, including numerous plays by Shakespeare, four by Beaumont and Fletcher, and Jonson's *The Alchemist*.

Despite the mourning for Prince Henry, it seems that the Christmas court was quite active. We have no precise dates for the plays presented, but some of the King's Men's plays must have been given then. The payments to the actors in the Chamber accounts are divided into two groupings, categorised by the patron: six plays were presented before the king, and fourteen before Prince Charles, Princess Elizabeth, and 'the Prince Pallatyne Elector'.[15] The former group is likely to consist of the plays presented, probably in the Hall, to the assembled court at Christmas and Shrovetide: the anonymous play *A Bad Beginning Makes a Good Ending*; Beaumont and Fletcher's *The Captain*; *The Alchemist*; *Cardenio* (a lost play by Shakespeare and Fletcher); *Henry IV, Part One* ('The Hotspurr'); and *Much Ado About Nothing* ('Benedicte and Betteris'). The majority of these are more likely to have been seen at Christmas, since Shrove was crowded with other events. We can date two performances in this Christmas season. On the night of New Year's Day, the company of the Queen's Revels presented Beaumont and Fletcher's play *Cupid's Revenge* before the king (one of the few plays by those dramatists not written for and owned by the King's Men), and the same play was performed again just over a week later for Prince Charles, on 9 January 1613. The two performances probably played in different theatres, and to audiences of different sizes.

Before looking at this question in more detail, we can note that comedy predominated among the Christmas performances of 1612–13; perhaps the Lord Chamberlain and the Master of the Revels deliberately chose plays which stayed clear of the sensitive matter of the death of princes. I take it that the lost *A Bad Beginning* was a comedy,[16] and, although *Henry IV, Part One* closes as an epic battle play, much of the action is dominated by the wit and exploits of the fat knight, Falstaff. *Cardenio* may have been rather different in style and in its staging demands, but *The Alchemist* and *Much Ado* can be played without much difficulty in virtually any space; *The Captain* includes several scenes which require a playing level above the stage, but is otherwise quite modest in its demands. For all its structural brilliance, *The Alchemist* requires only the entries to the stage as a physical setting; when the location suddenly changes from inside to outside Lovewit's house towards the end of the play, the playhouse entry door would have been used practically, to knock and beat at, but to play the scene in front of curtains or hangings would not have proved impossible. *Much Ado* requires some expedient for Benedick and Beatrice to conceal themselves in two 'eavesdropping' scenes, although this could have been fairly simply managed by conventional stage positioning. Nor need the 'monument of Leonato', at which Claudio laments the supposedly dead Hero in 5.3, have been physically realised; the verses which he hangs on the tomb could simply have been attached to some convenient part of the tiring house.

Cupid's Revenge, a tragedy, stands apart from the other plays not merely in genre. The play gives every sign of having been popular at court; it had been presented during the previous Christmas season, on 5 January 1612, probably in the Hall, and its reappearance a year later seems to indicate royal favour. The appeal of the play in the playhouses, I have argued elsewhere, had to do with its spectacle.[17] In two scenes Cupid descends from the heavens on a flying machine. If the play was staged at court in this fashion then the physical provisions of the stage would have been elaborate. It was certainly not impossible to construct a 'heavens' over a temporary stage, capable of supporting the stage machinery and the actor who was to descend in the flying device. Such stages had been built since the Elizabethan years, but the Works would not have made them as a matter of course, since they involved so much more carpenters' work. A temporary stage set up to create such effects would have resembled those at the outdoor playhouses, since the stage roof and ceiling would have to have been supported by posts on or at the sides of the stage platform.

The New Year performance is likely to have been put on in the Hall, but the subsequent showing of the play, after Twelfth Night and the end of Christmas proper, was probably elsewhere. Since the arrival of the Elector, he and the princess had been entertained with plays in smaller chambers. The Cockpit was prepared for entertainments four times between October and December 1612; the royal couple certainly saw a play there on 20 October, and, if the building continued to be used as a smaller, more private theatre for the younger members of the court, *Cupid's Revenge* was perhaps acted there for Prince Charles. Descent machinery was included in the converted theatre after 1630, but the walls of the building may have enclosed a stage of similar elaboration in the Jacobean years.

Among other plays known to have been performed before all or some of the king's children and his son-in-law, *The Tempest* also calls for a theatrical descent scene, when Juno comes down from heaven in act 4. The same play also requires an upper playing level, for Prospero to appear 'on the top', and such a space is required for scenes in *Philaster* and in *Othello*, acted again by the King's Men in this season. If these plays too were seen in the Cockpit, the size of the stage made for a temporary theatre there is likely to have been fairly similar to that at the Blackfriars, between which smaller playhouse and the Globe the King's Men had become accustomed to moving their plays, from and back to the Globe. The twelve-year-old Prince Charles, observing an active and exciting season of court theatre and festival in 1612–13, perhaps first saw the suitability for plays of the building he was later to convert into a permanent theatre.

The opening of that elegantly transformed space in 1630 seems an appropriate point to begin a consideration of the great variety of dramatic activity at the second Stuart court. It was to be something of a meeting place of theatrical traditions. Not only did the English troupes act their traditional repertory there, but Parisian actors also performed contemporary French plays in front of Jones's classical façade in 1635. Some have thought that painted scenery was used occasionally at the Cockpit; I find this unlikely, given the structure and character of the space, but it does seem that a specially decorated production of Fletcher's *The Faithful Shepherdess*, in which the King's Men wore the costumes designed by Jones for the royal production of *The Shepherd's Paradise* in 1633, was given a second performance on the Cockpit stage. The first show in the new theatre, on 5 November 1630, was a performance by the King's Men of Fletcher's *The Mad Lover*, which had been performed at court at least once before, in 1617, when Lady Ann Clifford noted that she watched the play with the Arundels (see chapter 5).

The play, as it was printed in the 1647 Folio edition of Beaumont and Fletcher's works, opens with a stage direction couched in the theatrical language of the playhouses: '*Flourish. Enter* Astorax *King of* Paphos, *his sister* Calis, *traine, and* Cleanthe, Lucippe *at one doore; At the other* Eumenes *a Souldier*'.[18] The traditional two symmetrically opposed doors from which distinct groupings of characters could move towards a meeting were in Fletcher's mind as he composed this opening effect; at the Cockpit, we observe in Jones's drawings (Plate 7), there were five entries to the stage, perhaps allowing the large group of Astorax's court to assemble more quickly, although the actors would have preserved the visual separation between the court and Eumenes by using distinct sectors of the curving tiring-house façade, on either side of the central door. In a performance of *The Mad Lover*, that central door, hung with curtains, was no doubt used for the episodes of concealment and revelation in act 5, when Calis visits the oracle of Venus. These scenes also include a divine appearance, when 'Venus *descends*', and '*ascends*' once more after a few lines of consolation. Such spectacle would have called for special structural preparations at court in 1617, whereas the Cockpit theatre had been planned to accommodate it. *The Mad*

Lover, unique among the plays we know of in the 1630–31 season in requiring the descent machinery, was perhaps chosen as an opening piece in order to show off the facilities of the new playhouse.

It is true that the payments to the property-maker John Walker, for making the elaborate folding cloth heavens and 'Cloudes' which concealed the flying throne, do not appear in the Works accounts until the year after the first season of the theatre's use. Such effects graced Jupiter's descent in *Cymbeline*, acted at court on 1 January 1634. Such decoration, however, was, I think, superficial. The machinery, the stage loft, and backstage access for stagehands and actors must have formed an integral part of Jones's adaptations to the building, although his drawings show very little of the structural detail behind and above the stage and tiring-house wall.

Yet the stage superstructure at the Cockpit was used no more often than it was in the playhouses; contemporary playwrights made infrequent call on the spectacular effect of ascents and descents. The plays by the King's Men at the Cockpit in 1630–31 represent the company's repertory as it had developed over the course of thirty-five years. The theatrical language of these plays, as in *The Mad Lover*, was that of the platform stage with tiring house at the rear. The rather unusual space at the Cockpit would have been employed as might any other place to which the company toured their plays, would have been and made to stand in for playhouse conditions as well as might be managed. At the Cockpit no corners need have been cut. The multiple entries allowed rather more flexibility in stage movement, and there was a permanent balcony space, centrally placed, above the stage, with backstage access via stairways. (We might also note that there is no sign that any part of the audience was accommodated behind the stage at the Whitehall Cockpit.)

The balcony would have been called on several times in the presentation of the King's Men's plays of the opening season. In *Volpone* (19 November 1630), Celia would have appeared there in the scene in which the disguised Volpone plays the mountebank Scoto. The façade would have given Jonson's fictional Venice an elegant character, and suggested that Corvino was a social climber, having bought a *palazzo* with his profits. Jonson would no doubt have approved of the *inamorata*'s appearance, in a scene of comic excess which very deliberately invokes the *commedia dell' arte*, above an inscription which reminded the observers of the serious ends of drama: 'PRODESSE ET DELECTARE' ('to benefit as well as to amuse'). The pedimented window, also used as an upper storey in *Philaster* (2.4; 14 December 1630), might have looked less convincing as 'walls', the military stronghold represented by the old Revels designation of 'battlement,' and employed as an acting position in many plays with historical subject matter. The balcony level is not used in the action of *Henry IV, Part One* (6 January 1631), but it is for a 'walls' scene in *The Maid's Tragedy* (5.2), when three actors would have been called on to appear together within the rather tight space of the central window. Their visual effect would have been further constrained by the heavy front to the balcony area, formed by the inscribed tablet, reclining carved figures, and the curved pediment of the doorway below. Actors would have been visible only from the waist up, and scenes calling for groups any larger than three to appear 'above'–though they are rare–would have looked very cramped on the Cockpit stage.

The Maid's Tragedy, acted at the Cockpit on 9 December 1630, also includes, towards the end of the play, a spectacular scene of murder in a bed, reminiscent of *Othello* but with quite a different ethos. Theatrically, the playhouse bed, whether at the Globe or the Blackfriars, would have served both plays. In *The Maid's Tragedy*, unlike *Othello*, the bed is removed from the stage following the one scene in which it is needed (5.1); the subsequent action takes place in other fictional locations. The actors' bed, transported from their theatre or borrowed with the help of the Revels Office, would therefore have been carried on to the Cockpit stage for the scene, and off it at the close. The large central door we see in Jones's drawings, both the highest and widest of the five entries from the tiring house, seems the most suitable point for moving large items on and off the stage. The strong effect of centrality created by the tiring-house façade, taken together with practical stage management, suggests where the bed scene in *The Maid's Tragedy* would have been played: at the very centre of the stage platform, the bed aligned with the central doorway and balcony window at the rear of the stage.

That the King's Men performed at the Cockpit on St Stephen's Night (in *The Duchess of Malfi*), on St John's Night (in *The Scornful Lady*), on 30 December (in *The Chances*), and on Twelfth Night (in *Henry IV, Part One*) indicates that those gathered for the Christmas court of 1630–31 saw plays exclusively in the relatively small space of the new permanent theatre. (The audiences, we have already noted, may not have been a great deal fewer in numbers than those for plays in the Hall at Whitehall; see chapter 5.) The same appears to be true of the following Shrovetide, 1631, and two years later the records suggest that most if not all of the plays at Whitehall were presented at the Cockpit. After November 1630, then, the conditions of court theatre had changed. Both actors and audiences became accustomed to a regular venue, the physical conditions of which remained substantially unchanged from one occasion to another. Concurrently, both the Works and the Revels had less to do: the seating, stage structure, and some of the light fixtures remained in place year round, ready for use after only the habitual 'making ready' the officers of the Chamber performed before any court room was employed.

The old tradition of temporary conversion did not die out, however. The Cockpit saw a great deal of activity while the court remained at Whitehall; when it travelled, as in the past, theatres were created to order in court chambers. Throughout the 1630s plays were performed for the king and queen in the small chambers at St James's Palace. These included plays previously staged at other court theatres—*Cupid's Revenge*, for example, performed at Whitehall in the Jacobean years; *Philaster*, played at the Cockpit and elsewhere; Jonson's *Epicœne*, acted at St James's in February 1636 and in April at the Cockpit; and *Julius Caesar*, performed on the necessarily small stage within the Presence Chamber at St James's in January 1637, and again, probably at the Cockpit, in November 1638. *Caesar*, with its crowd and battle scenes, would not have been easy to fit into a small theatre, although its emotional effect when played to a small audience close to the actors could have been very powerful. Other plays given at St James's call on visual effects which also would have been difficult to manage in a small space. Apart from the descent scenes in *Cupid's Revenge*, Fletcher's *A Wife for a Month*, performed two days after the former play in February 1637, includes an elaborate episode in which Cupid and the Graces descend and ascend in a '*Chariot*'. The low ceilings in the St James's chambers (about 16 feet high in their surviving state) would have prevented the use of descent machinery, so that the scenes were probably restaged as entries from the tiring house. Such simplification, or even cutting, must have been the actors' solution, while playing on tour, in solving difficulties posed by locations without the space or flexibility of their stages at the playhouses.

The constraints of height at St James's also affected lighting; unlike those in larger court theatres, performances there were not lit predominantly from overhead. The Revels accounts show that the workmen supplied the chamber with 'Wallers'[19]—wall sconces rather than hanging chandeliers. The Presence Chamber, only 20 feet wide, was capable of being effectively lit in this fashion, and perhaps the general effect of the illuminated room was not much dimmer than other spaces used for playing. The faces of the actors on the stage or playing area, lit from either side rather than relatively evenly from above, must have looked rather different at St James's, however.

Scenes in plays which call on an upper level must be thought of as being staged at St James's as they were written, despite the low ceilings. The Revels and the Works would have built solid, two-storey tiring houses, with backstage access to the upper floor, and a railed balcony forming part of the stage façade. Had they not done so, Fletcher's *The Tamer Tamed*, played as a companion piece to *The Taming of the Shrew* in 1633, could hardly have succeeded, and have been 'Very well likt'. In Fletcher's play Petruchio's second wife reduces him to obedience by leading a household rebellion and locking him out of the house: the upper level serves as a stronghold in a number of scenes which recall the older battle plays, in a mock-epic style. Such an older play performed at St James's in the same season uses the upper level in a rather different fashion: in *Richard III*, 3.7, Richard is paraded on the balcony before the gaze of the citizens, who stand on the stage below. The small temporary theatres at St James's, then, reproduced the necessary elements of platform stage and two-storey tiring house on a small scale, within which the actors gave interpretations of some very exuberant and expansive plays. They are unlikely to have acted in spaces smaller than the Presence Chamber at St James's, truly a chamber theatre.

The older traditional locations of the court chambers at Richmond and Hampton Court also served court theatrical activity in the 1630s. The entire Christmas court of 1636–37 was held at Hampton Court, as in 1603–04 and 1625–26, because of severe plague in London. The actors, prohibited from playing in their theatres from May 1636 until late in the summer of 1637, would have particularly welcomed their payments for court appearances in the interim; the King's Men in fact became resident players at Hampton Court, with a special weekly allowance paid between November 1636 and January 1637.[20] During that period they performed fourteen plays, many of them previously acted at court in other locations, but including the only verifiable performance of *Hamlet* before a court audience, on 24 January 1637. The Works account for this period has nothing to say about theatrical preparations, but it seems most likely that the Hall was used for the plays, as in the past. For the special conditions of the King's Men's performance of *The Royal Slave* (12 January 1637) a proscenium stage would have been set up, to accommodate the scenery. The Hall at Hampton Court was large enough to emulate the site of the original performances of the play – Christ Church Hall, Oxford – in the preceding August; it seems that the king and queen were interested in copying the first production as closely as possible. The preparation of a proscenium stage and fittings would have taken some days to get ready, as for the masques, although if seating for the Christmas plays was already in place the workmen would not have had to construct the entire theatre. The performance of *A King and No King* on 10 January, then, is likely to have taken place elsewhere, probably the Great Chamber, on a platform stage with a tiring house. Subsequently the scenic stage for *The Royal Slave* would have been taken down immediately after the performance was completed; two weeks later, *Hamlet* would have been performed as it might have been thirty-five years before, on a stage of the traditional English model.

In 1636 and 1637, the king and queen enjoyed both intimate performances at St James's and broader and more expansive performances in the large space of Hampton Court Hall, as the actors suited their actions and words to their physical surroundings. Several plays at Hampton Court had previously been presented in the more contained space, speaking both acoustically and visually, of the Whitehall Cockpit theatre: *Beggar's Bush*, *The Maid's Tragedy*, *A King and No King*, *Rollo*, and Lodowick Carlell's two-part play, *Arviragus and Philicia*. For the actors of the King's Men – used to shifting their repertory between the differing stages, acoustics, and lighting conditions of their two theatres – such expansion and contraction was a fact of professional life. If the smaller theatre at the Cockpit in Whitehall had become the usual venue for court plays in the 1630s, the court audiences at Hampton Court are likely to have seen and heard more of the kind of aural and visual emphasis the actors gave their plays at the Globe. While such a style may have suited the older repertory–*The Maid's Tragedy*, *Othello*, and *Hamlet*–more comfortably than the recently written plays, calculated for the audience of the Blackfriars, there may have been more of a two-way traffic of performance between the two theatres than is commonly thought. The large playhouse remained a valued source of income for the company, and plays continued to be performed there throughout the 1630s.

Habitual observers of court theatre, like King Charles himself, must have seen distinctly different versions of the more popular plays, as, over the years, they were acted with changing casts and in differing spaces within the palaces. Yet the physical characteristics of the staging of the old Globe play *Othello* at Hampton Court on 8 December 1636 are likely to have been very similar to those of the Jacobean court showing of the play, at Whitehall in 1604. Both performances took place in large halls, lit with the Revels candelabra, and acted on large platform stages with tiring houses built to reflect the physical requirements of the play: an area 'above', for Brabantio in the opening scene, and a large access point to the stage, to carry on the bed for the closing act. The 1636 performance, with an entirely different cast, perhaps a slightly different acting text, external changes in costuming, and subtler changes in the conventions of acting style which thirty years of active work are bound to have brought about, would have been unlike that of 1604, but in ways that lie beyond our calculation today. The general lines of the production, however, guided by 'the book' and by the traditions of a tightly organised repertory company, may have remained much the same. The notion of a radically different stylistic framework and governing concept for each new production of 'classic' plays is modern, and has grown more exaggerated in its effects over the course of the second half of the twentieth century.

Hence the *Hamlet* performed in Hampton Court Hall in January 1637 undoubtedly bore the imprint of its first productions, in which Shakespeare himself had acted. The text which the king and queen may have heard is of considerable interest–did the acting version of 1637 correspond to the text of the printed Folio, for example? Yet the chief features of the play are clear in any of its textual states, and they include action of considerable excitement and dynamism; the particular combination of rhetorical poetry and concrete physical actions which the play achieves seems suited to larger rather than smaller theatres. The formal duel scene at the end, particularly, calls on a good deal of stage space, and the play scene in the third act also benefits from the clear demarcation of groups of characters which a larger stage more easily allows.

Stages within Hampton Court Hall are likely to have been raised platforms as a matter of course, but *Hamlet* requires such a structure. The ghost enters and leaves the stage by means of the tiring-house entries, but, after having left Hamlet in 1.5, speaks from the space under the platform, 'the cellarage' as the prince very specifically calls it. The crucial scene set in the graveyard (5.1) is also written around the theatrical facility of the stage trap. The gravedigger jumps into it to continue his excavation, just before Hamlet and Horatio enter. Ophelia's corpse is lowered into it, and Laertes and Hamlet wrestle madly in it before being separated and pulled out. The funeral service and its chaotic disruption form another episode which benefits from ample stage space. That the play was acted within the large space of Hampton Court Hall was partly accidental; in a plague-free winter the performance would no doubt have taken place at the Cockpit. We can take it that as that theatre had a working flying machine it also possessed a stage cellar and a trap. So while the actors may have chosen plays for the court in 1636–37 to suit a larger space, the examples of *Richard III* and *Julius Caesar* at St James's show that they were able to adapt their scale to royal command. To perform *Hamlet* in the small space at St James's seems a daunting task, but the players would have attempted it, had the royal calendar called on them to do so.

Soon after the performance of *Hamlet*, the court returned to London, and the King's Men then gave a number of performances at St James's. In the few remaining seasons of court theatre, plays appear normally to have been given at the Cockpit when the court was at Whitehall. *Julius Caesar* was acted there in November 1638, after having been played on the small stage at St James's in

January of the preceding year, no doubt with more difficulty both on stage and off, from the actors' point of view. The court season of 1638–39 continued to make calls on the adaptability of the King's Men to differing physical conditions and modes of production. Apart from the series of plays from their playhouse repertory, presented at the Cockpit during November and December, on 20 and 22 December 1638 they played Lodowick Carlell's two-part play, *The Passionate Lovers*, before the king and queen at Somerset House.[21] This was an elaborate production with scenery, designed by Inigo Jones, acted in a theatre with a proscenium stage built within the Hall. The plays had first been staged there in the preceding July, so that the December performances were an expensive revival of a show in which the King's Men appeared amongst painted pastoral scenery very similar to that earlier used in *Florimène*.[22] The plays probably entered the repertory acted at Blackfriars (they are included in a list of pieces the company sought to protect as their property in 1641), but evidently not with the kind of scenic decoration provided for the two distinct court performances in 1638.

Christmas of 1638–39 was rather an odd one, since it seems that the entire court did not remain in one place; there was no masque, and though the king was at Whitehall during the three weeks before Christmas he had moved to Richmond by 28 December, and appears to have been away from Whitehall for about three weeks. Yet the chief court officers, including the Lord Keeper, the Earl Marshal (the Earl of Arundel), and the Lord Chamberlain, were at Whitehall in early January, before Twelfth Night.[23] The queen was in the final stages of pregnancy, and the news of the death of the young Duke of Savoy, the Queen's nephew, brought by the ambassador a few days after Christmas Day, was marked by some kind of official mourning.[24] In addition, theatrical entertainments at court had been numerous and lavish through November and the first three weeks of December (see appendix). Together these circumstances suggest that a full court season of revels was not held; probably the king and queen withdrew to Richmond to keep a smaller and quieter court in the company of their children. On 28 December 1638, when the King's Men performed Brome's *The Northern Lass* at Richmond, Princess Elizabeth, the royal couple's fourth surviving child, celebrated her third birthday.

All three plays presented during this period–*Beggar's Bush* on 1 January 1639, and *The Spanish Curate* on 7 January, in addition to *The Northern Lass*–are comedies, none of them with particularly complex demands for staging, and eminently adaptable to playing in spaces and to audiences of differing size. The title-page of the 1632 quarto edition of *The Northern Lass* announces that the play had been acted at both the Globe and the Blackfriars. So, at court in 1638–39, it was presented at the Cockpit on 29 November before the Richmond performance a month later; *The Spanish Curate* was also a repeat performance, the first performance having been given at the Cockpit on 6 December. While such repetition might signal royal favour, taken with the other indications of a rather improvised Christmas it indicates hasty, *ad hoc* arrangements: at short notice the actors provided plays which were ready to play and might be easily transported to Richmond. *Beggar's Bush* was undoubtedly a court favourite. First acted at court in the Christmas of 1622–23, it had been played in the opening season at the Whitehall Cockpit, and six years later at Hampton Court. An exuberant play with a large cast of colourful 'types' in the manner of *Bartholomew Fair*, calling for enthusiastic acting, its staging required nothing beyond the bare facilities of stage and tiring house. Its cheerful pastoral solutions to fictional political difficulties were perhaps a welcome release from the increasingly gloomy news from Scotland about the rebellion there.

All three plays at Richmond are likely to have been acted in the same place, the Great Chamber in the main suite of the royal apartments, which was prepared for plays before Prince Charles the following winter with 'seuerall Stages & Degrees' built by the Works.[25] The stage and tiring house within this relatively large chamber served plays which might be staged quite simply. *The Spanish Curate* includes a scene in which a character is carried on to the stage in a bed (4.5), but this seems more likely to have been some kind of invalid chair, like that of John of Gaunt in *Richard II*, rather than a large canopied bed. The scene, like similar episodes in *Volpone*, concerns a feigned death-bed, in which the 'dying' man blesses his heir with increasingly unlikely riches. Discovering the joke, the angry victim rushes off, subsequently arriving at his own house door, at which he vainly knocks for admission until eventually opening it himself with a key. The probable absence of a practical door in a court tiring house would not have defeated an ingenious actor; the right exasperated business could have provoked the expected laughter. In *The Northern Lass* a stage direction indicates that a character 'sings aboue' (2.3); there is no compelling dramatic necessity for this, and the direction rather indicates the place where music was commonly produced in the playhouses, as it may also have been in court theatres. A scene of concealment in the same play tells us that a character '*Withdrawes behind the hanging*' (3.4), an effect likely to have been easy to manage on court stages.

Thus until the end of the theatre at court the actors continued to perform and their patrons to watch in a variety of physical spaces, governed by a variety of theatrical conventions. Theatrical style was changing by 1642: the appearance during the preceding decade of the King's Men on proscenium stages with scenery was a sign of developments which were to be taken up on the professional stage in England twenty years later. Court life remained in many respects occasional: theatres were created to order at certain times of the year, and actors commanded to fill them with entertainment. As the court was not tied to one physical place so the actors continued to regard their repertory as portable and mobile, not created for any one theatre building. All their own plays were written for the flexible conventions of platform stage and tiring house, so that they might at a pinch be adapted to stages with painted wing scenery, as was *The Faithful Shepherdess* in the court production of 1634 at Somerset House. The extraordinary richness and variety of theatre at the English court before 1642 was built on the traditions both of the actors and of monarchs and their courtiers. Neither was to be the same thereafter.

Conclusion

At Saint James I was kept in Custody, a place much beloved of me by reason of my Child-hood spent there, and the many innocent recreations of my youth; At White-Hall I was Beheaded, the Scaffold being erected before the Doors of the Court, and I passed that place in which I was accustomed to be present at Masks and Showes, and at the entertainment of the Ambassadors of forrain Princes.
Richard Perrinchief, *A Messenger from the Dead* (London, 1658)

The theatricality of the ending of the life of King Charles I, executed on a raised wooden stage outside Inigo Jones's Banqueting House in January 1649, was much commented on, most famously in Marvell's poem, in which the scaffold becomes a 'memorable scene', with a noble performer acting a moving death.[1] The heir of James I was 'set on a stage' in a sense very ironically related to that phrase in *Basilikon Doron*, even if James himself may have been aware of the darker edge of his words. His own mother had ended her life on such a stage, built by the agents and servants of Queen Elizabeth.

It is easy enough to suggest that Charles was a self-deluded victim of theatricality, retreating from the considerable difficulties of his reign into the fantasy land of the masques, but such a judgement, or cliché, has only a very limited truth. Charles seems to have been well aware of the difference between theatre and real life, and if some of his attitudes to the latter were badly judged and unrealistic he also displayed determination and some courage in dealing with their consequences. His taste for the theatre was genuine, and formed part of his enthusiastic patronage of the arts. So, while the masques might be viewed politically as trivial escapism, their real significance in artistic terms was their animation of contemporary visual arts—the pictures of Rubens, Titian, and Mantegna brought to life in three dimensions, with characters emerging from landscapes and dancing to the best music of contemporary English composers. Royal magnificence was proclaimed not simply through a collection of beautiful pictures and sculptures, but by participation in an action conceived in their spirit. The costumed dancing of King Charles and Queen Henrietta Maria before their assembled court had a long ancestry, and a symbolism which still made sense to many in 1640.

The commercial theatre owed a great deal to the patronage of the court. This has long been part of historical understanding of the theatre of the English Renaissance, and none of the evidence presented in this book suggests that it should be revised. If the court had had more money to spend on actors and their plays, either in the 1570s or the 1630s, then the development of the companies and their repertories might have taken rather different paths; as it was, the arm's-length relationship between the crown and the actors produced competitive vigour in the business world in which the players were given licence and protection to operate. The 'choice of plays' which the Master of the Revels made each year for the Christmas and Shrove courts was one outcome of this system of indirect patronage. There was more wastage and failure than if plays and performances had been directly commissioned, but the court did not have to pay for it, and could benefit from the selective filter represented by the audiences in the playhouses.

The result was, especially from the 1590s onwards, that each Christmas and Shrovetide the court was in direct touch with some of the best products of the London theatre of the preceding year. Inevitably some excellent plays failed in production, some poor ones were 'cried up', and others simply were not chosen by the Master, but if we examine the titles of plays known to have been presented at court between 1600 and 1640 we find that many of those we most admire today were performed before the English monarchs and their leading courtiers soon after their first appearance in the playhouses. As members of the court had a first-hand acquaintance with the best contemporary plays, so they were familiar with the leading actors, who returned each year for the festival seasons, and whose faces, voices, gestures, and mannerisms would have been remembered and admired. Their reappearance in the context of new characters and fictional situations would have been anticipated with interest and pleasure, as it was in the playhouses. The actors' art, as well as that of the dramatists, was part of court culture, and a proper appreciation of it was undoubtedly the mark of the more discriminating courtiers. The affection and gratitude that good acting inspires no doubt led in some instances to relationships similar to that between Prince Hamlet and his visiting players, whom he greets as old friends. Whatever King James might have thought of Richard Burbage, his own Lord Chamberlain was so moved by the death of the actor, 'my old acquaintance', in

1619 that he could not bring himself to watch the King's Men perform without him.[2]

The cultural function of theatre at court changed considerably over the course of the years of this study. An admiration for theatre at the Elizabethan court of the 1580s is apparent in Sir Philip Sidney's *Defence of Poesie*, but Sidney admires the ideal of the drama rather than the theatrical reality of his own day, which he makes some fun of. By the early Jacobean years, the commercial theatre had been transformed, and the best plays written for it display a degree of theatrical sophistication and literary skill rarely equalled. The complaints Sidney voices about theatrical conventions were still heard–from Jonson in his bouts of impatience with the theatre, for example–but where Sidney could point only to *Gorboduc* as a relatively recent play which might pass muster in comparison with classical drama, Jonson's poem to Shakespeare's memory in the Folio of 1623 boldly proclaims England's famous dramatist to have surpassed anything produced in either tragedy or comedy by the ancient writers of Greece and Rome.

From our modern perspective, influenced by the great magnetic field generated by current reading, study, and performance of Shakespeare, it is perhaps difficult to see why monarchs and courtiers did not make more of or say more about the talented player and writer who worked for them. Jonson's poem, written at the end of James's reign, may be said to mark something of a change in attitude, in the direction of more cultural self-consciousness and of pride in the achievements of English theatre, in which the court of King Charles shared. Yet even in the early Jacobean years, Shakespeare was hardly neglected at court, and until his retirement his face would have been as well recognised there as was Burbage's. A leading member of one of the two principal acting companies, his plays were consistently selected for court performance; his 'flights', Jonson writes, pleased both 'Eliza, and our James'.[3]

Charles I inherited an accumulated tradition of court theatre, both in the form of the masques, enthusiastically promoted by his mother, and of visiting performances by the leading playing companies, which he had patronised directly while still Prince of Wales. His taste for the theatre owed a good deal to his upbringing, but his support for players, writers, and theatrical activity of many kinds combined with the similar interests of his wife to produce an unprecedentedly rich cultural ambience at the court, which his leading nobles emulated and shared. What I have called the later Stuart self-consciousness about theatrical tradition was upheld in the repertory of plays shown at court between 1625 and 1642, which included a good deal of the older drama, dating back in some cases to the 1590s, and the recurrent performance of favourite older plays. In the 1630s a group of 'classic' plays–especially by Beaumont and Fletcher, Shakespeare, and Jonson–was kept in performance by the King's Men and other troupes, and they appear to have been equally enjoyed at court and in the playhouses. Not only were plays watched at court, but also read, discussed, and indeed written and performed by court figures.

The physical presence of theatre at court was most marked in the 1630s: in that decade the distinctly theatrical spaces of the Cockpit and the Masquing House were created at Whitehall. Since medieval times, however, court chambers had functioned as theatres at certain periods of the year. Among the purposes of the larger rooms in royal courts, between 1558 and 1642, contemporaries would have recognised that of theatres as a matter of course. Even after the restructuring of the Revels Office, many members of the royal household spent some weeks of their time each year on preparation for theatrical events, from the intensive heavy labour of erecting wooden seating, platforms, and stage structures to the intricate needlework of spangled and jewelled costumes for the masques. Theatre business of one kind or another accompanied the festive seasons of the court.

The London actors of the sixteenth and seventeenth centuries, whom we think of first in relation to their playhouses–the Rose, the Fortune, the Blackfriars–and to the differing audiences which might be found at given playhouses during particular periods, also acted regularly in other theatre spaces for another distinct and select audience. For the King's Men in the Stuart years the court theatre became almost a third playhouse, in addition to the Globe and the Blackfriars; or rather a variety of playhouses, since to play in Hampton Court Hall would have been to act in a very large space before several hundred people, while a performance at St James's would have tested the actors' skill in reducing their range to intimate conditions. The conditions of court playing were not entirely predictable. After 1630, to play before the king at Whitehall could probably have been counted on to mean performing on the stage of the Cockpit, the idiosyncrasies of which the regularly patronised companies would have got to know well. Before that date, or at other palaces until the Civil War, even within one chamber, the area of the stage platform and the character of the tiring house might have varied somewhat from one occasion to the next.

Other things could have been relied on. The chief members of the audience–the king, queen, or other leading court figures patronising the occasion–would have been seated in full view, directly facing the front of the playing platform or area. The focus of the performance, accordingly, would have been primarily directed to that part of the auditorium. In any chambers larger than those at St James's the entire theatrical space—tiring house, stage, and audience—would have been evenly and relatively brilliantly lit from overhead, creating an effect quite different from that in indoor theatres like the Blackfriars, where artificial lighting was used more modestly and sparingly. The atmosphere created by light—a very important element in any theatrical performance—would have been distinct from that in any of the playhouses, and a performance of a given play at court would have had a third character, different from its appearance at either a large daylit theatre or an enclosed theatre lit by candles.

The considerable variation in the size of court theatres can be regarded on the one hand as of no great significance—to the actors. Even before the King's Men began the venture of running two quite distinct playhouses, and moving plays indifferently from one to the other, all actors had coped with taking their plays around the country from town to town, playing indoors and out, with more or less cramped or roomy stage conditions, and before audiences of varying size. Professional technique would have included the ability to adapt vocal level and speed of delivery to match the acoustical character of the space in which one happened to be playing, from an inn yard to a room in a large house. To the end of the period covered in this book, all actors remained touring players, with the improvisational skills required of touring players. Stages a few feet wider or narrower from one place to the next would not have called for long production meetings or further rehearsal. If the company knew the lines, stage positions, and costume changes required to play a piece, they might have played it in a wide variety of spaces.

The consequences of the size of the theatre for the experience of the audience is a different matter. Different kinds of court audience had different impressions of performance. *Hamlet* played with all the stops out in Hampton Court Hall, in order to cope with the sheer cubic space absorbing the actors' voices, and to reach an audience spread out over 4,000 square feet of floor area, would have had a very different kind of effect from *Richard III* played in the Presence Chamber at St James's, with its low ceiling and less than a quarter of the floor space at Hampton Court, and where the sinister humour and rising hysteria of the title character could have been presented very subtly and intriguingly to those watching. The monarch was always near the actors, and could see and hear well, but those attending Christmas plays in the Hall at Whitehall were enjoying royal hospitality, and could not be ignored. Actors who could play a wide range of plays to playhouse audiences numbering in the thousands, we must take it, would have been able to maintain contact with the whole of the audience even in the largest of court theatres.

The remarkable theatrical activity at the English court between 1558 and 1642 was unmatched anywhere in Europe. Other courts may have been more notable in their patronage of music, scholarship, and the visual arts (particularly so in the Elizabethan period) but nowhere else could show theatrical activity which combined the skills of English actors–acknowledged throughout continental Europe to be excellent–with the remarkable products of a sustained period of brilliant dramatic writing. Professional players performing at courts were known elsewhere in Europe–in Spain and Italy, for example–but nowhere else was seen such consistently outstanding achievement over many years. By comparison, the masques were distinctly imitative, their form based on the sixteenth-century *intermezzi* of the Medici festivals in Florence and on the *ballets de cour* of France. Jones's drawings for sets and costumes borrowed consistently from Italian and French designs; Busino thought he had heard far better music back in Venice than that performed at *Pleasure Reconciled to Virtue*. Disguised dancing had long been an English court tradition, but the devisers of the Stuart masques quite consciously copied and appropriated continental European styles. Jonson's texts ensured that such importation received a characteristically English stamp, but English court culture in general had little it need apologise for in the face of other European states. The theatre remained a valued part of its cultural life until the entire court changed forever in the 1640s.

Appendix

Performances at Court 1558–1642

The following chart lists all known performances of plays and masks/masques at royal palaces and houses between the accession of Queen Elizabeth I and the beginning of the Civil War. It does not include such quasi-theatrical material as speeches and shows of welcome, tournament pageants, and acrobatic displays by members of playing companies, nor does it record entertainments for the monarch or other members of the royal family which took place elsewhere—on visits to the universities or to houses of the aristocracy, for example.

Since the chief court festivals spanned the change in the calendar year, court years are here taken to run from July 1 to the following June 30; dates are given in the modern convention. The entries list as many details as are known for each occasion, under the categories of date, venue, sponsor, title, author, and performers. Abbreviations are used for the principal palaces: W (Whitehall); G (Greenwich); R (Richmond); HC (Hampton Court); SH (Somerset House); SJ (St. James's). Principal court chambers are abbreviated as H (Hall), GC (Great Chamber), BH (Banqueting House), and C (Cockpit). King, Queen, and Prince are abbreviated to K, Q, and P. In the 'author' column, any play on which Fletcher collaborated is listed under his name only, with the exception of *Cardenio*, which is listed as Shakespeare.

Date	Venue	Sponsor	Title	Author	Performers
1558–59					
6 January	W	Q	Play. Mask of Papists.		Q's Co.(?)
16 January	W	Q	Mask (of Almains & Palmers?).		
29 January	W	Q	Mask (of Moors?).		
5 February	W	Q	Mask of Swart Rutters.		
24 May	W	Q for French Ambassadors.	Mask of Astronomers.		
1559–60					
11 July	W	Q	Mask.		
31 December	W	Q	Play; Mask (of Clowns or Nusquams?).		Chapel Boys (?)
1 January	W	Q for Duke of Finland	Mask of Barbarians.		
6 January	W	Q	Masks of Patriarchs & of Italian Women.		
25 or 26 February	W	Q	Mask (of Nusquams or Clowns?).		
27 February	W	Q	Masks (of Diana, Actaeon, & Nymphs?).		
1560–61					
Christmas	W	Q	Plays (including *Cambyses*?) & Masks.	Preston	Dudley's Men, Paul's Boys

				Author	Company
1561–62					
28 October	W	Q for French Ambassadors	Mask of Wise & Foolish Virgins.		Dudley's Men, Paul's Boys
Christmas	W	Q	Plays.		
1 February	W	Q	Mask; Play(?) of 'Julyus Sesar'.		Paul's Boys
Shrovetide	W	Q	Play.		
1562–63					
Christmas	W	Q	Plays.		Dudley's Men, Paul's Boys
1563–64					
Christmas	W	Q	Plays.		
2 February	W	Q	Play.		
9 June	R	Q for French Ambassadors.	3 masks.		
1564–65					
Christmas	W/HC(?)	Q	4 plays (including *Damon & Pithias*?).	Edwards	Warwick's Men (2), Chapel Children, Paul's Boys
January	W/HC(?)	Q	*Miles Gloriosus*, *Heautontimorumenos*(?).	*Plautus* *Terence*	*Westminster Boys*
2 February	W	Q	Play.		Paul's Boys
18 February	W	Q	Play. Mask of Hunters & 9 Muses.		Sir Percival Hart's sons
4–6 March	W	Q	Mask of Satyrs and Tilters; *Massinissa & Sophonisba* (tragedy).		Gentlemen of Gray's Inn

Date	Venue	Sponsor	Title	Author	Performers
1565–66					
Christmas	W	Q	2 plays.		Paul's Boys
24–26 February	W	Q	Sapientia Solomonis. Gismond of Salerne.	Wilmot, etc.	Westminster Boys Gentlemen of the Inner Temple
		Q for Wedding of Earl of Southampton.	2 masks		
1566–67					
Christmas	W	Q	2 plays.		Paul's Boys
9–11 February	W	Q	2 plays.		Westminster Boys, Children of Chapel at Windsor
13 April	W	Q for Spanish Ambassadors.	Play.		
1567–68					
Christmas	W	Q	4 masks. *The King of Scots* (tragedy), *As Plain As Can Be, The Painful Pilgrimage, Jack and Jill, Six Fools, Wit and Will, Prodigality, Orestes.* Tragedy.		Lord Rich's Men (2), Paul's Boys (2), Westminster Boys Children of Chapel
29 February–2 March	W	Q	Play.		Children of Chapel at Windsor

1568–69

Date		Q		Company
26 December	Windsor(?)	Q	Play.	Lord Rich's Men
1 January	Windsor(?)	Q	Play.	Paul's Boys
22 February	W	Q	Play.	Children of Chapel at Windsor

1569–70

Date		Q		Company
27 December	Windsor	Q	Play.	Children of Chapel at Windsor
6 January	Windsor	Q	Play.	Children of Chapel
5 February	HC	Q	Play.	Lord Rich's Men

1570–71

Date		Q		Company
28 December	HC	Q	Play.	Paul's Boys
25–27 February	W	Q	3 plays.	Children of Chapel, Children of Chapel at Windsor, Paul's Boys

1571–72

Date		Q		Company
Christmas	W, H	Q	6 masks (prepared).	
27 December	W, H	Q	*Lady Barbara.*	Sir Robert Lane's Men
28 December	W, H	Q	*Iphigeneia.*	Paul's Boys
1 January	W, H	Q	*Ajax & Ulysses.*	Children of Chapel at Windsor
6 January	W, H	Q	*Narcissus.*	Children of Chapel
17 February	W, H	Q	*Cloridon & Radiamanta.*	Sir Robert Lane's Men
19 February	W, H	Q	*Paris & Vienna.*	Westminster Boys
15 June	W, BH 'on ye tarras'	Q for French ambassadors.	Mask of Apollo, the Muses, & Peace.	

Date	Venue	Sponsor	Title	Author	Performers
1572–73					
Christmas	HC	Q	Double mask of Fishermen and Fruitwives.		Leicester's Men (3). Paul's Boys
			Theagenes & Chariclea, Fortune.		Children of Chapel at Windsor
1 January	HC	Q	Play.		Children of Eton
6 January	HC	Q	Play.		Merchant Taylors Boys
1–3 February	G	Q	*Perseus & Andromeda* (?).		Sussex's Men
			Play.		Lincoln's Men
			Play.		
1573–74					
26 December	W	Q	Mask of Lanceknights.		Leicester's Men
			Predor & Lucia.		Paul's Boys
27 December	W	Q	*Alcmaeon.*		Leicester's Men
28 December	W	Q	*Mamillia.*		
1 January	W	Q	Mask of Foresters and Wild Men.		Westminster Boys
			Truth, Faithfulness, & Mercy.		Lord Clinton's Men
3 January	W	Q	*Herpetulus the Blue Knight & Perobia.*		

Date	Venue		Play	Company
6 January	W	Q	Mask of Sages. *Quintus Fabius.*	Children of Chapel at Windsor
2 February	HC, H	Q	*Timoclea at the Siege of Thebes by Alexander.*	Merchant Taylors Boys
21 February	HC, H	Q	*Philemon & Philecia.*	Leicester's Men
23 February	HC, H	Q	Masks of Warriors & of Ladies. *Perseus & Andromeda.*	Merchant Taylors Boys
1574–75				
11–13 July	Windsor	Q	Play.	Italian Players
Christmas	HC	Q	Masks of Pilgrims, of Mariners, & of Hobbyhorses.	
26 December	HC	Q	Play.	Leicester's Men, with boys
27 December	HC	Q	*Pretestus* (?).	Lord Clinton's Men.
1 January	HC	Q	*Panecia* (?).	Leicester's Men
2 January	HC	Q	Play.	Lord Clinton's Men
6 January	HC	Q	*Xerxes* (?).	Children of Chapel at Windsor
2 February	HC	Q	Play.	Paul's Boys
13 February	R	Q	Play.	Children of Chapel
14 February	R	Q	Play.	Warwick's Men
15 (?) February	R	Q	Play.	Merchant Taylors Boys
1575–76				
26 December	HC	Q	Play.	Warwick's Men
27 December	HC	Q	Play.	Children of Chapel at Windsor

227

Date	Venue	Sponsor	Title	Author	Performers
28 December	HC	Q	Play.		Leicester's Men
1 January	HC	Q	Play.		Warwick's Men
6 January	HC	Q	Play.		Paul's Boys
2 February	HC	Q	Play.		Sussex's Men
27 February	W	Q	Play.		Italian Players
4 March	W	Q	Play.		Leicester's Men
5 March	W	Q	Play.		Warwick's Men
6 March	W	Q	Play.		Merchant Taylors Boys
1576–77					
26 December	HC	Q	*The Painter's Daughter.*		Warwick's Men.
27 December	HC	Q	*Tooley.*		Lord Howard's Men
30 December	HC	Q	*The Collier.*		Leicester's Men
1 January	HC	Q	*The History of Error.*		Paul's Boys
6 January	HC	Q	*Mutius Scaevola.*		Children of Chapel & of Chapel at Windsor
2 February	HC	Q	*The Cynocephali.*		Sussex's Men
17 February	W	Q	*The Solitary Knight.*		Lord Howard's Men
18 February	W	Q	*The Irish Knight.*		Warwick's Men
19 February	W	Q	Mask of Boys.		
			Titus and Gisippus.		Paul's Boys
1577–78					
26 December	HC	Q	Play.		Leicester's Men
27 December	HC	Q	Play.		Children of Chapel

28 December	HC	Q	Play.	Warwick's Men
29 December	HC	Q	Play.	Paul's Boys
5 January	HC	Q	Play.	Lord Howard's Men
6 January	HC	Q	Play.	Warwick's Men
2 February	HC	Q	Play.	Sussex's Men
9 February	HC	Q	Play.	Warwick's Men
11 February	HC	Q	Play.	Lady Essex's Men
1578–79				
26 December	R	Q	*The Three Sisters of Mantua.*	Warwick's Men
27 December	R	Q	Play.	Children of Chapel
28 December	R	Q	*The Cruelty of a Stepmother.*	Sussex's Men
1 January	R	Q	*The Marriage of Mind and Measure.*	Paul's Boys
4 January	R	Q	*A Greek Maid.*	Leicester's Men
6 January	R	Q	*The Rape of the Second Helen.*	Sussex's Men
11 January	R	Q for French Ambassador	Mask of Knights and Amazons.	
1 March	W	Q	*The Knight in the Burning Rock.*	Warwick's Men
2 March	W	Q	*Loyalty and Beauty.*	Children of Chapel
3 March	W	Q	*Murderous Michael.*	Sussex's Men
1579–80				
26 December	W	Q	*The Duke of Milan & the Marquis of Mantua.*	Sussex's Men
27 December	W	Q	*Alucius.*	Children of Chapel
1 January	W	Q	*The Four Sons of Fabius.*	Warwick's Men
3 January	W	Q	*Scipio Africanus.*	Paul's Boys

Date	Venue	Sponsor	Title	Author	Performers
6 January	W	Q	Play.		Leicester's Men
2 February	W	Q	*Portio & Demorantes.*		Sussex's Men
14 February	W	Q	*The Soldan & the Duke of --.*		Derby's Men
16 February	W	Q	*Sarpedon.*		Sussex's Men
1580–81					
26 December	W, GC/H	Q	*Delight.*		Leicester's Men
27 December	W, GC/H	Q	Play.		Sussex's Men
1 January	W, GC/H	Q	Play.		Derby's Men
6 January	W, GC/H	Q	*Pompey.*		Paul's Boys
2 February	W	Q	Play.		Sussex's Men
5 February	W, GC/H	Q	Play.		Children of Chapel
7 February	W, GC/H	Q	Play.		Leicester's Men
1581–82					
26 December	W	Q	Play.		Paul's Boys
31 December	W	Q	Play.		Children of Chapel
26 February	G	Q for Wentworth-Cecil wedding	Play.		
27 February	G	Q	Play.		Children of Chapel.
1582–83					
26 December	Windsor	Q	*A Game of the Cards.*		Children of Chapel
27 December	Windsor	Q	*Beauty & Housewifery.*		Lord Hunsdon's Men
30 December	Windsor	Q	*The Rare Triumphs of Love and Fortune.*		Derby's Men

Date	Place		Play	Author	Company
5 January	Windsor	Q	Mask.		Ladies & Boys
6 January	Windsor	Q	Ferrar.		Sussex's Men
1583–84					
10 February	R	Q	Telomo.		Leicester's Men
12 February	R	Q	Ariodante & Genevora.		Merchant Taylors Boys
26 December	W	Q	Play.		Q's Men
29 December	W	Q	Play.		Q's Men
1 January	W	Q	Campaspe.	Lyly	Oxford's Boys
6 January	W	Q	Play.		Children of Chapel
2 February	W, GC	Q	The Arraignment of Paris (?).	Peele	Children of Chapel
3 March	W	Q	Sappho & Phao.	Lyly	Oxford's Boys
			Play.		Q's Men
1584–85					
26 December	G, GC/H	Q	Phyllida & Corin.		Q's Men
27 December	G, GC/H	Q	Agamemnon & Ulysses.		Oxford's Boys
3 January	G, GC/H	Q	Felix & Philiomena.		Q's Men
6 January	G, GC/H	Q	Five Plays in One.		Q's Men
23 February	SH	Q	'Antick' Play. Comedy.		Q's Men
1585–86					
26 December	G, GC/H	Q	Play.		Q's Men
27 December	G, GC/H	Q	Play.		Admiral's Men
1 January	G, GC/H	Q	Play.		Q's Men.
6 January	G, GC/H	Q	Play.		Admiral's & Chamberlain's Men
13 February	G	Q	Play.		Q's Men

Date	Venue	Sponsor	Title	Author	Performers
1586–87					
26 December	G	Q	Play.		Q's Men
27 December	G	Q	Play.		Leicester's Men
1 January	G	Q	Play.		Q's Men
6 January	G	Q	Play.		Q's Men.
26 February	G	Q	Play.		Paul's Boys
28 February	G	Q	Play.		Q's Men
1587–88					
26 December	G, GC/H	Q	Play.		Q's Men
1 January	G, GC/H	Q	Gallathea.	Lyly	Paul's Boys
6 January	G, GC/H	Q	Play.		Q's Men
2 February	G	Q	Endymion.	Lyly	Paul's Boys
18 February	G	Q	Play.		Q's Men
20 February	G	Q	Play.		Mr Evelyn's Men
28 February	G, H (?)	Q	The Misfortunes of Arthur.	Hughes, etc.	Gentlemen of Gray's Inn
1588–89					
26 December	R, GC	Q	Play.		Q's Men
27 December	R, GC	Q	Play.		Paul's Boys
29 December	R, GC	Q	Play.		Admiral's Men
1 January	R, GC	Q	Play.		Paul's Boys
12 January	R, GC (?)	Q	Play.		Paul's Boys
9 February	W	Q	Play.		Q's Men
11 February	W	Q	Play.		Admiral's Men

1589–90

Date				Play		Company
26 December	R, GC	Q		Play.		Q's Men
28 December	R, GC	Q		Play.		Paul's Boys
1 January	R, GC	Q		Play.		Paul's Boys
6 January	R, GC	Q	Lyly	Midas (?).		Paul's Boys
1 March	G, GC	Q		Play.		Q's Men
3 March	G, GC	Q		Play.		Admiral's Men

1590–91

Date			Play		Company
26 December	R, GC	Q	Play.		Q's Men
27 December	R, GC	Q	Play(s?).		Lord Strange's Men & Admiral's Men
1 January	R, GC	Q	Play.		Q's Men
3 January	R, GC	Q	Play.		Q's Men
6 January	R, GC	Q	Play.		Q's Men
14 February	G, GC	Q	Play.		Q's Men
16 February	G, GC	Q	Play(s?)		Lord Strange's Men & Admiral's Men

1591–92

Date			Play		Company
26 December	W, GC	Q	Play.		Q's Men
27 December	W, GC	Q	Play.		Lord Strange's Men
28 December	W, GC	Q	Play.		Lord Strange's Men
1 January	W, GC	Q	Play.		Lord Strange's Men
2 January	W, GC	Q	Play.		Sussex's Men
6 January	W, GC	Q	Play.		Hertford's Men
9 January	W, GC (?)	Q	Play.		Lord Strange's Men
6 February	W, GC	Q	Play.		Lord Strange's Men
8 February	W, GC	Q	Play.		Lord Strange's Men

Date	Venue	Sponsor	Title	Author	Performers
1592–93					
26 December	HC	Q	Play.		Pembroke's Men
27 December	HC	Q	Play.		Lord Strange's Men
31 December	HC	Q	Play.		Lord Strange's Men
1 January	HC	Q	Play.		Lord Strange's Men
6 January	HC	Q	Play.		Pembroke's Men
1593–94					
6 January	HC	Q	Play.		Q's Men
1594–95					
26 December	G, GC	Q	Play.		Chamberlain's Men
27 December	G, GC	Q	Play.		Chamberlain's Men
28 December	G, GC	Q	Play.		Admiral's Men
1 January	G, GC	Q	Play.		Admiral's Men
6 January	G, GC	Q	Play.		Admiral's Men
26 January	G (?), GC (?)	Q for Derby–Vere wedding	Play.		Chamberlain's Men
3 March	W, H	Q	*Proteus & the Adamantine Rock.*		Gentlemen of Gray's Inn
1595–96					
26 December	R	Q	Play.		Chamberlain's Men
27 December	R	Q	Play.		Chamberlain's Men
28 December	R	Q	Play.		Chamberlain's Men
1 January	R	Q	Play.		Admiral's Men
4 January	R	Q	Play.		Admiral's Men

6 January	R	Q	Play.	Chamberlain's Men
22 February	W (?)	Q	Plays.	Chamberlain's Men, Admiral's Men, Admiral's Men
24 February	W (?)	Q	Play.	Admiral's Men
1596–97				
26 December	W, GC	Q	Play.	Chamberlain's Men
27 December	W, GC	Q	Play.	Chamberlain's Men
1 January	W, GC	Q	Play.	Chamberlain's Men
6 January	W, GC	Q	Play.	Chamberlain's Men
6 February	R	Q	Play.	Chamberlain's Men
8 February	R	Q	Play.	Chamberlain's Men
1597–98				
26 December	W	Q	Play.	Chamberlain's Men
27 December	W	Q	Play.	Admiral's Men
1 January	W	Q	Play.	Chamberlain's Men
6 January	W, H (?)	Q	Mask of the Passions.	Gentlemen of Middle Temple
26 February	W	Q	Play.	Chamberlain's Men
27 February	W	Q	Play.	Chamberlain's Men
1598–99				
26 December	W	Q	Play.	Chamberlain's Men
27 December	W	Q	Play.	Admiral's Men
1 January	W	Q	Play.	Chamberlain's Men
6 January	W	Q	Play.	Admiral's Men

Date	Venue	Sponsor	Title	Author	Performers
18 February	R	Q	Play.		Admiral's Men
20 February	R	Q	Play.		Chamberlain's Men
1599–1600					
26 December	R	Q	Play.		Chamberlain's Men
27 December	R	Q	Old Fortunatus (?).	Dekker	Admiral's Men
1 January	R	Q	The Shoemakers' Holiday.	Dekker	Admiral's Men
6 January	R	Q	Play.		Chamberlain's Men
3 February	R	Q	Play.		Chamberlain's Men
5 February	R	Q	Play.		Derby's Men
1600–1					
26 December	W, GC	Q	Play.		Chamberlain's Men
28 December	W, GC	Q	Play.		Admiral's Men
1 January	W, GC	Q	Plays.		Paul's Boys, Derby's Men
6 January	W, H	Q	'A Showe with musycke & speciall songes'.		Children of Chapel,
			Play(s) (?).		Chamberlain's Men, Admiral's Men, Derby's Men Men
2 February	W, GC	Q	Play.		Admiral's Men
22 February	W	Q	Play.		Children of Chapel
24 February	W	Q	Play.		Chamberlain's Men

1601–2

26 December	W, GC/H	Q	Play.	Chamberlain's Men
27 December	W, GC/H	Q	Plays.	Chamberlain's Men, Admiral's Men
1 January	W, GC/H	Q	Play.	Chamberlain's Men
3 January	W, GC/H	Q	Play.	Worcester's Men
6 January	W, GC/H	Q	Play.	Children of Chapel
10 January	W	Q	Play.	Children of Chapel
14 February	W, GC	Q	Plays.	Chamberlain's Men, Children of Chapel

1602–3

29 August	Oatlands	Q	Play.	Flaminio Curtesse & Italian actors
26 December	W, GC (?)	Q	Play.	Chamberlain's Men
27 December	W, GC (?)	Q	Play.	Admiral's Men
1 January	W, GC (?)	Q	Play.	Paul's Boys
3 January	W, GC (?)	Q	Play.	Worcester's Men
6 January	W, GC (?)	Q	Play.	Hertford's Men
2 February	R, GC	Q	Play.	Chamberlain's Men
6 March	R, GC	Q	Play.	Admiral's Men
8 March (?)	R, GC	Q	Play.	Admiral's Men

1603–4

26 December	HC, H	K	Play (among those presented was *The Fair Maid of Bristow*).	K's Men
27 December	HC, H	K	Play.	K's Men
28 December	HC, H	K	Play.	K's Men

Date	Venue	Sponsor	Title	Author	Performers
30 December	HC, H	P Henry	Play.		K's Men
1 January	HC, H	K	Masque of Indian and Chinese Knights.		Lords
		P Henry	Play.		K's Men
		K	*A Midsummer Night's Dream* (?).	Shakespeare	K's Men
2 January	HC, H	P Henry	Play.		Q's Men
4 January	HC, H	P Henry	Play.		P's Men
6 January	HC, H	K	Masque of Scots.		
8 January	HC, H	K	*The Vision of the Twelve Goddesses.*	Daniel	Q, Ladies & Gentlemen
13 January	HC	P Henry	Play.		Q's Men
15 January	HC	P Henry	Play.		P's Men
21 January	HC	K	Play.		P's Men
22 January	HC	P Henry	Play.		P's Men
2 February	HC, H	K	Play.		K's Men
19 February	W, H	K	Play.		K's Men
20 February	W, H	K	Play.		P's Men
21 February	W, H	K	*The Phoenix* (?).	Middleton	Paul's Boys
			Play.		Children of Q's Revels
1604–5					
1 November	W, BH	K	*Othello.*	Shakespeare	K's Men
4 November	W, BH (?)	K	*The Merry Wives of Windsor.*	Shakespeare	K's Men
23 November	W, GC/H	Q	Play.		P's Men

Date		Title	Author	Company
24 November	W, GC/H P Henry	Play.		P's Men
14 December	W, GC/H P Henry	Play.		P's Men
19 December	W, GC/H P Henry	Play.		P's Men
26 December	W, H K	*Measure for Measure.*	Shakespeare	K's Men
27 December	W, H (?) K for Herbert-Vere Juno & Hymenaeus. wedding			Lords
28 December	W, GC/H K	*The Comedy of Errors.*	Shakespeare	K's Men
30 December	W, GC/H K	*How to Learn of a Woman to Woo.*	Heywood	Q's Men
1 January	W, GC/H K	*All Fools.*	Chapman	Children of Q's Revels
3 January	W	K (?), Spanish Ambassador	Play.		Children of Q's Revels
6 January	W, BH K	*The Masque of Blackness.*	Jonson	Q & Ladies
7 January	W, GC/H K	*Henry V.*	Shakespeare	K's Men
8 January	W, GC/H K	*Every Man Out of His Humour.*	Jonson	K's Men
15 January	W P Henry	Play.		P's Men
22 January	W P Henry	Play.		P's Men
2 February	W, GC/H K	*Every Man in His Humour.*	Jonson	K's Men
5 February	W P Henry	Play.		P's Men
10 February	W, GC/H K	*The Merchant of Venice.*	Shakespeare	K's Men
11 February	W, GC/H K	*The Spanish Maze.*		K's Men
12 February	W, GC/H K	*The Merchant of Venice*(repeat).	Shakespeare	K's Men
19 February	W P Henry	Play.		P's Men
1605–06				
1 December	W P Henry	Play.		P's Men

239

Date	Venue	Sponsor	Title	Author	Performers
Christmas	W	K, etc.	Plays.		K's Men (10, undated); Paul's Boys (2, undated)
27 December	W, GC	K	Play.		Q's Men
30 December	W, GC	P Henry	Play.		P's Men
1 January	W, GC	K	Play.		P's Men
4 January	W, GC	P Henry	Play.		P's Men
5 January	W, H (?)	K for Essex–Howard wedding	*Hymenaei.*	Jonson	Gentlemen & Ladies
3 March	W, H	K	Play.		P's Men
4 March	W, H	K	Play.		P's Men
1606–7					
July–August	G	K for K of Denmark	Plays.		K's Men (2, undated)
29 July	G	K for K of Denmark	Play.		Children of Blackfriars
30 July	G	K for K of Denmark	*Abuses.*		Paul's Boys
7 August	HC	K for K of Denmark	Play.		K's Men
26 December	W, GC	K	*King Lear.*	Shakespeare	K's Men
28 December	W, GC	K	Play.		P's Men
29 December	W, GC	K	Play.		K's Men

1 January	W, GC	K	Play.		Children of Blackfriars
4 January	W, GC	K	Play.		K's Men
6 January	W, H	K for Hay-Denny wedding	*The Masque at Lord Hay's Marriage.*	Campion	Gentlemen
8 January	W	H (?)	Play.		K's Men
13 January	W	K	Play.		K's Men
24 January	W	K (?)	Play.		P's Men
30 January	W, H	K (?)	Play.		P's Men
1 February	W, H	K	Play.		P's Men
2 February	W, H	K	*The Devil's Charter.*	Barnes	P's Men
5 February	W	K	Play.		K's Men
11 February	W	K	Play.		K's Men
15 February	W	K (?)	Play.		P's Men
27 February	W	K	Play.		K's Men
1607–08					
19 November	W	K	Play.		P's Men
26 December	W, H	K	Play.		K's Men
27 December	W, H	K	Play.		K's Men
28 December	W, H	K	Play.		K's Men
30 December	W, H	K	Play.		P's Men
2 January	W, H	K	Play.		K's Men
3 January	W, H	K	Play.		P's Men
4 January	W, H	K	Play.		P's Men
6 January	W, H	K	2 plays.		K's Men
7 January	W, H	K	Play.		K's Men

Date	Venue	Sponsor	Title	Author	Performers
9 January	W, H	K	Play.		K's Men
10 January	W, BH	K	*The Masque of Beauty*.	Jonson	Q & Ladies
17 January	W, C (?)	K	2 plays.		K's Men
26 January	W, C (?)	K	Play.		K's Men
2 February	W, H	K	Play.		K's Men
7 February	W, H	K	Play.		K's Men
9 February	W, BH	K for Haddington-Radcliffe wedding	*The Masque at Lord Haddington's Marriage*.	Jonson	Scottish & English Gentlemen
1608–09					
Christmas	W, H, C	K, etc.	Plays.		K's Men (12, undated); Q's Men (5, undated); P's Men (3, undated); Children of Blackfriars (3, 1 undated)
1 January	W, H	K	*A Trick to Catch the Old One*.	Middleton	Children of Blackfriars
4 January	W, C	K	Play.		Children of Blackfriars
2 February	W, BH	K	*The Masque of Queens*.	Jonson	Q & Ladies
1609–10					
Christmas & following	W, GC, H, C	K, etc.	Plays.		K's Men (13, undated, including *Mucedorus*); Children of Whitefriars (5, undated)

242

Date				Author	Company
27 December	W, H	K	Play.		Q's Men
28 December	W, H	K	Play.		P's Men
31 December	W, H	K	Play.		P's Men
7 January	SJ	K, P Henry	Play.		P's Men
24 January	W	K	Play.		P's Men
9 February	W (?)	P Henry, etc.	Play.		Duke of York's Men
5 June	W, BH	K, P Henry	*Tethys' Festival.*	Daniel	Q. Princess Elizabeth, P Charles, & Ladies
1610–11					
10 December	W, C (?)	P Henry	3 plays.		Q's Men
12 December	W, C (?)	P Henry, etc.	Play.		Duke of York's Men
13 December	W	K	Play.		Children of Q's Revels
19 December	W	K	Play.		P's Men
20 December	W, C (?)	P Henry, etc.	Play.		Duke of York's Men
Christmas & following	W	K, etc.	Plays.		K's Men (15, undated)
27 December	W	K	Play.		Q's Men
28 December	W	K	Play.		P's Men
1 January	W, BH	K	*Oberon the Fairy Prince.*	Jonson	P Henry & Gentlemen
14 January	W, H	K	Play.		P's Men
15 January	W, H	P Henry, etc.	Play.		Duke of York's Men
16 January	W, H	K	Play.		P's Men
2 February	W	K	Play.		Children of Q's Revels
3 February	W, BH/H (?)	K	*Love Freed from Ignorance & Folly.*	Jonson	Q & Ladies

Date	Venue	Sponsor	Title	Author	Performers
14 April	W, BH (?)	P Henry	Play.		Children of Q's Revels
1611–12					
31 October	W, BH (?)	K	Play.		K's Men
1 November	W, BH (?)	K	The Tempest.	Shakespeare	K's Men
5 November	W	K	The Winter's Tale.	Shakespeare	K's Men
9 November	W (?)	P Henry, etc.	Play.		K's Men
19 November	W (?)	P Henry, etc.	Play.		K's Men
16 December	W, C (?)	P Henry, etc.	Play.		K's Men
26 December	W, BH (?)	K	A King & No King.	Fletcher	K's Men
27 December	W, BH (?)	K	Greene's Tu Quoque.	Cooke	Q's Men
28 December	W, BH (?)	K	Play.		P's Men
29 December	W, BH (?)	K	The Almanac.		P's Men
31 December	W, C (?)	P Henry, etc.	Play.		K's Men
1 January	W, BH (?)	K	The Twins' Tragedy.	Niccols	K's Men
5 January	W, GC (?)	K (?)	Cupid's Revenge.	Fletcher	Children of Q's Revels
6 January	W, BH	K	Love Restored.	Jonson	Gentlemen
7 January	W, C (?)	P Henry, etc.	Play.		K's Men
12 January	G	Q & P Henry	The Silver Age.	Heywood	K's Men & Q's Men
	W (?)	P Charles & Princess Elizabeth	Play.		Duke of York's Men
13 January	G	Q & P Henry	The Rape of Lucrece.	Heywood	K's Men & Q's Men
15 January	G/W (?)	P Henry, etc.	Play.		K's Men
19 January	G/W (?)	P Henry, etc.	Play.		Lady Elizabeth's Men

21 January	G/W (?)	P Henry, etc.	Play.		Q's Men
23 January	W (?)	P Henry, etc.	Play.		Q's Men
28 January	W (?)	P Charles & Princess Elizabeth	Play.		Duke of York's Men
2 February	W	K	*Greene's Tu Quoque.*	Cooke	Q's Men
5 February	W, C (?)	P Henry	Play.		P's Men.
9 February	W (?)	Princess Elizabeth & P Charles	Play.		K's Men
13 February	W (?)	P Charles & Princess Elizabeth	Play.		Duke of York's Men
19 February	W (?)	P Henry, etc.	Play.		K's Men
20 February	W (?)	P Henry, etc.	2 plays.		K's Men
23 February	W, GC	K	*The Nobleman.*	Tourneur	K's Men
24 February	W (?)	P Charles & Princess Elizabeth	*Hymen's Holiday.*	Rowley	Duke of York's Men
25 February	W, GC	K	*The Proud Maid's Tragedy.*		Lady Elizabeth's Men
28 February	W (?)	P Henry, etc.	Play.		K's Men
29 February	W (?)	P Henry	Play.		P's Men
11 March	W (?)	P Henry, etc.	Play.		Lady Elizabeth's Men
28 March	W (?)	Princess Elizabeth	Play.		K's Men
3 April	W (?)	P Henry, etc.	Play.		K's Men
11 April	W (?)	Princess Elizabeth	Play.		P's Men
16 April	SJ	P Henry, etc.	Play.		K's Men
26 April	W (?)	P Henry	Play.		K's Men
1612–13					
20 October	W, C	Princess Elizabeth	Play.		Lady Elizabeth's Men

Date	Venue	Sponsor	Title	Author	Performers
November	W	P Charles, etc.	*The Coxcomb.*	Fletcher	Children of Q's Revels
Christmas & following (undated)	W	K	*The Alchemist,*	Jonson	K's Men
			Cardenio,	Shakespeare	
			A Bad Beginning Makes a Good Ending,		
			Much Ado About Nothing,	Shakespeare	
			1 Henry IV,	Shakespeare	
			The Captain,	Fletcher	
			The Maid's Tragedy,	Fletcher	
			A King & No King,	Fletcher	
		P Charles, Princess Elizabeth, & Elector Palatine	*Philaster* (twice ?),	Fletcher	K's Men
			The Knot of Fools,		
			The Merry Devil of Edmonton,	Dekker, etc.	
			Much Ado About Nothing,	Shakespeare	
			The Winter's Tale,	Shakespeare	
			Othello,	Shakespeare	
			Julius Caesar,	Shakespeare	

Date			Play	Author	Company
1 January	W	K	*The Tempest,*	Shakespeare	Children of Q's Revels
9 January	W (?)	P Charles	*2 Henry IV* (?),	Shakespeare	Children of Q's Revels
14 February	W, BH	K for wedding of Princess Elizabeth & Elector Palatine	*The Twins' Tragedy, / The Nobleman. / Cupid's Revenge. / Cupid's Revenge. / The Lords' Masque.*	Niccols / Tourneur / Fletcher / Fletcher / Campion	Gentlemen & Ladies
15 February	W, H	K, as above	*Masque of the Middle Temple & Lincoln's Inn.*	Chapman	Gentlemen of the Inns
16 February	W, H (?)	K, as above	Play.		K's Men
20 February	W, BH	K, as above	*Masque of the Inner Temple & Gray's Inn.*	Beaumont	Gentlemen of the Inns
25 February	W, C (?)	P Charles, Princess Elizabeth, & Elector Palatine	*The Dutch Courtesan.*	Marston	Lady Elizabeth's Men
27 February	W, C (?)	P Charles, etc.	*The Widow's Tears.*	Chapman	Children of Q's Revels
1 March	W, C (?)	P Charles, etc.	*Raymond Duke of Lyons.*		Lady Elizabeth's Men
2 March	W	K	*1 The Knaves.*		P's Men
5 March	W	K	*2 The Knaves.*		P's Men
8 June	G	K for Ambassador of Savoy	*Cardenio.*	Shakespeare	K's Men
1613–14					
1 November	W	K	Play.		K's Men
4 November	W (?)	P Charles	Play.		K's Men

Date	Venue	Sponsor	Title	Author	Performers
5 November	W	K	Play.		K's Men
15 November	W	K	Play.		K's Men
16 November	W (?)	P Charles	Play.		K's Men
12 December	SJ (?)	P Charles	*The Dutch Courtesan.*	Marston	Lady Elizabeth's Men
24 December	W, H (?)	K	Play.		K's Men
26 December	W, BH	K for Somerset–Howard wedding	*The Masque of Squires.*	Campion	Gentlemen
27 December	W, H (?)	K	Play.		K's Men
29 December	W, BH	K for Somerset–Howard wedding	*The Irish Masque.*	Jonson	Gentlemen
1 January	W, H (?)	K	Play.		K's Men
3 January	W, BH	K for Somerset–Howard wedding	*The Irish Masque* (repeat).	Jonson	Gentlemen
4 January	W, H (?)	K	Play.		K's Men
5 January	W, H (?)	K	Play.		Q's Men
6 January	W, BH	K for Somerset–Howard wedding	*The Masque of Flowers.*	Gentlemen of Gray's Inn	
10 January	W (?)	P Charles	Play.		K's Men
25 January	W	K	*Eastward Ho.*	Chapman, etc.	Lady Elizabeth's Men

Date	Place	For whom	Performance	Author	Company
2 February	W, BH	K	Play.		K's Men
3 February	SH, Temporary Courtyard Theatre	Q for K & Roxborough–Drummond wedding	*Hymen's Triumph.*	Daniel	
4 February	W (?)	P Charles	Play.		K's Men
8 February	W	K	Play.		K's Men
10 February	W (?)	P Charles	Play.		K's Men
18 February	W (?)	P Charles	Play.		K's Men
6 March	W, BH	K	Play.		K's Men
8 March	W, BH	K	Play.		K's Men
1614–15					
24–30 July	SH, W (?), G (?)	K of Denmark	Plays.		
1 November	W, BH	K	*Bartholomew Fair.*	Jonson	Lady Elizabeth's Men
Christmas & following	W, BH, H, SH	K, etc.	Plays.		K's Men (8, undated), Q's Men (3, undated), P's Men (6, undated), Elector Palatine's Men (3, undated)
6 January	W, BH	K	*Mercury Vindicated from the Alchemists at Court.*	Jonson	Gentlemen
8 January	W, BH	K	*Mercury Vindicated* (repeat).	Jonson	Gentlemen
19–21 February	W	Spanish Ambassador	Masque(s?)		

Date	Venue	Sponsor	Title	Author	Performers
1615–16					
November–May	W, H, BH,C; SJ, Council Chamber	K, etc.	Plays.		K's Men (13, undated), Q's Men (6, undated), P's Men (4, undated)
17 December	SH, H (?)	Q	Play.		Q's Men
21 December	SH, H (?)	Q	Play.		K's Men
1 January	W, BH	K	*The Golden Age Restored.*	Jonson	Gentlemen
6 January	W, BH	K	*The Golden Age Restored* (repeat).	Jonson	Gentlemen
12 March	Royston, Presence Chamber	K	*Susenbrotus.*	Chappell	Cambridge Students
1616–17					
October–January	SJ, W	P Charles	Plays.		P's Men (13, undated)
November– December (?)	G, GC Queen's Side.	Q	Play.		
November	G, H	Q	Masque.		
November– February	SH	Q	Play.		
25 December	W, BH, H, C	K, etc.	Plays.		K's Men (11, undated)
	W, BH (?) K		*Christmas His Masque.*	Jonson	K's Men (?)

Date			Event	Title	Author	Company
28 December	W (?)	P Charles	Play.			P's Men
1 January	W	K (?)	Play.			K's Men
5 January	W, H (?)	K		*The Mad Lover.*	Fletcher	
6 January	W, BH	K		*The Vision of Delight.*	Jonson	Q & Lords
			Play (?)			Q & Lords
19 January	W, BH	K		*The Vision of Delight* (repeat).	Jonson	Q & Lords
19 February	SH, H	Q	Masque ('or antique').			French Musicians
4 March	SH, Presence Chamber	K & Q	Play.			Anthony Cossart & French Company
5–11 March	W	K	Play.			Cossart & Company
March & preceding		Q, P Charles	Plays.			Q's Men (3, undated)
4 May	G	Q		*Cupid's Banishment.*	White	Young Ladies
1617–18						
6 September (?)	Woodstock, Masquing Room	K	Masque.			
29 September	HC, H (?)	K for Villiers–Coke wedding	Masque.			
October–February	W, GC, H,BH, C SJ	K, P Charles	Plays.			K's Men (15, undated), Q's Men (2, 'at Christmas')
6 January	W, BH	K		*Pleasure Reconciled to Virtue.*	Jonson	P Charles & Gentlemen
17 February	W, BH	K		*For the Honour of Wales.*	Jonson	P Charles & Gentlemen

Date	Venue	Sponsor	Title	Author	Performers
19 February	W, BH	K	The First Antimasque of Mountebanks.		Gentlemen of Gray's Inn
6 April	W	K	Twelfth Night.	Shakespeare	K's Men
7 April	W	K	The Winter's Tale.	Shakespeare	K's Men
3 May	W	K	The Merry Devil of Edmonton.	Dekker, etc.	K's Men
1618–19					
July–August (?)	HC, H	Q (?)	Play.		
September	W, GC	K, etc. (?)	3 plays.		
1 November	W, H (?)	K	Play.		P's Men
30 November	W	Sir John Digby	Play.		
November–Christmas	W, H, C	K	Plays.		K's Men (8, undated)
1 January	W, H (?)	K	Play.		P's Men
3 January	W, H (?)	K	Play.		Palsgrave's Men
6 January	W, BH	K	Masque.		P Charles & Lords
Candlemas (early February)	W	K	3 plays.		
8 February	W, H	K	Masque (repeat).		P Charles & Lords
20 May	W, GC	Duke of Lennox for French Ambassador	Pericles.	Shakespeare	K's Men

1619–20					
November–March	W, GC Queen's Side, etc.	K	Plays.		K's Men (10, undated), P's Men, (4, undated)
2 January	W	K	*The Two Merry Milkmaids.*	I. C.	Robert Lee's Company (formerly Q's Men)
6 January	W, H (?)	K	*News from the New World. Discovered in the Moon.*	Jonson	P Charles & Lords
10 January	SH, H (?)	P Charles	'Running Masque'.		Duke of Buckingham & Lords
29 February	W, H (?)	K	*News from the New World. Discovered in the Moon* (repeat).	Jonson	P Charles & Lords
4 March	SH	P Charles for Lords	Play.		
April (?)	HC	K	Play.		
1620–21					
29 September	W	K	Play.		
October–March	W, GC, GC Queen's Side, H	K, P Charles	Plays.		K's Men (9, undated), P's Men (2 undated)
6 January	W, H	K	Masque.		P Charles & Lords
11 February	W, H	K	Masque (repeat).		P Charles & Lords
13 February	W, H	K	Masque.		Gentlemen of Middle Temple

Date	Venue	Sponsor	Title	Author	Performers
1621–22					
26 August	Woodstock, H	K	*Technogamia.*	Holyday	Oxford Students
2 September	Windsor	K	*The Gypsies Metamorphosed.*	Jonson	Ladies & Gentlemen
5 November	W	K	*The Woman's Plot.*		K's Men
26 November	W	P Charles	*The Woman Is Too Hard for Him.*	Massinger	K's Men
Christmas (?)	SJ, Council Chamber	P Charles	Plays.		
26 December	W, H (?)	K	*The Island Princess.*	Fletcher	K's Men
27 December	W, H (?)	K	*The Man in the Moon Drinks Claret.*		P's Men
29 December	W, H (?)	K	*The Witch of Edmonton.*	Dekker, etc.	P's Men
30 December	W, H (?)	K	*Grammercy Wit.*		Company of Revels
1 January	W, H (?)	K	*The Pilgrim.*	Fletcher	K's Men
6 January	W, BH	K	*The Masque of Augurs.*	Jonson	P Charles & Gentlemen
24 January	W	K	*The Wild Goose Chase.*	Fletcher	K's Men
5 February	W	P Charles (?)	*The Coxcomb.*	Fletcher	K's Men
6 May	W, BH	K	*The Masque of Augurs* (repeat).	Jonson	P Charles & Gentlemen
1622–23					
September–Christmas (?)	SJ, Council Chamber	P Charles	Plays.		
26 December	W, H	K	*The Spanish Curate.*	Fletcher	K's Men

27 December	W, H	K	*Beggars' Bush.*	Fletcher	K's Men
29 December	W, H	K	*The Pilgrim.*	Fletcher	K's Men
1 January	W, H	K	*The Alchemist.*	Jonson	K's Men
6 January	W, H (?)	K	*A Vow & a Good One.*		P's Men
19 January	W, BH	K	*Time Vindicated to Himself & to His Honours.*	Jonson	P Charles & Gentlemen
December(?)– January	W, GC Queen's Side/H	K	2 plays.		Lady Elizabeth's Men
2 February	W, BH	K	*Twelfth Night.*	Shakespeare	K's Men
February– March (?)	W	K	Plays.		K's Men (4, undated)
1623–24					
29 September	HC, GC/ Presence Chamber	K	*The Maid in the Mill.*	Fletcher	K's Men
1 November	SJ	P Charles	*The Maid in the Mill.*	Fletcher	K's Men
5 November	W, H (?)	P Charles	*The Spanish Gypsy.*	Middleton	Q of Bohemia's Men
Christmas & following	W	K	Plays.		K's Men (3–8, undated)
26 December	W, H	K	*The Maid in the Mill.*	Fletcher	K's Men
27 December	W, H	P Charles	*The Bondman.*	Massinger	Q of Bohemia's Men
28 December	W, H	K	*The Buck Is a Thief.*		K's Men
1 January	W, H	P Charles	*The Lovers' Progress.*	Fletcher	K's Men
4 January	W, H	P Charles	*The Changeling.*	Middleton	Q of Bohemia's Men
6 January	W, H	P Charles	*More Dissemblers Besides Women.*	Middleton	K's Men

Date	Venue	Sponsor	Title	Author	Performers
18 January	W, H (?)	Duchess of Richmond	*The Winter's Tale.*	Shakespeare	K's Men
1624–25					
2 November	W	Lord Chamberlain 'for the ladies'	*Rule a Wife & Have a Wife.*	Fletcher	K's Men
26 December	W	P Charles	*Rule a Wife & Have a Wife.*	Fletcher	K's Men
27 December	W	P Charles	*Volpone.*	Jonson	K's Men
28 December	W	P Charles	*Cupid's Revenge.*	Fletcher	K's Men
1 January	W	P Charles	*1 Henry IV.*	Shakespeare	K's Men
6 January	W	P Charles	*Greene's Tu Quoque.*	Cooke	Q of Bohemia's Men
9 January	W, BH	K	*The Fortunate Isles & Their Union.*	Jonson	P Charles & Gentlemen
12 January	W	K (?)	*Play.*		K's Men
12 February	New-market	K	*Play.*		Cambridge Students
March (?)	W	K (?)	*Play.*		K's Men
1625–26					
Christmas	HC, H	K Charles	*Plays.*		K's Men (10, undated)
21 February	SH, H	K	*L'Artenice.*	Racan	Q & Ladies
1626–27					
6 November	W	K (?)	'The Duke's Play'.		
16 November	SH, Presence Chamber	Q for French Ambassador	*Masque.*		

Date	Venue		Title	Author	Company
19 November	W	Q (?)	'The Queen's Play'.		K's Men (12, undated)
Christmas–Shrove	W, GC/H K		Plays.		
14 January	W, BH/SH (?)		Masque.		K & Q, etc
April–June	W, H	K (?)	2 plays.		
1627–28					
August–September	Nonsuch	K & Q (?)	Play.		K's Men (10, undated)
29 September–31 January	W, GC, H, BH	K	Plays.		K's Men (10, undated)
2 February	W, H	K	Play.		
15 April	W	K	*The Dumb Bawd of Venice.*	H. Shirley	K's Men
1628–29					
August–September (?)	HC, GC	K & Q (?)	Play.		
29 September–February	W, GC, H, BH	K	Plays.		K's Men (16, undated)
6 April	W, GC/H/BH	K	*The Lovesick Maid.*	Brome	K's Men
1629–30					
29 September	HC	K	'Comedy'.		
29 October–February	W, GC/H K & Q		Plays.		Q's Men (10, undated)
1 November	W	K	Play.		
Christmas	W, GC/H, K SH		Plays.		K's Men (12, undated)

Date	Venue	Sponsor	Title	Author	Performers
22 February (?)	W, BH (?)	K	Masque.		
1630–31					
September–October	HC, H (?)	K & Q	3 plays.		Q's Men
30 September	HC, H (?)	K & Q	*The Inconstant Lady.*	Wilson	K's Men
3 October	HC, H (?)	K & Q	*Alphonsus Emperor of Germany.*		K's Men
17 October	HC, H (?)	K & Q	*A Midsummer Night's Dream.*	Shakespeare	K's Men
24 October	HC, H (?)	K & Q	*The Custom of the Country.*	Fletcher	K's Men
November–February	W, C (?)	K & Q	Plays.		Q's Men (13, undated)
5 November	W, C	K & Q	*The Mad Lover.*	Fletcher	K's Men
7 November	W, C (?)	K & Q	*Rollo.*	Fletcher	K's Men
19 November	W, C	K & Q	*Volpone.*	Jonson	K's Men
28 November	W, C (?)	K & Q	*Beauty in a Trance.*	Ford	K's Men
9 December	W, C	K & Q	*The Maid's Tragedy.*	Fletcher	K's Men
14 December	W, C	K & Q	*Philaster.*	Fletcher	K's Men
26 December	W, C	K & Q	*The Duchess of Malfi.*	Webster	K's Men
27 December	W, C	K & Q	*The Scornful Lady.*	Fletcher	K's Men
30 December	W, C	K & Q	*The Chances.*	Fletcher	K's Men
6 January	W, C	K & Q	*1 Henry IV* (?).	Shakespeare	K's Men
9 January	W, BH	Q	*Love's Triumph through Callipolis.*	Jonson	K & Gentlemen

Date	Place	For	Play	Author	Company
3 February	W, C (?)	K & Q	*The Fatal Dowry.*	Massinger	K's Men
15 February	W, C	K & Q	*The Merry Devil of Edmonton.*	Dekker, etc.	K's Men
17 February	W, C	K & Q	*Every Man in His Humour.*	Jonson	K's Men
21 February	W, C	K & Q	*Rollo.*	Fletcher	K's Men
22 February	W, BH	K	*Chloridia.*	Jonson	Q & Ladies
May	W (?)		Masque (rehearsed, if not performed).		
1631–32					
October	HC, H	K	Plays.		K's Men (1, undated), Q's Men (1, undated)
Christmas	W, C (?)	K	Plays.		K's Men (10, undated), Q's Men (8, undated), Children of K's Revels (3, undated)
8 January	W, BH	Q	*Albion's Triumph.*	Townshend	K & Gentlemen
14 February	W, BH	K	*Tempe Restored.*	Townshend	Q & Ladies
March (?)	New-market, Q's Presence Chamber	K & Q (?)	'Comedy'.		
3 May	W, C	Lord Chamberlain for K & Q	Play.		K's Men
1632–33					
September–October (?)	HC	K	Plays.		K's Men (2, undated)

Date	Venue	Sponsor	Title	Author	Performers
Christmas, etc.	W, C, SH	K & Q	Plays.		K's Men (20, undated, May–March), Q's Men (14, undated, November–February)
9 January	SH, Paved Court Theatre	K	*The Shepherd's Paradise.*	Montagu	Q & Ladies
5 March	SH, Paved Court Theatre	K	Masque.		Q & Ladies
1633–34					
September (?)	HC (?)	K	3 plays.		P's Men
16 November	SJ, Presence Chamber	K & Q	*Richard III.*	Shakespeare	K's Men
19 November	SJ, Presence Chamber	K & Q	*The Young Admiral.*	Shirley	Q's Men
26 November	SJ, Presence Chamber	K & Q	*The Taming of the Shrew.*	Shakespeare	K's Men
28 November	SJ, Presence Chamber	K & Q	*The Tamer Tamed.*	Fletcher	K's Men

Date			Play	Author	Company
10 December	W, C (?)	K & Q	*The Loyal Subject.*	Fletcher	K's Men
16 December	W, C	K & Q	*Hymen's Holiday.*	W. Rowley	Q's Men
Christmas, etc.	W	K & Q	Plays.		K's Men (11, undated, May–April), Q's Men (2, undated, November–March)
1 January	W, C	K & Q	*Cymbeline.*	Shakespeare	K's Men
6 January	SH, Presence Chamber	Q for K & Nobles	*The Faithful Shepherdess.*	Fletcher	K's Men
12 January	W, C	K & Q	*The Guardian.*	Massinger	K's Men
14 January	W, C	K & Q	*A Tale of a Tub.*	Jonson	Q's Men
16 January	W, C	K & Q	*The Winter's Tale.*	Shakespeare	K's Men
28 January	W, C	K & Q	*The Wits.*	Davenant	K's Men
30 January	W, C	K & Q	*The Night Walker.*	Fletcher	Q's Men
3 February	W, BH	K & Q	*The Triumph of Peace.*	Shirley	Gentlemen of the Inns of Court
6 February	W, C	K & Q	*The Gamester.*	Shirley	Q's Men
18 February	W, BH	Q	*Coelum Britannicum.*	Carew	K & Gentlemen
7 April	W, C	K & Q	*Bussy D'Ambois.*	Chapman	K's Men
8 April	W, C	K & Q	*The Faithful Shepherdess* (repeat).	Fletcher	K's Men
May	W	K & Q	Play(s ?).		K's Men (14, undated, May–March)

261

Date	Venue	Sponsor	Title	Author	Performers
1634–35					
16 September–24 October	HC, H (?)	K & Q	Plays.		K's Men (5, undated), Q's Men (1, undated), P's Men (3, undated)
22 (?) October	HC, H (?)	K & Q	Play.		Juan Navarro & Spanish Players
9 November	W, C	K & Q (?)	*Catiline.*	Jonson	K's Men
19 November	SH	K & Q	*Love's Mistress.*	Heywood	Q's Men
20–26 November	SH	K & Q	*Love's Mistress* (repeat).	Heywood	Q's Men
Christmas, etc.	W	K & Q	Plays.		K's Men (14, undated, May–March), Q's Men (7, undated)
8 January	W	K for Herbert–Villiers Wedding	Plays.		
January	W, C/SJ	K & Q (?)	Play(s?).		P's Men (1–2, undated)
10 February	W, BH	K	*The Temple of Love.*	Davenant	Q & Ladies
11, 12, & 14 February	W, BH	K (?)	*The Temple of Love* (repeats).	Davenant	Q & Ladies
17 February	W, C	K & Q	*La Melise.*	Du Rocher	Josias Floridor & French Players
February	W, C/SJ	K & Q (?)	Play(s?).		P's Men (1–2, undated)
30 March	W, C	K & Q	*Le Trompeur Puni.*	Scudéry	Josias Floridor & French Players

Date	Venue	Auspices	Title	Author	Company
15/16 April	W, C	K & Q	*Alcimedon.*	Durier	Josias Floridor & French Players
May	W, C/SJ	K & Q (?)	Plays.		K's Men (8, undated, May–March), (P's Men (1–2, undated)
1635–36					
12 August	SH (?)	Q	Play.		Q's Ladies
September–October	HC	K & Q (?)	Plays.		K's Men (4, undated), Q's Men (4, undated), Company of K's Revels (2, October).
19 November	W, H (?)	Q for K	French play.		Q's Ladies
November	W, C (?)	K	Play.		Juan Navarro & Spanish Players
21 December	W, H	Q for K	*Florimène.*		Q's Ladies
December	W, C (?)	K	Tragedy.		Josias Floridor & French Players
Christmas, etc.	W	K & Q	Plays.		K's Men (8, undated, May–March), Q's Men (5, undated), Beeston's Boys (1, undated)
18 February	SJ	K & Q	*Epicoene.*	Jonson	K's Men
22/25 February	SJ	K & Q	*The Duke's Mistress.*	Shirley	
24 February	SJ	K & Q	*The Proxy.*		Company of K's Revels
28 February	SJ	K & Q	*The Knight of the Burning Pestle.*	Beaumont	Beeston's Boys
18 April	W, C	K & Q	*1 Arviragus & Philicia.*	Carlell	K's Men

Date	Venue	Sponsor	Title	Author	Performers
19 April	W, C	K & Q	*2 Arviragus & Philicia.*	Carlell	K's Men
21 April	W, C	K & Q	*Epicoene.*	Jonson	K's Men
1636–37					
12 September	R, H (?)	K & Q	*The King & Queen's Entertainment at Richmond.*		P Charles & Gentlemen
17 November	HC, H (?)	K & Q	*The Coxcomb.*	Fletcher	K's Men
19 November	HC, H (?)	K & Q	*Beggars' Bush.*	Fletcher	K's Men
29 November	HC, H (?)	K & Q	*The Maid's Tragedy.*	Fletcher	K's Men
6 December	HC, H (?)	K & Q	*The Loyal Subject.*	Fletcher	K's Men
26 December	HC, H (?)	K & Q	*1 Arviragus & Philicia.*	Carlell	K's Men
27 December	HC, H (?)	K & Q	*2 Arviragus & Philicia.*	Carlell	K's Men
1 January	HC, H (?)	K & Q	*Love & Honour.*	Davenant	K's Men
5 January	HC, H (?)	K & Q	*The Elder Brother.*	Fletcher	K's Men
10 January	HC, H (?)	K & Q	*A King & No King.*	Fletcher	K's Men
12 January	HC, H	K & Q	*The Royal Slave.*	Cartwright	K's Men
17 January	HC, H (?)	K & Q	*Rollo.*	Fletcher	K's Men
24 January	HC, H (?)	K & Q	*Hamlet.*	Shakespeare	K's Men
31 January	SJ	K & Q	*Julius Caesar.*	Shakespeare	K's Men
7 February	SJ	K & Q	*Cupid's Revenge.*	Fletcher	Beeston's Boys
9 February	SJ	K & Q	*A Wife for a Month.*	Fletcher	K's Men
14 February	SJ	K & Q	*Wit without Money.*		Beeston's Boys
16 February	SJ	K & Q	*The Governor.*	Formido (?)	K's Men
21 February	SJ	K & Q	*Philaster.*	Fletcher	K's Men

264

1637–38

Date	Location	Audience	Play	Author	Company
30 September	HC	K & Q	Play.		K's Men
November–December	SJ, Presence Chamber	P Charles	2 plays.		P's Men
Christmas, etc.	R, GC (?)	P Charles (?)	Play.		P's Men
	W	K & Q	Plays.		K's Men (12, undated, October–February, including *Aglaura*, Suckling, & *The Lost Lady*, Berkeley)
7 January	W, Masquing House	Q	*Britannia Triumphans.*	Davenant	K & Lords
3 February	W, C (?)	K & Q (?)	Play.		K's Men
6 February	W, Masquing House	K	*Luminalia.*	Davenant (?)	Q & Ladies
26 March	W, C	K & Q	*The Lost Lady.*	Berkeley	K's Men
27 March	W, C	K & Q	*Bussy D'Ambois.*	Chapman	K's Men
3 April	W, C	K & Q	*Aglaura.*	Suckling	K's Men
29 May	W, C	K, Q, P Charles (?)	*1 Henry IV* (?).	Shakespeare	K's Men
31 May	W, C	K & Q	*The Unfortunate Lovers.*	Davenant	K's Men

1638–39

Date	Location	Audience	Play	Author	Company
26 July	SH, H	K & Q	1 *The Passionate Lovers.*	Carlell	K's Men
28 July	SH, H	K & Q	2 *The Passionate Lovers.*	Carlell	K's Men

Date	Venue	Sponsor	Title	Author	Performers
30 September	HC, H (?)	K & Q	*The Unfortunate Lovers.*	Davenant	K's Men
October (?)	HC	K & Q	5(?) plays.		K's Men
6 November	R, GC (?)	P Charles (?)	*The Merry Devil of Edmonton.*	Dekker, etc.	K's Men
8 November	W, C	K & Q	*Volpone.*	Jonson	K's Men
13 November	W, C	K & Q	*Julius Caesar.*	Shakespeare	K's Men
15 November	W, C	K & Q	*The Merry Wives of Windsor.*	Shakespeare	K's Men
20 November	W, C	K & Q	*The Fair Favourite.*	Davenant	K's Men
22 November	W, C	K & Q	*The Chances.*	Fletcher	K's Men
27 November	W, C	K & Q	*The Custom of the Country.*	Fletcher	K's Men
29 November	W, C	K & Q	*The Northern Lass.*	Brome	K's Men
6 December	W, C	K & Q	*The Spanish Curate.*	Fletcher	K's Men
11 December	W, C	K & Q	*The Fair Favourite* (repeat).	Davenant	K's Men
18 December	W, C	K & Q	Play.		K's Men/Q's Men (?)
20 December	SH, H	K & Q	*1 The Passionate Lovers.*	Carlell	K's Men
22 December	SH, H	K & Q	*2 The Passionate Lovers.*	Carlell	K's Men
Christmas, etc.	W, R	K & Q	Plays.		Q's Men (7, undated, 1638–39)
27 December (?)	W, C/R	K & Q (?)	Play.		K's Men/Q's Men (?)
28 December	R, GC (?)	K & Q	*The Northern Lass.*	Brome	K's Men
1 January	R, GC (?)	K & Q	*Beggar's Bush.*	Fletcher	K's Men
7 January	R, GC (?)	K & Q	*The Spanish Curate.*	Fletcher	K's Men
1639–40					
14 October	R, GC	P Charles for Duke of York	Play.		

Date	Venue	Audience	Play	Author	Company
November–December	R, GC	P Charles	5 plays.		P's Men (3, undated), etc.
Christmas, etc.	W, R	K & Q	Plays.		K's Men (20, undated, August–February), Q's Men (7, undated, 1638–39)
21 January	W, Masquing House	Q Mother, Marie de Medici, & royal children	*Salmacida Spolia.*	Davenant	K & Q, etc
January	R, GC	P Charles	2 plays.		
11 February	W, C (?)	K & Q	Play.		K's Men
16–18 February	R, GC	P Charles	Play.		
18 February	W, Masquing House	Court	*Salmacida Spolia* (repeat).	Davenant	K & Q, etc.
9 April	W, H	K & Q	*The Queen of Aragon.*	Habington	Servants of Lord Chamberlain
10 April	W, H	K & Q	*The Queen of Aragon* (repeat).	Habington	Servants of Lord Chamberlain
May–June (29 May?)	R, GC	P Charles	Play.		
1640–41					
October–March	R, GC	P Charles, etc.	Plays.		
November–February	W (?)	K, Q, P Charles	Plays.		K's Men (up to 16, undated)
1641–42					
6 January	W, C	P Charles	*The Scornful Lady.*	Fletcher	K's Men.

Notes

Introduction

1 John Guy, 'Introduction. The 1590s: the Second Reign of Elizabeth I?' in John Guy, ed., *The Reign of Elizabeth I. Court and Culture in the Last Decade* (Cambridge, 1995), pp. 1–2.

2 C. H. McIlwain, ed., *Political Works of James I* (Cambridge, MA, 1918), p. 43.

3 See Alan Young, *Tudor and Jacobean Tournaments* (London, 1987).

4 See *HKW*, vol. IV, pp. 222–25; Sydney Anglo, *Spectacle, Pageantry, and Early Tudor Policy*. 2nd edn (Oxford, 1996); Gordon Kipling, *The Triumph of Honour* (Leiden, 1977).

5 See *ES*, vol. I, chapters 10 and 11, 'The Actor's Quality' and 'The Actor's Economics'. For more recent commentary on the relationship between actors and patrons, see J. Leeds Barroll, *Politics, Plague, and Shakespeare's Theater* (Ithaca, 1991), and, on conditions in the mid sixteenth century, William Ingram, *The Business of Playing* (Ithaca, 1992).

1 The royal administration

1 My account of the court in this chapter relies on those of Chambers, *ES*, vol. I, pp. 1–105; D. M. Loades, *The Tudor Court* (London, 1987); and David Starkey, D. A. L. Morgan, John Murphy, Pam Wright, Neil Cuddy and Kevin Sharpe, *The English Court: From the Wars of the Roses to the Civil War* (London, 1987).

2 See *MSC II. 3* (Oxford, 1931), pp. 413–15.

3 See Neil Cuddy, 'The Revival of the Entourage: the Bedchamber of James I, 1603–1625' in Starkey *et al.*, *English Court*, pp. 173–91.

4 The nominal successor to Buc was Sir John Astley, but if he acted as Master at all he can have done so only for a short period. Though retaining the title of the post, he came to some arrangement to deputise his responsibilities and all the practical exercise of the job to Sir Henry Herbert. See Richard Dutton, *Mastering the Revels* (London, 1991), pp. 218–35.

5 *ES*, vol. I, pp. 71–105. A recent survey of the earlier career of the Office, and an account of its changing functions, is to be found in W. R. Streitberger, *Court Revels, 1485–1559* (Toronto, 1994).

6 On Kirkham, see *MSC XIII* (Oxford, 1986), appendix II, p. 163.

7 Streitberger, *Court Revels*, p. 15.

8 The standard account of the Office of the Works is *HKW*, where many original accounts and other records are cited. A selection of the Works entries relating to theatrical preparations is published in *MSC X* (Oxford, 1975 [1977]).

9 For a general view of the bureaucracy of the court as it was organised under Charles I, the organisation of its various departments, and allowances and wages paid to various officers, see G. E. Aylmer, *The King's Servants*, rev. edn (London, 1974).

10 Ibid., p. 207.

11 See Dutton, *Revels*, chapter 2.

12 See W. R. Streitberger, 'Introduction' to *MSC XIII*, pp. xvi–xxiii.

13 *MSC XIII*, p. 99.

14 Streitberger, *Court Revels*, pp. 161–65.

15 These were published in modern facsimile at the start of this century: Feuillerat, *Elizabeth*, and Feuillerat, *Edward and Mary*.

16 Streitberger, *Court Revels*, pp. 201–2.

17 Ibid., p. 227.

18 Feuillerat, *Elizabeth*, pp. 5–17.

19 See W. R. Streitberger, *Edmond Tyllney, Master of the Revels and Censor of Plays* (New York, 1986).

20 See Ingram, *Business*.

21 Patent of Commission cited in *ES*, vol. IV, pp. 285–87.

22 Ibid., p. 285.

23 *MSC XIII*, p. 12.

24 See Dutton, *Revels*, chapters 6 and 8.

25 Ibid., pp. 219–20.

26 Ibid., p. 220.

27 Herbert's records have recently been collected and edited by N. W. Bawcutt, *The Control and Censorship of Caroline Drama. The Records of Sir Henry Herbert, Master of the Revels 1623–73* (Oxford, 1996), superseding the older edited collection by J. Q. Adams; see chapter 5.

28 See Ingram, *Business*, pp. 67–72.

29 On a particularly splendid banqueting house erected at Greenwich for the occasion of a treaty signed with French ambassadors, see Simon Thurley, 'The Banqueting and Disguising Houses of 1527', in D. Starkey, ed., *Henry VIII. A European Court in England*, (London, 1991) (hereafter cited as *Henry VIII*), pp. 64–69.

30 Holinshed's account of 1587 cited in *HKW*, vol. IV, p. 320.

31 See John Orrell, *The Theatres of Inigo Jones and John Webb* (Cambridge, 1985).

32 The surviving plan of and accompanying notes on the theatre were identified by John Orrell, 'The Theatre at Christ Church, Oxford, in 1605', *Shakespeare Survey*, 35 (1982), 129–40; see also Orrell, *Theatres*, chapter 2.

33 Orrell, *Theatres*, p. 29.

2   Royal places

1 *HKW*, vol. IV, pp. 222–34.

2 See Thurley, *Palaces*, pp. 1–27.

3 See ibid., pp. 113–20.

4 See, e.g., T. J. King, *Shakespearean Staging, 1599–1642* (Cambridge, MA, 1971); Richard Southern, *The Staging of Plays before Shakespeare* (London, 1973); D. F. Rowan, 'The Players and Playing Places of Norwich' in John H. Astington, ed., *The Development of Shakespeare's Theater* (New York, 1992), pp. 77–94; Richard Beadle, ed., *The Cambridge Companion to English Medieval Theatre* (Cambridge, 1994); Alan Somerset, '"How Chances It They Travel?" Provincial Touring, Playing Places, and the King's Men', *Shakespeare Survey*, 47 (1994), 45–60.

5 See Thurley, *Palaces*, chapters 7 and 8.

6 See *Royal Commission on Historical Monuments (England). London. Volume II. West London* (London, 1925), p. 127; *Survey of London*, vol. XIII, *St Margaret Westminster, Part II* (London, 1930), pp. 145–47, plates 54 and 55; Richard Trench and Ellis Hillman, *London under London* (London, 1984), pp. 210–11.

7 For a discussion of the character of the room, see below (and Plate 5); also John H. Astington, 'A Drawing of the Great Chamber at Whitehall in 1601', *Records of Early English Drama Newsletter*, 16,1 (1991), 6–11.

8 *The Dramatic Works of Richard Brome*, 3 vols. (London, 1873), vol. I, p. 322; *The City Wit*, 3.2.

9 *Finetti Philoxenis* (London, 1656), p. 138.

10 *HKW*, vol. IV, pp. 303–43.

11 Ibid., pp. 286–88.

12 See Thurley, *Palaces*, pp. 85–111.

13 Coloured reproductions of the whole and of details of this painting may be seen in ibid., pp. 212–15.

14 *Survey of London*, vol. XIII, pp. 51–53.

15 See Orrell, *Theatres*, chapter 7.

16 PRO E351/3267.

17 See *HKW*, vol. IV, pp. 319–38.

18 On the history of the Cockpit see *Survey of London*, vol. XIV, *The Parish of St. Margaret, Westminster, Part III* (London, 1931), pp. 23–29, 101–3; *JCS*, vol. VI, pp. 267–84; John H. Astington, 'Inigo Jones and the Whitehall Cockpit', in

G. R. Hibbard, ed., *The Elizabethan Theatre VII* (Port Credit, 1980), pp. 46–64; John H. Astington, 'The Whitehall Cockpit: The Building and the Theater', *English Literary Renaissance*, 12 (1982), 301–18; Orrell, *Theatres*, chapter 5.

19 Modern theatre historians have debated the matter of whether the baiting rings, which were present in Southwark before playhouses were located there, were 'ancestors' of the 'wooden O' theatres, but one theatre was certainly built expressly to double as a baiting ring: the Hope, of 1613. See *ES*, vol. II, pp. 448–71.

20 See *MSC X*, pp. 39–43; *JCS*, vol. VI, pp. 271–73.

21 See *HKW*, vol. IV, pp. 96–123, with plates, and plates in G. H. Chettle, *The Queen's House, Greenwich* (London, 1937); Thurley, *Palaces*, pp. 35, 49.

22 See Starkey, *Henry VIII*; Anglo, *Spectacle*.

23 *HKW*, vol. IV, pp. 98, 100–3.

24 PRO E351/3240.

25 PRO E351/3214, 3221, 3229, 3237, 3240.

26 *MSC X*, p. 12.

27 Ibid., p. 13.

28 See *HKW*, vol. IV, pp. 222–34, plates 18 and 19.

29 Transcription by Francis Grose, *The Antiquarian Repertory*, vol. II (London, 1808), p. 315; contractions silently expanded.

30 W. H. Hart, 'The Parliamentary Surveys of Richmond, Wimbledon, and Nonsuch, in the County of Surrey, A.D. 1649', in *Surrey Archaeological Collections*, vol. V (London, 1871), p. 77.

31 Ibid., p. 78.

32 PRO E351/3233.

33 PRO E351/3272.

34 E.g., PRO E351/3221, 3265.

35 Grose, *Repertory*, p. 316.

36 *HKW*, vol. IV, pp. 126–47. A fold-out drawing opposite p. 146 shows the palace in its fullest state of architectural development in the Tudor period.

37 See Thurley, *Palaces*, pp. 51–54.

38 Ibid., pp. 120–22.

39 *HKW*, vol. IV, pp. 241–52.

40 See Roy Strong, *Henry Prince of Wales and England's Lost Renaissance* (London, 1986).

41 Jean Puget de la Serre, *Histoire de l'Entrée de la Reyne Mere du Roy Tres-Chrestien dans la Grande Bretaigne* (London, 1639).

42 See John H. Astington, 'Staging at St James's Palace in the Seventeenth Century', *Theatre Research International*, 11 (1986), 199–213.

43 *MSC X*, p. 26.

44 Ibid., p. 47.

45 PRO E351/3245.

46 PRO E351/3265.

47 Cited in E. Sheppard, *Memorials of St James's Palace*, 2 vols. (London, 1894), vol. I, p. 181.
48 *HKW*, vol. IV, pp. 252–71, plate 20.
49 PRO E351/3228: accounts for the repairing of roofs over these chambers in 1593–94.
50 PRO E351/3229.
51 *HKW*, vol. IV, pp. 254–59.
52 PRO E351/3246: dimensions given in payment to a carpenter for reboarding the floor of the Hall.
53 Orrell, *Theatres*, chapter 6.
54 *MSC X*, p. 47.
55 See W. H. St John Hope, *Windsor Castle. An Architectural History*, 3 vols. (London, 1913); *HKW*, vol. III, pp. 302ff.
56 *JCS*, vol. I, pp. 310–11. Prince Charles's Men travelled with the king during July and August 1634, when he visited Nottinghamshire and Derbyshire.
57 *ES*, vol. I, p. 157.
58 *MSC X*, p. 43.
59 *MSC VI* (Oxford, 1961 (1962)), pp. 34–35.
60 *HKW*, vol. IV, pp. 237–40.
61 *MSC X*, p. 26.
62 Ibid., p. 43.
63 Ibid., pp. 28, 32.
64 Quoted in *HKW*, vol. II, p. 1010; see also vol. IV, pp. 349–55.

3 Royal theatres

1 *MSC XIII*, p. 9.
2 *ES*, vol. II, pp. 8–23, 475–515.
3 Peter Meredith and John F. Tailby, eds., *The Staging of Religious Drama in Europe in the Later Middle Ages: Texts and Documents in English Translation* (Kalamazoo, 1983), p. 64.
4 A coloured reproduction may be seen, e.g., in Phyllis Hartnoll, *The Concise History of the Theatre* (New York, 1968), p. 38.
5 *HKW*, vol. IV, 2, p. 286: account of 1493.
6 See Astington, 'Staging at St James's Palace in the Seventeenth Century', *Theatre Research International*, 11 (1986), 199–213.
7 See Janet Loengard, An Elizabethan Lawsuit: John Brayne, his Carpenter, and the Building of the Red Lion Theatre', *Shakespeare Quarterly*, 35 (1984), 298–310; *ES*, vol. II, pp. 435–43.
8 *MSC X*, p. 13.
9 See Alan Nelson, *Early Cambridge Theatres* (Cambridge, 1994), chapter 2, on Queens' College's stage and galleries.
10 *MSC X*, p. 5.

11 PRO E351/3226.

12 PRO E351/3227.

13 PRO E351/3326.

14 PRO E351/3322.

15 PRO E351/3273. Fir, alder, and ash poles, from 20 to 40 feet in length, were all used as uprights in construction scaffolding. Poles were frequently lashed together, and the joints tightened with wedges. At Hampton Court in 1533, 'bast [bark fibre] ropes for the scaffold makers' were bought. See L. F. Salzman, *Building in England Down to 1540. A Documentary History* (Oxford, 1952), pp. 318–20.

16 The scantlings, or minimum measurements, of building timbers varied over time, but joists were at least 7in. x 3in. in section, and rafters 5in. x 4in. See Salzman, *Building*, p. 238.

17 *MSC X*, p. 33.

18 All citations from Orrell, 'The Theatre at Christ Church'.

19 [A]fter some small time of repose in the Councell Chamber, passing over the then ruinous wooden Terras, at the instant that he was entring the first great doore next that of the Guard Chamber, the weight of the over thronging multitude next about him, pressing down part of the Plancks and Joyces under him, that it suddainly fell, and with all the Earle of Arundell, the Lord Gray, and others, with great danger, and some hurt (particularly to one youth, who under the ruins had his arme and shoulder broken) the Ambassador having received but halfe a fall of the nether parts of his Body onely, his Servants next him staying and holding him by the upper, as he was at the instant of entring under the doore. The danger, and feare of it past, he was received at the Presence doore by the Lord Chamberlain.

   Finetti Philoxenis, p. 63

20 Orrell, *Theatres*, p. 30.

21 *MSC X*, p. 40.

22 Ibid., p. 21.

23 This argument is presented by Richard Hosley in a series of pieces published in the 1960s and 1970s: 'The Origins of the Shakespearian Playhouse', *Shakespeare Quarterly*, 15, 2 (1964), 29–39; 'Three Renaissance English Indoor Playhouses', *English Literary Renaissance*, 3 (1973), 166–82; and in two accounts of the playhouses published in Kenneth Muir and S. Schoenbaum, eds., *A New Companion to Shakespeare Studies* (Cambridge, 1971), pp. 15–34, and J. Leeds Barroll, Alexander Leggatt, Richard Hosley, and Alvin Kernan, eds., *The Revels History of Drama in English, Volume III, 1576–1613* (London, 1975), pp. 121–235.

24 See the evidence presented by Alan Nelson in *Cambridge*, 2 vols. (Toronto, 1989), and argued in his book *Early Cambridge Theatres*, cited above.

25 O & S, vol. II, pp. 630–59.

26 See Busino's account of a masque performance, cited below.

27 *MSC X*, p. 43.

28 The surviving plans for an unknown indoor theatre by Inigo Jones, currently being realised in three dimensions at the Bankside Globe complex, have been connected with the Cockpit in Drury Lane by John Orrell. (See *Theatres*, chapter 3.) Though such an identification remains speculative–since most of Jones's work was for the court, the plans may represent one proposal for the kind of theatre established in the Cockpit in 1630–it seems thoroughly likely that Jones's theatre is representative of the contemporary indoor playhouses of London.

29 On privacy at the Caroline court see Kevin Sharpe, 'The Image of Virtue: The Court and Household of Charles I, 1625–1642', in Starkey, *English Court*, pp. 226–60.

30 *MSC X*, p. 18.

31 *MSC VI*, pp. 96–97.

32 *MSC X*, p. 19.

33 Ibid., p. 20.

34 Quotations from Jonson's masques conform to the text of Stephen Orgel, ed., *Ben Jonson: The Complete Masques* (New Haven, 1969).

35 *MSC X*, p. 21.

36 Ibid., p. 22.

37 *MSC X*, p. 31.

38 *MSC II.3*, p. 333.

39 Ibid., p. 19.

40 All quotations from Shakespeare conform to the text of G. Blakemore Evans, ed., *The Riverside Shakespeare*, 2nd edn (Boston, 1997).

41 In Jonson's play *Epicœne* (1609–10), the pretentious Mistress Otter claims to have been present at 'the lord's masque' when 'it dropped all my wire and my ruff with wax candle, that I could not go up to the banquet' (3.2.62–65).

42 *MSC XIII*, p. 10.

43 *MSC X*, p. 42.

44 See *ES*, vol. I, chapter 5.

45 Ibid., pp. 159–60, 168–69.

46 Candlemas–Shrove 1574 and Twelfth Night 1583; see Feuillerat, *Elizabeth*, pp. 213, 218.

47 See Young, *Tournaments*, pp. 54–58.

48 A comprehensive record of entertainments in this wider sense is to be found in John Nichols, *The Progresses and Public Processions of Queen Elizabeth*, 3 vols. (London, 1823).

49 *MSC X*, p. 6.

50 Reproductions abound, but see, e.g., Andrew Gurr, *The Shakespearean Stage 1574–1642*, 3rd edn (Cambridge, 1992), p. 133, with discussion, pp. 131–36.

51 Various continental and classical analogies are considered by Chambers in *ES*, vol. III, pp. 1–21.

52 Feuillerat, *Elizabeth*, pp. 303, 306–8.

53 See William Tydeman, *The Theatre in the Middle Ages* (Cambridge, 1978), pp. 70–73.

54 The play was staged by Warwick's Men; for their possible connection with the playhouse, see William Ingram, 'The Playhouse at Newington Butts: A New Proposal', *Shakespeare Quarterly*, 21 (1970), 385–98.

55 See, e.g., John Wasson, 'Professional Actors in the Middle Ages and Early Renaissance', *Medieval and Renaissance Drama in England*, 1 (1984), 1–11; Ingram, *Business*.

56 See R. Mark Benbow, 'Dutton and Goffe versus Broughton: A Disputed Contract for Plays in the 1570s', *Records of Early English Drama Newsletter*, 2 (1981), 3–9.

57 PRO E351/3321.

58 Feuillerat, *Elizabeth*, p. 390.

59 *ES*, vol. IV, p. 102.

60 *MSC X*, p. 12.

61 Feuillerat, *Elizabeth*, pp. 390–91.

62 The Revels records quoted above also include the payment 'to a painter for painting of a battlement' (Feuillerat, *Elizabeth*, p. 391).

63 See *ES*, vol. IV, pp. 197–225.

64 *MSC X*, p. 16.

65 John Stow, *Annales*, cited in *JCS*, vol. VI, p. 255.

66 PRO E351/3243.

67 *JCS*, vol. VI, p. 257.

68 Ibid., p. 286.

69 See Barroll, *Politics*.

70 *ES*, vol. IV, pp. 117–18.

71 See Erica Veevers, *Images of Love and Religion. Queen Henrietta Maria and Court Entertainments* (Cambridge, 1989).

72 *JCS*, vol. I, pp. 51–53.

73 Ibid., vol. VI, pp. 284–87.

74 See *MSC II.3*, p. 393; and *Ceremonies*, p. 282.

75 *Ceremonies*, p. 288.

76 See Orrell, *Theatres*, chapter 6.

77 *JCS*, vol. I, p. 51.

78 Dimensions from Orrell, *Theatres*.

79 *MSC VI*, pp. 152–54.

80 *MSC X*, p. 55.

4 Artists and artisans

1 Edward Croft-Murray, *Decorative Painting in England, 1537–1837*, 2 vols. (London, 1962), vol. I, p. 17.

2 John Peacock, *The Stage Designs of Inigo Jones* (Cambridge, 1995), pp. 252–53.

3 Quoted in Ellis Waterhouse, *Painting in Britain 1530–1790* (London, 1953), p. 4.

4 Eric Mercer, 'The Decoration of the Royal Palaces from 1553–1625', *Archaeological Journal*, 110 (1953–54), 150–63: 152.

5 See the excellent recent survey by Anthony Wells-Cole, *Art and Decoration in Elizabethan and Jacobean England* (New Haven, 1997).

6 Feuillerat, *Edward and Mary*, p. 132.

7 See J. R. Hale, *Artists and Warfare in the Renaissance* (New Haven, 1990), chapter 2.

8 See Roy Strong, *The English Icon. Elizabethan and Jacobean Portraiture* (London, 1969).

9 *Henry VIII*, p. 61.

10 Waterhouse, *Painting*, p. 8.

11 Feuillerat, *Edward and Mary*, pp. 32, 55, 101, 132.

12 See Croft-Murray, *Decorative Painting*, plates 17–20; Thurley, *Palaces*, pp. 216–20.

13 See Timothy Mowl, *Elizabethan and Jacobean Style* (London, 1993), p. 149; Wells-Cole, *Art and Decoration*, pp. 30–32.

14 Streitberger, *Court Revels*, p. 20.

15 Roy Strong, *The Elizabethan Image* (London, 1969), pp. 22–24.

16 Croft-Murray, *Decorative Painting*, vol. I, p. 182.

17 See L. Rostenberg, *English Publishers in the Graphic Arts* (New York, 1963).

18 A. M. Hind, *Engraving in England in the Sixteenth and Seventeenth Centuries. Part II. The Reign of James I* (Cambridge, 1955), pp. 245ff.

19 See R. Malcolm Smuts, 'Art and the Material Culture of Majesty in Early Stuart England', in Smuts, ed., *The Stuart Court and Europe* (Cambridge, 1996), pp. 86–112.

20 E351/3145.

21 *Henry VIII*, p. 53.

22 E351/2947.

23 E351/2948 (1628–30).

24 See Anglo, *Spectacle*. The relationship between such a circular structure and the later playhouses is discussed by Richard Hosley in 'The Theatre and the Tradition of Playhouse Design', in Herbert Berry, ed., *The First Public Playhouse* (Montreal, 1979), pp. 60–79.

25 Feuillerat, *Elizabeth*, pp. 163–68.

26 Quoted in *HKW*, vol. IV, p. 320.

27 E351/3218.

28 E351/3219.

29 E351/3223.

30 E351/3239.

31 E351/3240.

32 For other examples see John Ronayne, 'Decorative and Mechanical Effects Relevant to the Theatre of Shakespeare', in C. Walter Hodges, S. Schoenbaum, and Leonard Leone, eds., *The Third Globe* (Detroit, 1981), pp. 190–221.

33 Quoted in ibid., p. 199.

34 E351/3237.

35 See *JCS*, vol. VI, p. 278; Glynne Wickham, *Early English Stages 1300–1660*, vol. II, part 2 (London, 1972), p. 120; *MSC X*, p. 43; Orrell, *Theatres*, p. 97.

36 Strong, *Image*, p. 52; see also Karen Hearn, ed., *Dynasties. Painting in Tudor and Jacobean England 1530–1630* (London, 1995), pp. 102–8.

37 See Hearn, *Dynasties*, pp. 173–75, 184–85, 190–91.

38 E351/3259.

39 E351/3263.

40 Feuillerat, *Elizabeth*, p. 158.

41 Ibid., pp. 119, 129, 145, 200, 218, 266, 320–21.

42 Ibid., p. 179.

43 Ibid., p. 218.

44 Ibid., p. 370.

45 Ibid., p. 239.

46 Sir Philip Sidney, *The Defence of Poesie*, ed. Wolfgang Clemen (Heidelberg, 1950), p. 33. See discussion in *ES*, vol. III, pp. 40–41.

47 Feuillerat, *Elizabeth*, p. 338.

48 Ibid., p. 365.

49 Ibid.

50 Ibid., p. 336.

51 *MSC XIII*, p. 43.

52 Feuillerat, *Elizabeth*, p. 241.

53 Ibid., pp. 303–9.

54 Ibid., p. 240.

55 Barnard Hewitt, ed., *The Renaissance Stage* (Coral Gables, 1958), p. 34.

56 See the account of the Ascension at Florence in 1439, for example: Meredith and Tailby, *Staging of Religious Drama*, pp. 245–47.

57 Feuillerat, *Elizabeth*, p. 237.

58 Inventory of Philip Henslowe, quoted in Gurr, *Shakespearean Stage*, pp. 187–88.

59 *MSC XIII*, p. 12.

60 *MSC X*, p. 29.

61 *MSC XIII*, p. 70.

62 *MSC II.3*, p. 387.

63 *MSC XIII*, p. 106.

64 *MSC X*, p. 25.

65 Ibid., p. 41.

66 See John H. Astington, '*The King and Queenes Entertainement at Richmond*', *Records of Early English Drama Newsletter*, 12, 1 (1987), 12–18.

67 *Vitruvius. The Ten Books of Architecture*, trans. M. H. Morgan (New York, 1960 [1914]), p. 150.

68 'An Expostulation with Inigo Jones', ll. 31–41. All quotations from Jonson's poetry conform to the text of *Ben Jonson*, ed. Ian Donaldson (Oxford, 1985).

69 Allardyce Nicoll, *Stuart Masques and the Renaissance Stage* (New York, 1968 [1938]), pp. 129–37.

70 Peter Thornton, *Seventeenth-Century Interior Decoration in England, France, and Holland* (New Haven, 1978), p. 268.

71 *MSC XIII*, p. 141. Accounts for 1635–38.

72 Thornton, *Decoration*, pp. 268–81.

73 *MSC X*, p. 54.

74 Ibid., pp. 22, 50.

75 See O & S, vol. II, pp. 736–62.

76 A famous sixteenth-century feat of engineering was the moving of the Vatican obelisk in 1585–86, effected by enormous numbers of ranked capstans pulled by horses and manpower. See Domenico Fontana, *Della Trasportatione dell' Obelisco Vaticano* (Rome, 1590).

77 Mercer, 'Decoration of Royal Palaces', 150–51.

78 *MSC II.3*, p. 348. Account for 1627–28.

79 See Pierre Dan, *Le Trésor des merveilles de la maison royale de Fontainebleau* (Paris, 1642), pp. 319–20.

80 W. G. Thomson, *A History of Tapestry* (London, 1930 [1906]), pp. 192–96.

81 *Ceremonies*, p. 279.

82 Quoted in Thomson, *Tapestry*, pp. 314–29.

83 *JCS*, vol. IV, p. 655.

84 See R. A. Foakes, *Illustrations of the English Stage 1580–1642* (London, 1985), pp. 80–81; John H. Astington, 'The *Messalina* Stage and Salisbury Court Plays', *Theatre Journal*, 43 (1991), 141–56.

85 Thomson, *Tapestry*, p. 338.

86 O & S, vol. I, pp. 234–35.

87 Peacock, *Stage Designs*, pp. 144–47. For Rabel, see *The Court Ballet of Louis XIII*, ed. Margaret M. McGowan (London, n. d. [1986]).

88 O & S, vol. I, p. 283.

89 *JCS*, vol. IV, p. 670.

90 Feuillerat, *Elizabeth*, pp. 136–38.

91 Ibid, p. 146.

92 Ibid., p. 22.

93 Ibid., p. 27.

94 Ibid., p. 320.

95 Ibid., p. 321.

96 Gurr, *Shakespearean Stage*, pp. 194–98.

97 O & S, vol. I, pp. 313–16.

98 Ibid., vol. II, pp. 439, 444–45.

99 Ibid., vol. I, pp. 191–92.

100 Ibid., pp. 277–78.

101 Ibid., p. 283.

102 Ibid., vol. II, p. 543.

5 Royal audiences

1 O & S, vol. II, p. 729.

2 John Orrell, *The Quest for Shakespeare's Globe* (Cambridge, 1983), p. 129.

3 Quoted in *WS*, vol. II, p. 342.

4 Andrew Gurr, *Playgoing in Shakespeare's London*, 2nd edn (Cambridge, 1996), pp. 20–28.

5 R. Malcolm Smuts, *Court Culture and the Origins of a Royalist Tradition in Early Stuart England* (Philadelphia, 1987), pp. 3–4.

6 Neil Cuddy, 'The Revival of the Entourage: The Bedchamber of James I, 1603–1625', in Starkey, *English Court*, pp. 173–225: p. 179.

7 Caroline M. Hibbard, 'The Role of a Queen Consort. The Household and Court of Henrietta Maria, 1625–1642', in Ronald G. Asch and Adolf M. Birke, ed., *Princes, Patronage, and the Nobility* (Oxford, 1991), pp. 393–414.

8 See Barroll, *Politics*, pp. 49–59.

9 Aylmer, *Servants*, pp. 322–29; Lawrence Stone, *The Crisis of the Aristocracy 1558–1641* (Oxford, 1965).

10 Guy, *The Reign of Elizabeth I*, p. 2.

11 See G. W. Bernard, ed., *The Tudor Nobility* (Manchester, 1992), 'Introduction', p. 20.

12 Penry Williams, 'Court and Polity under Elizabeth I', in John Guy, ed., *The Tudor Monarchy* (London, 1997), pp. 362–63.

13 Ibid., p. 364.

14 See, e. g., Barbara K. Lewalski, 'Lucy, Countess of Bedford: Images of a Jacobean Courtier and Patroness', in Kevin Sharpe and Steven N. Zwicker, eds., *Politics of Discourse* (Berkeley and Los Angeles, 1987).

15 Norman E. McClure, ed., *The Letters of John Chamberlain*, 2 vols. (Philadelphia, 1939) (hereafter cited as *Letters*), vol. II, p. 50.

16 Pam Wright, 'A Change in Direction: The Ramifications of a Female Household, 1558–1603', in Starkey, *English Court*, pp. 147–72: p. 158.

17 Ibid., p. 158.

18 *ES*, vol. II, pp. 102–3.

19 Quoted in *ES*, vol. IV, p. 114.

20 See Gurr, *Playgoing*.

21 *Diary*, p. 47.

22 Ibid., p. 3.

23 *ES*, vol. II, p. 99; vol. IV, p. 315.

24 A. R. Braunmuller, 'Robert Carr, Earl of Somerset, as Collector and Patron', in Linda Levy Peck, ed., *The Mental World of the Jacobean Court* (Cambridge, 1991), pp. 230–50;

Graham Parry, *The Golden Age Restor'd. The Culture of the Stuart Court 1603–1642* (Manchester, 1981), chapter 6.

25 O & S, vol. I, p. 282.

26 *Ceremonies*, p. 119.

27 *Diary*, p. 47; my emphasis.

28 See the Lord Chamberlain's stipulations about the numbers expected at the performance of *Luminalia* in 1640: *Ceremonies*, p. 242.

29 O & S, vol. I, p. 282.

30 *Letters*, vol. I, p. 250.

31 Ibid., p. 251.

32 *MSC XIII*, p. 59, etc.

33 *JCS*, vol. III, p. 200.

34 *Letters*, vol. II, pp. 466, 468.

35 *The Magnificent Marriage of the Two Great Princes* (London, 1613), as quoted in John Nichols, *The Progresses, Processions, and Magnificent Festivities of King James the First*, 4 vols. (London, 1828), vol. II, pp. 549–51. *Letters*, vol. I, pp. 418, 424.

36 Quoted in *JCS*, vol. IV, p. 918.

37 A 'turnstile' was used for an entertainment at York House, the Duke of Buckingham's residence, in November 1626: see *The Survey of London. Volume XVIII. The Strand* (London, 1937), p. 55.

38 *MSC II.3*, p. 375.

39 *Ceremonies*, pp. 149, 195–96.

40 O & S, vol. I, pp. 282–83.

41 See Martin Butler, 'Entertaining the Palatine Prince: Plays on Foreign Affairs 1635–1637', *English Literary Renaissance*, 13 (1983), 319–44.

42 *Ceremonies*, p. 196.

43 *MSC X*, p. 32.

44 *Ceremonies*, pp. 277–78.

45 *Letters*, vol. II, p. 47.

46 Quoted in *JCS*, vol. V, p. 1158.

47 See Streitberger, *Court Revels*, pp. 80–81, 257.

48 O & S, vol. I, p. 284.

49 Ibid., p. 206.

50 Giovanni Battista Gabaleone, envoy of Savoy. See John Orrell, 'The London Court Stage in the Savoy Correspondence, 1613–1675', *Theatre Research International*, 4 (1979), 79–94: 85–86.

51 Nichols, *Progresses of King James*, vol. II, p. 587.

52 Quoted in *JCS*, vol. II, p. 678.

53 O & S, vol. I, p. 384.

54 *Diary*, p. 101.

55 *Letters*, vol. II, p. 240.

56 Quoted in *WS*, vol. II, p. 346.

57 *Ceremonies*, p. 195.

58 *Diary*, p. 101.

59 *Herbert*, pp. 142, 149.

60 *Letters*, vol. II, p. 539.

61 *Herbert*, p. 157.

62 *JCS*, vol. III, p. 217.

63 On 29 December 1601; quoted in *WS*, vol. II, p. 327.

64 *MSC XIII*, p. 9.

65 *Letters*, vol. I, p. 426.

66 *JCS*, vol. IV, pp. 590, 594.

67 *MSC X*, p. 32.

68 *Herbert*, p. 185.

69 Ibid., pp. 191–92.

70 Ibid., p. 187.

71 Ibid., p. 207.

72 Charles, Prince Palatine, in a letter; quoted in *JCS*, vol. III, p. 113.

73 *Herbert*, p. 196.

74 *JCS*, vol. III, p. 136.

75 *Herbert*, pp. 180, 184.

76 Ibid., p. 148.

77 Quoted in O & S, vol. I, p. 279.

78 *Letters*, vol. I, pp. 391, 416.

79 Quoted in *JCS*, vol. IV, p. 671.

80 *Letters*, vol. II, p. 49.

81 Ibid., p. 677.

82 G. E. Bentley's claim that Mildmay 'records his attendance . . . at four court masques' (*JCS*, vol. II, p. 381) is mistaken. Mildmay watched the *procession* of *The Triumph of Peace* from the window of a house in the Strand, as many other members of the public did; he then records the second performance in his diary, but simply as an event of note. The record in his account book 'for the Masque of his Ma 00-00-06' at the time of *Coelum Britannicum* does not mean that he was in the audience. Keith Sturgess places him there, and writes that he 'expended sixpence on the visit' (*Jacobean Private Theatre* [London, 1987], p. 190) but does not suggest what it bought. Tickets were not for sale, and sixpence would hardly have gone very far as a bribe. What it *would* buy, and did buy, I believe, was the published text of the masque, a quarto of twenty leaves, which Mildmay perhaps acquired directly from the shop of the publisher, Thomas Walkley, near York House, not far from Whitehall. Had Mildmay attended the performance he would have written about it in his journal.

83 Edward Sherburn, quoted in O & S, vol. I, p. 279.

84 *Ceremonies*, p. 272.

85 See the account of Bulstrode Whitelocke, cited below (note 87). 'The Dancers, Masquers, Anti-Masquers, and Musicians, did before-hand practise in the place where they were to present the Masque, and the Scenes were artificially prepared at the lower end of the Banquetting-house' (O & S, vol. II, p. 540).

86 O & S, vol. II, p. 538; *Ceremonies*, p. 149.

87 O & S, vol. II, p. 543.

88 Quoted in *JCS*, vol. V, p. 1157.

89 O & S, vol. II, p. 539.

90 *Herbert*, p. 187.

91 Ibid.

6 Royal occasions

1 *JCS*, vol. VII, p. 62; *MSC VI*, p. 152.

2 As quoted in the Malone Society edition of *The Rare Triumphs of Love and Fortune* (Oxford, 1930), p. vi.

3 E. K. Chambers suggests that the gods sit in a balcony throughout the play to watch the romantic action, but the indications of the text are not at all convincing on this score, and he does not seem to have calculated the consequences of such staging for casting the play: *ES*, vol. III, p. 45.

4 See G. K. Hunter and David Bevington, eds., *Campaspe, Sappho and Phao* (Manchester, 1991).

5 *MSC X*, p. 11.

6 See *The Life and Works of George Peele*, gen. ed. Charles T. Prouty, 3 vols. (New Haven, 1952–70), vol. III, pp. 7–12.

7 Hunter and Bevington, *Campaspe*, 2.2.137.

8 Ibid., pp. 184–85.

9 *MSC X*, p. 12.

10 Ibid.

11 See David Bevington's discussion in his Revels edition of *Endymion* (Manchester, 1996), pp. 50–57.

12 Dudley Carleton wrote that 'The first holy days we had every night a public play in the great hall'; quoted in Barroll, *Politics*, p. 27.

13 Quoted in *WS*, vol. II, p. 329.

14 *ES*, vol. IV, p. 12. Chambers suggests that Jonson's *Sejanus* may also have been part of the 1603–4 repertory of the King's Men, although the evidence seems to me ambiguous, at best. The play was published in 1605 after its failure in the theatre, alluded to in the dedication. Had there been a court performance one might expect Jonson to have proclaimed it in print, but he speaks only of a text 'which was acted on the publike Stage'.

15 *MSC VI*, p. 55.

16 Compare the title *All's Well That Ends Well*. A play called *An Ill Beginning has a Good End* was assigned to John Ford in 1660, but variant or approximate titles for plays are very common in the written records of the period. Could it be that the King's Men acted Shakespeare's *All's Well* at court in 1612–13?

17 John H. Astington, 'The Popularity of *Cupid's Revenge*', *Studies in English Literature 1500–1900*, 19 (1979), 215–27.

18 All quotations from Beaumont and Fletcher plays in this chapter conform to the text of *The Dramatic Works in the Beaumont and Fletcher Canon*, gen. ed. Fredson Bowers, 10 vols. (Cambridge, 1966–96).

19 *MSC XIII*, p. 128.

20 *JCS*, vol. I, p. 53.

21 See *MSC X*, pp. 53–54; *MSC II.3*, pp. 388–89; *Ceremonies*, p. 257. Reading the Works accounts in the context of *The Passionate Lovers* tells us a little more about Inigo Jones's designs for the play, first produced in the preceding summer: see O & S, vol. II, pp. 724–27. Since 'Soape' and 'Baserope' were among the supplies, there presumably was machinery to change the scenery. That the dates of the later performance are correct and that Carlell's play was not mounted at the Cockpit are confirmed by Finet, who speaks of the two-part 'comedy' at Somerset House having been 'made by one of the Kings servants'. Carlell was a Groom of the Privy Chamber in the court of the queen and Gentleman of the Bows and Lime-Hounds in the King's Chamber.

22 See O & S, vol. II, pp. 724–27; John Orrell, 'Amerigo Salvetti and the London Court Theatre, 1616–1640', *Theatre Survey*, 20 (1979), 1–26: 24–25.

23 See *Privy Council Registers*, 11 vols. (London, 1967–68), vols. IV and V.

24 See Orrell, 'Salvetti,' 25; *CSPV*, 1636–39.

25 *MSC X*, p. 55.

Conclusion

1 'An Horatian Ode upon Cromwell's Return from Ireland' (written in 1650), l. 58.

2 *JCS*, vol. I, p. 6.

3 'To the Memory of My Beloved, The Author, Mr William Shakespeare, And What He Hath Left Us' (1623), ll. 73–74.

Select bibliography

Anglo, Sydney, *Spectacle, Pageantry, and Early Tudor Policy*, 2nd edn (Oxford, 1996).

Asch, Ronald G., and Adolf M. Birke, eds., *Princes, Patronage, and the Nobility* (Oxford, 1991).

Astington, John H., ed., *The Development of Shakespeare's Theater* (New York, 1992).

Aylmer, G. E., *The King's Servants*, rev. edn (London, 1974).

Barroll, J. Leeds, *Politics, Plague, and Shakespeare's Theater* (Ithaca, 1991).

Bawcutt, N. W., ed., *The Control and Censorship of Caroline Drama. The Records of Sir Henry Herbert, Master of the Revels 1623–73* (Oxford, 1996).

Beadle, Richard, ed., *The Cambridge Companion to English Medieval Theatre* (Cambridge, 1994).

Bentley, G. E., *The Jacobean and Caroline Stage*, 7 vols. (Oxford, 1941–68).

Birch, Thomas, *The Court and Times of James I* (London, 1848).

  The Court and Times of Charles I (London, 1848).

Campbell, Lily B., *Scenes and Machines on the English Stage During the Renaissance* (Cambridge, 1923).

Chambers, E. K., *The Elizabethan Stage*, 4 vols. (Oxford, 1923).

  William Shakespeare. A Study of Facts and Problems, 2 vols. (Oxford, 1930).

Colvin, H. M., gen. ed., *The History of the King's Works*, 6 vols. (London, 1963–82).

Croft-Murray, Edward, *Decorative Painting in England, 1537–1837*, 2 vols. (London, 1962).

Dutton, Richard, *Mastering the Revels* (London, 1991).

Feuillerat, Albert, *Documents Relating to the Office of the Revels in the Time of Queen Elizabeth* (Louvain, 1908).

  Documents Relating to the Revels at Court in the Time of King Edward VI and Queen Mary (Louvain, 1914).

Foakes, R. A., *Illustrations of the English Stage 1580–1642* (London, 1985).

Gent, Lucy, ed., *Albion's Classicism. The Visual Arts in Britain, 1550–1660* (New Haven, 1995).

Gurr, Andrew, *The Shakespearean Stage 1574–1642*, 3rd edn (Cambridge, 1992).

Playgoing in Shakespeare's London, 2nd edn (Cambridge, 1996).

Guy, John, ed., *The Reign of Elizabeth I. Court and Culture in the Last Decade* (Cambridge, 1995).

    The Tudor Monarchy (London, 1997).

Hewitt, Barnard, ed., *The Renaissance Stage* (Coral Gables, 1958).

Howarth, David, *Images of Rule. Art and Politics in the English Renaissance, 1485–1649* (London, 1997).

Ingram, William, *The Business of Playing* (Ithaca, 1992).

Kernan, Alvin, *Shakespeare the King's Playwright. Theater in the Stuart Court, 1603–1613* (New Haven, 1995).

King, T. J., *Shakespearean Staging, 1599–1642* (Cambridge, MA, 1971).

Kipling, Gordon, *The Triumph of Honour* (Leiden, 1977).

Loades, D. M., *The Tudor Court* (London, 1987).

Loomie, Albert J., ed., *Ceremonies of Charles I. The Notebooks of John Finet 1628–1641* (New York, 1987).

Malone Society, *Collections, Volume II, Part III: Dramatic Records: The Lord Chamberlain's Office*, ed. E. K. Chambers (Oxford, 1931), pp.321–416.

    Collections, Volume VI: Dramatic Records in the Declared Accounts of the Treasurer of the Chamber 1558–1642, ed. David Cook and F. P. Wilson (Oxford, 1961 (1962)).

    Collections, Volume X: Dramatic Records in the Declared Accounts of the Office of the Works 1560–1640, ed. F. P. Wilson and R. F. Hill (Oxford, 1975 (1977)).

    Collections, Volume XIII: Jacobean and Caroline Revels Accounts, 1603–1642, ed. W. R. Streitberger (Oxford, 1986).

McClure, Norman E., ed., *The Letters of John Chamberlain*, 2 vols. (Philadelphia, 1939).

McGowan, Margaret M., *L'Art du ballet de cour en France 1581–1643* (Paris, 1963).

McGowan, Margaret M., ed., *The Court Ballet of Louis XIII* (London, n. d.[1986]).

Mercer, Eric, 'The Decorations of the Royal Palaces from 1553–1625', *Archaeological Journal*, 110 (1953–54), 150–63.

Meredith, Peter, and John F. Tailby, eds., *The Staging of Religious Drama in Europe in the Later Middle Ages: Texts and Documents in English Translation* (Kalamazoo, 1983).

Mulryne, J. R., and M. Shewring, eds., *Theatre and Government under the Early Stuarts* (Cambridge, 1993).

Nagler, Alois M., *Theatre Festivals of the Medici 1539–1637* (New Haven, 1964).

Nelson, Alan, *Early Cambridge Theatres* (Cambridge, 1994).

Nichols, John, *The Progresses and Public Processions of Queen Elizabeth*, 3 vols. (London, 1823).

    The Progresses, Processions, and Magnificent Festivities of King James the First, 4 vols. (London, 1828).

Nicoll, Allardyce, *Stuart Masques and the Renaissance Stage* (New York, 1968 [1938]).

Orgel, Stephen, and Roy Strong, eds., *Inigo Jones. The Theatre of the Stuart Court*, 2 vols. (Berkeley and London, 1973).

Orrell, John, 'The Theatre at Christ Church, Oxford, in 1605', *Shakespeare Survey*, 35 (1982), 129–40.

    The Quest for Shakespeare's Globe (Cambridge, 1983).

    The Theatres of Inigo Jones and John Webb (Cambridge, 1985).

Parry, Graham, *The Golden Age Restor'd. The Culture of the Stuart Court 1603–1642* (Manchester, 1981).

Peacock, John, *The Stage Designs of Inigo Jones* (Cambridge, 1995).

Peck, Linda Levy, ed., *The Mental World of the Jacobean Court* (Cambridge, 1991).

Sackville-West, V., ed., *The Diary of Lady Ann Clifford* (London, 1923).

Salzman, L. F., *Building in England Down to 1540. A Documentary History* (Oxford, 1952).

Sharpe, Kevin, *Criticism and Compliment. The Politics of Literature in the England of Charles I* (Cambridge, 1987).

Sharpe, Kevin, and Steven N. Zwicker, eds., *Politics of Discourse* (Berkeley and Los Angeles, 1987).

Sharpe, Kevin, and Peter Lake, eds., *Culture and Politics in Early Stuart England* (London, 1994).

Smuts, R. Malcolm, *Court Culture and the Origins of a Royalist Tradition in Early Stuart England* (Philadelphia, 1987).

Smuts, R. Malcolm, ed., *The Stuart Court and Europe* (Cambridge, 1996).

Southern, Richard, *The Staging of Plays before Shakespeare* (London, 1973).

Starkey, David, ed., *Henry VIII. A European Court in England* (London, 1991).

Starkey, David, D. A. L. Morgan, John Murphy, Pam Wright, Neil Cuddy and Kevin Sharpe, *The English Court: From the Wars of the Roses to the Civil War* (London, 1987).

Stone, Lawrence, *The Crisis of the Aristocracy 1558–1641* (Oxford, 1965).

Streitberger, W. R., *Court Revels, 1485–1559* (Toronto, 1994).

Strong, Roy, *The Elizabethan Image* (London, 1969).

    The English Icon. Elizabethan and Jacobean Portraiture (London, 1969).

    Art and Power: Renaissance Festivals 1450–1650 (Berkeley, 1984).

Thomson, W. G., *A History of Tapestry* (London, 1930 [1906]).

Thornton, Peter, *Seventeenth-Century Interior Decoration in England, France, and Holland* (New Haven, 1978).

Thurley, Simon, *The Royal Palaces of Tudor England* (New Haven, 1993).

Veevers, Erica, *Images of Love and Religion. Queen Henrietta Maria and Court Entertainments* (Cambridge, 1989).

Waterhouse, Ellis, *Painting in Britain 1530–1790* (London, 1953).

Wells-Cole, Anthony, *Art and Decoration in Elizabethan and Jacobean England* (New Haven, 1997).

Young, Alan, *Tudor and Jacobean Tournaments* (London, 1987).

Index

.